An Introduction to Paraconsistent Logics

Manuel Bremer

An Introduction to Paraconsistent Logics

PETER LANG
Frankfurt am Main · Berlin · Bern · Bruxelles · New York · Oxford · Wien

Bibliographic Information published by Die Deutsche Bibliothek
Die Deutsche Bibliothek lists this publication in the Deutsche Nationalbibliografie; detailed bibliographic data is available in the internet at <http://dnb.ddb.de>.

ISBN 3-631-53413-2
US-ISBN 0-8204-7671-4

www.peterlang.de

[W]hen you have eliminated the impossible, whatever remains,
however improbable, must be the truth.
As a rule the more bizarre a thing is the less mysterious it proves to be.
(Sherlock Holmes)

Contents

Part III: Discussions, Alternatives, Perspectives

1 | Introduction

This book provides an introduction to paraconsistent logics and to the philosophy of paraconsistency accompanying the logics. At least it provides a first overview including the main fields of paraconsistent logics, their basic characteristics, motivations and areas of application.
Paraconsistent logics are logics that allow for inconsistency. This "allowing for inconsistency" and what "inconsistency" can mean is spelled out formally. There are some variations within the field of paraconsistency how far this "allowing for inconsistency" should go.[1]
Allowing for inconsistency of whatever kind makes paraconsistent logics definitely *non-classical*, even more so – one is inclined to say – than are the many valued logic approaches, which although possessing a plenty of maybe not so obvious additional truth-values for formulas nevertheless aim at a consistent logic of the interaction of these many truth-values.
Nonetheless such paraconsistent logics are worth considering:
• Logical systems are worth considering *in their own right*, since so we learn about very abstract structural properties of logics and the concepts employed within them (e.g., negation, necessity, consistency ...).
• Some non-classical logics are especially of interest from a philosophical perspective, since only by them some *philosophical* problems can be solved or even be stated.

Paraconsistent Topics

This introduction argues from a philosophical perspective why (some) paraconsistent logics are interesting or even the best candidates for treating some specific philosophical problems.
This philosophical perspective is responsible for the focus laid on matters of semantic motivation and intuitive justification of some paraconsistent logics. Assessments and discussions try to meet philosophical scruples and several misgivings when hearing of paraconsistency.
Although logic is seen from the point of view of its philosophical use, various formal systems are described, compared and employed.
At the rate that the literature on paraconsistent logic and its various (supposed and real) applications is increasing it is, of course, not possible

---

1 The name "Paraconsistent Logic" is said to have originated with the Brazilian logician Miro Quesada (cf. Arruda 1989).

to deal with all approaches and all topics, but the topics dealt with here should at least give a first understanding of paraconsistent logics and their application, the major approaches and some trends in the discussion around paraconsistency.

So – as always in introductions – knowing what is dealt with here may not be sufficient for understanding all of the literature, but for much of the lietrature it is necessary.

This introduction is written for:

• *Philosophers* who have heard of these new systems, having some idea what they might be good for, but are still looking for a readable more general introduction.

• *Information scientists* interested in the treatment of inconsistent data and their consequence relation.

• *Mathematicians* who care about the foundational problems of set theory, or have even heard of "inconsistent arithmetic" or such things.

• *Linguists* interested in formal methods and the philosophical foundations of semantics or the theory of formal languages.

• *Anyone interested in the paradoxes* of semantics, set theory ...

It is assumed that the reader has mastered a course in classical (or as I rather say "standard") **F**irst **O**rder **L**ogic, has heard at least in general about meta-logical properties of logical systems (like *soundness*) and about the idea of modal logics and their semantics (possible worlds...)

It is surely helpful if the reader has some background knowledge in the philosophy of logic and language (especially semantics), or such philosophical fields as epistemology, ontology or meta-ethics.

Apart from this first chapter which contains some definitions and some historical remarks on paraconsistency the lectures are divided into three parts:

• *Foundations*. This part presents the basic philosophical motivation for paraconsistent logics, introduces some methodological guidelines for developing or choosing paraconsistent logics and describes the different ways (i.e. systems) how one can develop paraconsistent logics. Chapter 2 presents the idea of semantic closure as one of the main motivations for paraconsistency. On the formal side this part of the book introduces the main approaches and systems within the field of paraconsistent logic. Chapter 4 deals with the basic logic **LP** and its extensions. **LP** provides a good starting point to see the workings of setting up a paraconsistent semantics and a corresponding proof theory or a corresponding decision procedure. Chapter 5 deals with Relevant Logics as one of the major versions of paraconsistent logics. Chapter 6 presents a paraconsistent sequential calculus as an alternative to the controversial semantics of Relevant Logics. Chapter 7 deals with the adaptive approach to logic, which also covers the idea of logics which are adaptive to the occurrence or recognition of inconsistency in a premise set. Chapter 8 introduces the Brazilian approach to paraconsistency, which was made famous by the work of Newton da Costa. Chapter 9 then collects some more paraconsistent logics that do not simply fall into one of the categories of the foregoing chapters. Some of these logics are applied in Part II. All logics in Part I are assessed in the light of the methodological criteria derived in Chapter 3 from more philosophical motivations for paraconsistency.

• *Applications*. This part employs some of the paraconsistent logics or extensions thereof to deal with topics in set theory, meta-logic, semantics, epistemology, and meta-ethics. Chapter 10 shows that the standard way of providing a Tarski-style theory of truth for a language can be adapted to provide a theory of truth for a language in that language itself, i.e. to provide semantic closure. One of the main motivations for paraconsistency is thus shown viable. One other main motivation for paraconsistency is to preserve naïve set theory with unrestricted Comprehension. Chapter 11 covers some approaches to paraconsistent set theory. Chapter 12 continues on these more meta-logical themes by introducing inconsistent versions of arithmetic, so that even mathematics can be done paraconsistently. Chapter 13 reflects on the consequences that paraconsistency has for meta-logic, especially the famous limitative theorems of meta-logic. Chapter 14 and 15 concern more real life applications of paraconsistency. Chapter 14 presents paraconsistent versions of Deontic Logic which are able to deal with the presence of normative conflicts in moral or legal systems. Chapter 15 deals with paraconsistent models and interpretations of scientific theories that turn out or are known to be inconsistent. The system of our beliefs is also a candidate for an inconsistent set that needs a paraconsistent logic.

• *Discussions, Alternatives, Perspectives*. This part confronts the whole approach with some problems (like the strange idea of having an ontology of inconsistent objects, some so called "hypercontradictions") and discusses some alternatives to paraconsistent logics. Chapter 16 meets the challenge of hypercontradictions (contradictions that are as devastating to paraconsistency as ordinary contradictions are to standard logic). Chapter 17 discusses the question of whether we can understand what an ontology of inconsistent objects would be. In this context Meinong's famous ontology of possible and impossible objects is presented. Chapter 18 asks whether there are not simpler ways to meet the main motivations for paraconsistency than paraconsistency itself. Such alternatives may include other non-standard set theories and approximations to semantic closure. Chapter 19 gives a short overview on the relation between paraconsistency and programming, since the inconsistency of databases seems to be a paradigmatic area needing paraconsistent logics and techniques. Chapter 20 brings several features of different paraconsistent logics together. The question put in this chapter is what a truly universal logic should be and what it might look like.

Each chapter contains a list of *further readings*; here the primary sources of the chapter are given and texts with which you might continue on the topic in question (general references are listed at the end of the book).
Almost all chapters
• contain at the end some *questions* on the topic of that chapter inviting you to reflect on some of the issues or to grasp the crucial points more clearly.
• contain at the end some more formal *exercises* asking you to employ the methods just dealt with.

The chapters in Part I are more or the less self-contained, the chapters in Part II obviously presuppose the PL-systems introduced in Part I.

Notation and Usage

I use mostly standard notation: $\forall$ $\exists$ $\neg$ $\wedge$ $\vee$ $\cap$ $\cup$ $\supset$ $\subset$ $\subseteq$ $\in$ $\notin$ $\neq$ $\equiv$ $\varnothing$ $\Box$ $\Diamond$ ...
"$\rightarrow$" is used for a conditional stronger than "$\supset$".
"$\Rightarrow$" is used at the meta-level (e.g., in stating rules).
"A", "B"... are meta-language expressions for object language formulas: "p", "q" ... [2]
Capital Greek letters mostly denote sets (of sentences). A great "Σ" is used for sums. "Δ" is used as truth operator.
If there is some relation to Relevant logics I write "Relevantly" with a capital "R" (to distinguish from ordinary talk like "not relevant").
By "logic", if not indicated otherwise, a proof system/theory *and* a corresponding semantics is meant. If the difference between syntax and semantics is important "proof system/theory" as usual means the systematisation of the relation of derivability, $\vdash$, in contrast to the

2 This distinction is under discussion here, so later expressions are translated into themselves at the meta-level.

semantic consequence relation, $\models$. "$\vdash$" and "$\models$" are used with subscripts if a distinction between logics is needed in the context.
By *proven equivalents* A and B it is meant: $\vdash A \equiv B$
By *provably equivalent* in contrast it is meant that $A \vdash B$ and $B \vdash A$.[3]
Given *Modus Ponens* and the Deduction Theorem in some logical system, the proven equivalents are provably equivalent, but many paraconsistent logics lack either one or both of these!

Paraconsistency Is Contra-Intuitive?

Consistency seems to belong to *the* most basic assumptions of logic and epistemology. How could anyone dare to put it into question? Can something that contains contradictions *make sense* at all?
Even our ordinary concept of logical consequence is often based on the concept of consistency: A statement A follows from a set of statements Γ if the closure of $\Gamma \cup \{\neg A\}$ is inconsistent.
But logical consequence can be defined without invoking consistency:

> A statement A follows from a set of statements Γ if in case that all $B \in \Gamma$ are true, A is true.

Maybe one can introduce whole logical systems without relying on the concept of consistency (or consistency in a narrow sense).
Furthermore, there are also powerful intuitions that speak against the treatment of inconsistency in standard logics, and powerful arguments that something might be wrong with the standard accounts how to avoid the inconsistencies that arise with the semantic paradoxes.
There are quite different ways in which inconsistency can arise:
A set of statements is *simply inconsistent* iff it contains for some A both A and $\neg A$ as elements; i.e. $(\exists A)(A \in \Gamma \wedge \neg A \in \Gamma)$.
A set of statements is *syntactically absolute inconsistent* (or *trivial*) iff it contains all A (or a given language) whatsoever, i.e. $(\forall A)(A \in \Gamma)$. We also say that a set of statements is *syntactically absolute inconsistent* (or *trivial*) iff its set of consequences (given some specified logic) is *syntactically absolute inconsistent* (or *trivial*); i.e. $(\forall A)\ \Gamma \vdash A$.
A set of statements is *semantically absolute inconsistent* (or *trivial*) iff it makes all statements A true (given some specified semantics). We also say that a set of statements is *semantically absolute inconsistent* (or *trivial*) iff its set of consequences (given some specified interpretation) is *semantically absolute inconsistent* (or *trivial*); i.e. $(\forall A)\ \Gamma \models A$.

---

[3] This distinction becomes important for the validity of (respective versions of) replacement of equivalents in some logical system.

A set of statements is *explicitly inconsistent* iff $(A \wedge \neg A) \in \Gamma$.
A set Γ may be simply inconsistent without being explicitly so, and be explicitly inconsistent without being absolutely inconsistent.

Paraconsistency Defined

A logic is *paraconsistent* iff a set of statements can be simply or explicitly inconsistent without being trivial with respect to the concepts of $\vdash$ and $\models$ defined by that logic.
The decisive property is: $(\exists A)(A \in \Gamma \wedge \neg A \in \Gamma) \wedge (\exists B)\ \Gamma \nvdash B$
Triviality is certainly bad: If everything is true all distinctions disappear, nothing can be asserted in distinction to anything else. Triviality has to be avoided. This requirement does not carry over to inconsistency if inconsistency and triviality can be kept apart.
Logics that cannot distinguish between inconsistency and triviality are called *explosive*, since a simple inconsistency causes a set (of consequences) to explode by containing all sentences of the language. Paraconsistent Logics (short: "PLs") can, therefore, also be characterized as being *non-explosive*.

ex contradictione qoudlibet

Standard logics (i.e. **FOL**, but also Intuitionistic and Minimal Logic, systems based on them, and many Many Valued Logics) are explosive by principles/rules that cause explosion. The most (in-)famous is *ex contradictione qoudlibet* (sometimes called "principle of explosion"):

$$A, \neg A \vdash B$$

or

$$(A \wedge \neg A) \vdash B$$

i.e. given a (simple) inconsistency any formula B whatsoever can be derived. The proof in the standard prepositional calculus (short: "**PC**") is:

1.<1>	p	PREM
2.<2>	$\neg p$	PREM
3.<1>	$p \vee q$	$(\vee I)$, 1
4.<1,2>	q	$(\vee E)$, 2, 3

Avoiding explosion means giving up as theorems formula like:

(1) $p \wedge \neg p \supset q$

and

(2) $p \supset (\neg p \supset q)$

both proven in variants of the proof above with ($\wedge$E) or ($\supset$I) used. Avoiding such theorems and rules like *ex contradictione qoudlibet* requires changing the logic in such a way that they are no longer derivable.
Given the proof above this means dropping one of the rules employed, i.e. ($\vee$I) or ($\vee$E), or inventing some new restrictions on a derivation being a *proper* derivation (like the restrictions used in the context of ($\forall$I) and ($\exists$E) in standard first order logic).
Many paraconsistent logics give up ($\vee$E), the so called *Disjunctive Syllogism*. Some lay down further requirements on proofs (typically such that the consequence should be *relevantly* related to the premises). Some combine these procedures.
In any case such revisions should be justified by:

- their effectiveness in blocking explosion
- their power in blocking further contra-intuitive theorems
- showing that not too much is being given up (the simplest paraconsistent logic is such that *nothing* can be derived at all from some premise set Γ!)

Weak Paraconsistency

The *weak* paraconsistent approach says that we need a paraconsistent logic to deal with inconsistencies, especially with inconsistent theories, although weak paraconsistency sees inconsistencies still as something bad that should be *avoided* and has to be avoided in the end.
The main motivation for weak paraconsistency lays in the fact that many of our theories (or systems of belief) are simply inconsistent. Nevertheless we do not conclude everything from them.
Sometimes we discover that our system of beliefs *was* inconsistent (say by believing that Schuhmacher did not win at Monza, that a Ferrari driver won, that Barricello did not win and knowing in general that every Formula I team has two pilots only); we correct ourselves, but we do not remember that at the time of inconsistency we believed every statement whatsoever (e.g. that John Paul II won at Monza). Probably our current belief system *is* inconsistent, but we do not feel inclined to believe everything. Applied to our ordinary reasoning, therefore, explosion is a *highly contra-intuitive* logical principle.
The argument concerning belief systems may be circumvented if one claims that ordinary belief is not deductively closed. That is, at least, controversial, but an ideal reasoner should aspire to closure.

In case of scientific theories, however, the theory *as a structure* can be considered. And here theories that are inconsistent are not always considered to be trivial. Weak paraconsistency claims that this often was and often is the case in all the sciences.
An often cited example is Bohr's theory of the atom: It stated that an electron can revolve around the kernel without giving off energy, and at the same time it made use of Maxwell's equations, which imply that an accelerated electron (like the one revolving around the kernel) has to give off energy. The theory, so, is inconsistent. Nevertheless nobody claimed arbitrary things like the electron receiving energy and so on.
Weak paraconsistency tries to model these cases.
Weak paraconsistency does *not* claim that the logic of completed science has to be a paraconsistent one.

Strong Paraconsistency

The strong paraconsistent approach says that contradictions are not things that happen, but can be avoided. According to strong paraconsistency (some) contradictions are unavoidable. Some contradictions can even be proven. Some contradictions, therefore, have to be considered as being *true*!
Dialetheism is the claim that there are true contradictions (called "dialetheias" by Routley and Priest).
Of course, dialetheism is the philosophically more controversial and challenging position. Its justification needs even closer scrutiny than that of weak paraconsistency. Its main motivations are the idea of semantic closure and universality (including mostly the adherence to naïve set theory).
Note that weak and strong paraconsistency can agree widely on the logics under investigation, since both try to avoid explosion. Their difference concerns the (ultimate) *truth* of contradictions.
If dialetheism claims that some contradictions can be proven and weak paraconsistency denies the (ultimate) truth of contradictions that can only mean that weak paraconsistency has to reject the systems and logics that allow these proofs.
That might mean that weak paraconsistency has the shortcomings of *both* worlds: Having neither the strength of **FOL** nor semantic universality (or other benefits of dialetheism).
Dialetheism, on the other hand, has to do some serious explanation *how* it can be that there are true contradictions and whether this implies that there

are inconsistent *objects* (apart from sentences which are true and false at the same time)!

This introduction sides with dialetheism and tries to impart some understanding of its motivations, working and use.

The Prehistory and History of Paraconsistency

Philosophers and scientists contradict each other and themselves quite often, but that does not make them dialetheists or adherents of PL.

Some philosophers have countenanced views sympathetic to the occurrence of true contradictions, for example Cusanus with respect to the properties of God. Hegel is famous for the ubiquity of contradictions in his writings, contradictions in human thought or world history. Meinong proposes an ontology of inconsistent objects.

The mere support of true contradictions does not entail that the corresponding philosophers think there is a *logic* of contradictions.

Hegel might be considered an exception in as much as his dialectic in his main work *Die Wissenschaft der Logik* [The Science of Logic] is supposed to proceed by developing and cancelling contradictions. Hegel, however, did not know much logic. The dialectic proceeds as a "logic" of concepts. Even under adherents of Hegel it is still unclear how it really proceeds, and whether there is a general method present that could in principle be formalized.

The history of paraconsistency begins with those who really develop logical systems that deal with the occurrence of contradictions.

The earliest work are some articles by Vasilev (about 1910) where he proposes a syllogism allowing for S to be P and non-P. This might be true, according to Vasilev, in some imaginated, but not in the real world. Jaskowski in 1948 published a first paper on the logic of discussions ("Discursive Logic"). In a discussion people may contradict each other. Someone taking down notes cannot simply build the conjunction of everything said, since this would often result in $A \wedge \neg A$. Jaskowski developed a logic that takes as given what each speaker says without ending in triviality [see Chap. 3].

Da Costa in the 1960s developed a new type of inconsistency tolerant logics. Ansenjo did related work in 1954. [Chap. 8 deals with them.]

The first system of Relevant Logic was given by Orlov in 1929. Relevant Logic as we know it was developed in the USA and in Australia by Anderson, Belnap, Dunn, Routley, Meyer et. al. in the 1960s [see Chap. 5, but many systems here are Relevant Logics].

The Present of Paraconsistency

Today paraconsistency is a rapidly developing field of non-standard logic. Three World Conferences on Paraconsistency, several readers and a plenitude of papers are witness to that.

There are three main camps of paraconsistent logic and a lot of work not within exactly one of these:

• the Brazilian approach related to the work of Newton Da Costa and championed by Walter Carnielli and his co-workers [see Chap. 8];
• the Adaptive approach championed in Ghent by Diderik Batens and his team [see Chap.7];
• the Relevant approach and his relatives championed by the co-authors of Richard Routley (Sylvan): Ross Brady, Robert Meyer, and especially Graham Priest, who for the wider philosophical audience has become *the* author/speaker of the field [see Chap. 4 – 6].

Within an introductory text it is difficult to do justice to all recent developments and ideas, but it may be hoped that some are covered and the rest at least require covering the ground presented here.

Further Reading

The whole book draws heavily in many chapters on the following resources:

• Bremer, Manuel. *Wahre Widersprüche.* Eine Einführung in die Parakonsistente Logik. Sankt Augustin, 1998.
• Graham Priest's books and papers; I especially recommend: *In Contradiction.* A Study of the Transconsistent. Dordrecht, 1987. A book with Priest's perspective on the history of paraconsistency is (Priest 1995).
• Priest, Graham/Routley, Richard. *On Paraconsistency.* Research Report 13. Australian National University 1983; a newer concise overview from Priest's perspective is: Priest, Graham. "Paraconsistent Logic", in: Gabbay, D./Guenthner, F. (Eds.) *Handbook of Philosophical Logic.* 2nd Edition.
• On the history of paraconsistency also consult these resources; on Hegel see (Bremer 1998, Chap. 6.1); on Vasiliev (Bazhanov 1998).
• For some background on the different fields of philosophical logic and formal semantics we touch upon on the way an excellent help are the essays in: Goble, Lou (Ed.) *The Blackwell Guide to Philosophical Logic.* Oxford, 2001.

2 | Semantic Closure

For the weak paraconsistent program the mere occurrence of inconsistency and inconsistent theories is enough as a motivation. But what is the motivation and justification of the strong paraconsistent program? The (accidental) occurrence of inconsistencies is certainly not enough to believe in true contradictions. The main motivation for strong paraconsistency (dialetheism) is *universality* as a feature of language and cognition.

Universality means that we are aiming at – and supposedly capable of – a theory of, say, language *in general*, that is not just of this or that language or languages of this or that formal structure. And this theory is expressed in language, so that at least some language can be its own meta-language (with respect to all interesting properties of that language, semantics included).

Universality means as well that we use fundamental concepts like "set" unrestricted (i.e. not only for sets of some sort, given in sets of another kind). That means there is a universal set corresponding to "set".

Syntactic Closure and Self-Reference

A language can talk consistently about its own *syntax*. This presupposes expressive resources to name expressions/terms of the language and to represent syntactic properties. Once a language contains a basic system of arithmetic (the system **Q**) this is feasible.

Within such a language L one can give a general structural description of what is a well-formed expression, what expressions are generalizations, and one can even define what counts as a derivation or a proof in that language. *Being provable in L* as a syntactic property of a formula can be defined within language L.

Even if there was a hierarchy of language levels in L, given that the levels have some index there are formula that consistently talk about all such indices or talk about indices that are above the level such a formula is on. Syntactic hierarchies in contrast to semantic hierarchies are not strictly downwards, even in standard logic.[4]

---

[4] There was a time Rudolf Carnap thought such syntactic descriptions were the core of philosophy; see his *Die logische Syntax der Sprache* (1933).

Semantic Closure Defined

A language L is semantically closed iff L is able to talk about its own semantics. The meanings of the terms of L can be given within L then.

If a language is semantically closed it can not only talk about its own expressions (by suitable names or quotation marks), but it can also apply semantic properties to these terms, and even to the terms that express semantic properties.

Given that a language L has names for its terms, one can build the name for an open formula "F( )", and one can then insert that very name into the open formula itself, given rise to the self-application of formulas and properties.[5]

Examples are equivalents to more intuitive expressions like

(1) Sentence number (1) is well-formed.

(2) This sentence contains five words.

(3) The third sentence displayed in this list is true.

The sentences in the examples above are often called "self-referential". There are, however different types of self-referentiality:

(a) *temporal back reference*: x refers to itself in that phase 2 of (enduring) x refers to phase 1 [Example: a talk];

(b) *partial self-referentiality*: x refers by part y of x to part z of x [Example: a name in a language L referring to another term of L];

(c) *partially mediated self-reference*: x refers by some part y of x to x as a whole and thereby also to the part y referring [Example: the expression "language" refers to the whole and thereby to itself as well];

(d) *performative self-reference*: some x refers in a process to itself such that the reference is guaranteed successful [Example: the pronoun "I" taken to mean "the one speaking now"];

(e) *total self-referentiality*: some x is structured in a way that it can only exist as this self-referential structure, and has no parts not being part of that structure [Example: traditional model of the *Ego* ("*the* I")].

Type (c) is the one we are concerned with here: Some formula refers to itself by a description/name occurring in that formula.

---

5 This is the informal content of the *Diagonalization Theorem*; cf. (Smullyan 1992), p.24; in formal contexts the naming proceeds by arithmetization.

The Liar

Given semantic closure and self-referentiality, a sentence/formula expressing some semantic property can ascribe that property to itself. (Such a sentence/formula is called a "fixed point".)
An infamous example is the Liar:

(1) Sentence (1) is false.

The Liar is a fixed point for the predicate "( ) is false", or – in some other version – of "( ) is not true".[6]
Now consider (1): If (1) is true, then (1) is false, because the general term in (1) "( ) is false" should apply to the singular term "sentence 1". If (1) is false, then (1) is true, because (1) is just saying that it is false. So we get:

$\text{True}(1) \equiv \text{False}(1)$

or given that we have a two-valued logic where "false" is just the opposite of "true":

$\text{True}(1) \equiv \neg\, \text{True}(1)$

So (1) is an *antinomy*: a sentence A where we have a proof for A and ¬A.[7] Usually this means we also have a proof of A ∧ ¬A.
As an example let's walk through the two proofs in case of the Liar: [Proof of ¬A]. If (1) is true, then (1) is false (by simple properties of being true). This is inconsistent, i.e. the assumption of (1) being true leads to inconsistency, so by the rule of Negation-Introduction (¬I) we get that (1) cannot be true
[Proof of A]. If (1) is false, then (1) is true, just saying that it is false. This is once again inconsistent, i.e. the assumption of (1) being false leads to inconsistency so by (¬I) we get that (1) cannot be false.
[Proof of A ∧ ¬A]. Taking the two proofs together by Conjunction-Introduction (∧I) we get:

(1) is true and (1) is false.

Given standard logic from "True(1) ≡ ¬True(1)" we can easily derive an explicit inconsistency "True(1) ∧ ¬True(1)":

[6] This goes back to antiquity, a Cretan saying "I am lying now."
[7] Let's call A a "paradox" just in case A is a surprising and mostly unwanted result/theorem, not necessarily an antinomy. This is just a convention of usage here, in the literature "paradox" is used in a wider and in a narrower sense at the same time.

1.<1> $True(1) \equiv \neg True(1)$	PREM
2.<1> $(True(1) \supset \neg True(1)) \wedge (\neg True(1) \supset True(1))$	Df. $\equiv$,1
3.<1> $True(1) \supset \neg True(1)$	$(\wedge E)$,2
4.<1> $\neg True(1) \supset True(1)$	$(\wedge E)$,2
5.<5> $True(1)$	PREM
6.<1,5> $\neg True(1)$	$(\supset E)$, 3, 5
7.<1> $\neg True(1)$	$(\neg I)$, $\underline{5}$, 6
8.<8> $\neg True(1)$	PREM
9.<1,8> $True(1)$	$(\supset E)$, 4, 8
10. <1> $\neg\neg True(1)$	$(\neg I)$, $\underline{8}$, 9
11.<1> $True(1)$	$(\neg E)$, 10
12.<1> $True(1) \wedge \neg True(1)$	$(\wedge I)$, 7, 11 ■

Proofs are given here often in standard Natural Deduction fashion. In (5) a premise is introduced for reduction, and discarded (written "$\underline{5}$") given the contradiction between (5) and (6). The same for (8).

The Liar is a case of bad semantic self-referentiality. There are also harmless semantically self-referential sentences, like:

(2) Sentence (2) is true.

Consider (2):
If (2) is true, then the general term "( ) is true" applies to the singular term "sentence (2)" and so (2) is true. No contradiction occurs.
If (2) is false, then (2) is not true, i.e. (in two-valued logic) (2) is false. No contradiction occurs. It seems that we can either assume (2) to be true or to be false. (2) is underdetermined in that we cannot reason from the falsehood of one of these assumptions to the truth of its opposite.
So by *fiat* we say that (2) is true, and call it "the truth-sayer".
There are more harmless semantically self-referential sentences, like

(3) Sentence (3) is meaningful.

The Liar is the basic case of bad semantic self-referentiality. It bears its badness on its sleeve. It is not hidden. Within a language that is semantically closed semantic self-reference may be hidden, however.
It need not be the case that one sentence refers to itself directly (as in the case of the Liar). There may be situations of cross-reference the result of which is a Liar-like situation. Consider:

(4) Sentence (5) is true.

(5) Sentence (4) is false.

Given that (5) refers to (4) the self-attribution of falsehood in (4) is delayed, so to speak, through (5). We get a version of the Liar. Now, however, we may not recognize it so easily. Suppose today you only utter a single statement

(6) What the pope declares today is true.

and *as a contingent matter of fact* he only says that day:

(7) Everything N.N. says today is false.

The Dialetheist's Agenda

The Liar is an antinomy. Dialetheism claims that it cannot be prevented, since a natural language is a semantically closed language. Since, furthermore, the antinomy can be proved, it has to be true.

So the dialetheist has to show three things:

(I) The contradictions can be proven in a sound non-standard logic, if we use a semantically closed language.

(II) We have to use a semantically closed language.

(III) There is no satisfactory alternative to accepting the antinomies. [i.e. the attempts to prevent them either fail or have consequences worse than dialetheism]

Convention (T)

(ad I)

To reason from the provability of an antinomy to its truth we need at least one correct/sound paraconsistent logical system. We will see several such systems in the next chapters. Besides that the reasoning about the Liar employs some properties of negation and Tarski's convention

(T) "p" is true (in L) if and only if p.

ascribing truth to the name of a sentence/statement[8] is true just in case we can use that sentence truly, i.e. it is true. This convention is not tied to a specific theory of truth, since it may be taken either as a minimal condition, a statement of correspondence or a disquotational analysis. Whatever truth is, the adequacy of (T) seems to be beyond doubt. It is neither tied to the underlying logic being 2- or many-valued.

---

8 For the discussions here there is no important difference between statements, sentences and closed formula. So whereas strictly speaking only a sentence used in an *assertoric utterance* to make a *statement* is true or false I keep to the loose common standard of talking of the truth of sentences.

(T) formulates a part of our ordinary understanding of truth. It should be part of the semantics of a semantically closed language.
Relating Convention (T) and the Liar we have for the Liar:

(8) "(1) is false" is true (in L) if and only if (1) is false.

and given that the Liar just is the sentence "(1) is false" and falsity is not truth we get:

(9) (1) is true (in L) if and only if (1) is not true.

There is room for debate how to take the "if and only if" in (T). So far we have taken it as a simple bi-conditional "≡". In many systems of paraconsistent logic it will be a stronger bi-conditional (maybe disallowing for some detachments allowed for "≡").

Negation

True contradictions are said to be sentences such that A and ¬A are true. How is that compatible with our concept of negation? How can we justify that "¬" behaving thus still expresses *negation*?
An intuitive acceptable concept of negation should support:

(MN)(i) If A is false, then the negation of A is true.
(ii) If A is true, then the negation of A is false.

These conditions seem to express the idea that the negation of a sentence A expresses the opposite of A.
Note that the two conditions are not expressed as bi-conditionals. So they do not give us *Tertium Non Datur* [nothing requires A to have a value at all in (i) or (ii)].
If "false" and "not true" are the same, then the two conditions just give us the ordinary truth table:

A	¬A
T	F
F	T

Take the Liar again, using the instance (9) of convention (T) and the two conditions on negation we can reason thus:
• Given (9) if "True(1)" is true, then "¬True(1)" is true. If "True(1)" is false, then because of (i) "¬True(1)" is true, and so, because of (9), "True(1)" is true. So: *in both cases* are "True(1)" and "¬True(1)" *both* true. That is meant by true contradictions.
• Both of them, however, are also *false* (not-true) at the same time: If "True(1)" is false, then because of (9) "¬True(1)" is false. If "True(1)" is true, then because of (ii) "¬True(1)" is false, and so is "True(1)" given (9).

That is also meant by true contradictions. Contradictions are true in as much as they are true and false at the same time.[9]

When does some connective "¬" codify negation? What does the concept of negation entail anyway?
The negation in many paraconsistent logics does separate falsity from non-truth. Nevertheless there are paraconsistent logics (e.g. **LP**) the negation of which satisfies the conditions (i) and (ii). These negations (respectively the connective "¬") can claim to capture our intuitive concept of negation. They do so at least to an significant degree; there may be other requirements on negation, but which should these be?
Some claim that *ex contradictione qoudlibet* is essential to a real negation. Then certainly many paraconsistent logics have no negation at all. But *ex contradictione qoudlibet* obviously is highly *counter*intuitive.
Some claim that certain logical truths define "real" negation, maybe *Tertium Non Datur* or negation-introduction:

$$A \supset \neg A \vdash (\neg A)$$

or maybe contraposition:

$$A \supset B, \neg B \vdash (\neg A)$$

All this, however, is controversial. Some of these theorems hold in some systems of paraconsistent logic [see also the next chapter.].

Are Natural Languages Closed?

(ad II) in the dialetheist's agenda:
The natural languages we use seem to be semantically closed. We can express the antinomies in these languages. Natural languages have the resources of naming and corresponding self-reference. Semantic properties can be expressed in natural languages. *Prima facie* natural languages, therefore, are the very paradigm of universal languages.
If somebody wants to deny this he has the burden of proof. Our ordinary conception of our language had to be seriously mistaken then! Usually the arguments against the semantic closure are based just on the antinomies.
One may further claim that neither do we speak nor do we need semantically closed languages in any science.
I will argue against this in (ad III).
Independent from that philosophy cannot restrict itself to non-universal languages. The language of philosophy has to be semantically closed.

[9] Following common usage again I will use (λ) from now on as the name of the Liar if not indicated otherwise.

Philosophy does not want to deal only with the structure or conditions of talking in some specific language or languages of some kind, but aims at a theory of the basic structures and conditions of having a language *in general*. This requires the corresponding resources to express the universal claims.

There may not be a hierarchy of languages so that we always talk in a *last* meta-language the semantic properties of which cannot be made clear, except in a further turn of the screw (a new meta-language ...).

Universal theories of meaning, truth, knowledge etc. were not to have if we can talk only from some meta-language "down" to some distinct object-language. A general statement like

(K) Knowledge is true belief.

would be not well-*formed*.

But these are the very theories that philosophy is after. And notwithstanding their lip-service to hierarchy solutions of the antinomies most philosophers propose their *general* theories of meaning, truth, belief, reference, knowledge etc. They are right to do the latter, since we have such universal concepts.

There seems to be *no* crucial difference between formal languages and natural languages with respect to the properties being of interest here (i.e. semantic and structural properties), although formal languages have no native speakers, mostly no pragmatics, no socio-linguistics ...

We can investigate and formalize the logical structures of any natural languages. That is one of the central tenets of logic and formalization.

We not only talk about properties of all (natural) languages, it seems even incoherent whether there could be two completely incommensurable languages. Such a system could never be identified as a language at all. Our concept of language, therefore, involves unity and universality. There has to be a set of properties defining what a language is. These properties are preserved in change or translation.

Elucidating these properties and making them explicit from our intuitive understanding of language(s) is the traditional understanding of (transcendental) philosophy (of language). Without semantic closure we would not be *able* to elucidate a concept that we seem to have!

Assessing the Alternatives

So I take it that we need semantic closure. No-one, but dialetheism seems to be able to deliver it. [ad (III) of the dialetheist's agenda]:

Their are two major alternatives to paraconsistent treatments of the antinomies:

(IIIa) many-valued semantics or truth-value gaps,

(IIIb) the hierarchy of semantic meta-languages (in Tarskian style).
Both fail, but for different reasons.
(IIIa)-type solutions solve some antinomies, but the linguistic resources they employ in their formal framework are sufficient to generate new versions of the antinomies.
(IIIb)-type solutions result in an outrageous pragmatic self-contradiction.
Let us turn to (IIIa) first:
It has been claimed that the problems with the antinomies show that the crucial sentence has no truth value whatsoever or some further value besides "true" and "false".
One may criticize this move as *ad hoc*: a further truth value is assumed just to avoid the antinomies. Since there are more general arguments to the failure of bivalence (arguments from referential failure, vagueness, indeterminacy) a proponent of this view can defend himself as merely applying a framework that is around to solve other problems with bivalence to the problem of the antinomies.
Antinomies, however, are no problem tied to bivalence. If the Liar sentence (λ) is taken as neither true nor false the reasoning concerning sentence (1) does not go through. That is right. The problem is that the *linguistic framework* employed to solve this antinomy is sufficiently rich to allow for new versions of the old antinomies, like the Liar.
What is a "linguistic framework"?
I take a linguistic framework to consist of both the language defined as well as its meta-linguistically expressed distinctions and semantics. Three-valuedness, for example, is part of some linguistic framework, given the interpretation of formulas in some semantics.
Antinomies can be avoided by having no logic at all. Keeping our power to infer from premises usually some distinctions are introduced to argue that the antinomies lack some crucial property or are on the wrong side of some crucial border. That is the basic outline for a "solution" to the paradox.
A general *hypothesis* against this is:

> A linguistic framework rich enough to avoid some the antinomies, generates its own versions of them.

This hypothesis is rather vague, but it can be illustrated on several versions to deal with antinomies.
The task of paraconsistent frameworks is to defuse antinomies, keep a sufficiently rich logic and not generate some "hypercontradiction".
With respect to three-valued approaches, one can introduce a *strengthened* Liar, (λ‘). If the (old) Liar (λ) is neither true nor false, it is not true. A three-valued framework has two values (say "false" and "undetermined")

opposite to "true". But now we can *say* that (λ) is not true. This gives us a strengthened Liar:

(λ‘) (λ‘) is not true.

We argue again by cases:
(a) If (λ‘) is true, then (λ‘) is not true (by convention (T), see above)
(b) If (λ‘) is false, then (λ‘) is not true, because falsity is opposed to truth, and being non-true is what (λ‘) says of itself, so (λ‘) is true.
(c) If (λ‘) is undetermined, then (λ‘) is not true, so (λ‘) is true.
Since:

(P3) Not-True(A) ≡ False(A) ∨ Undetermined(A)

we get by Dilemma [that both alternatives (b), (c) of the right side of (P3) applied to (λ‘) imply "True(λ‘)"] a *new antinomy*:

(10) True(λ‘) ≡ Not-True(λ‘)

A framework involving three truth values involves the implicit or explicit validity of some principle like (P3). Even if "Not-True" is not *introduced* as a truth-value within the semantics, the semantic framework has *the expressive power* to introduce this notion. What we do here is to re-introduce a bifurcation within the realm of the truth-values. "Not-True" works like the notion of falsity in ordinary bivalent semantics. (This forced bifurcation is always available.)
The strengthened Liar, therefore, might reside on the language level at which we can express "Not-True", and given the framework there has to be *some* such level. The only way out would be to resort to some strict separation of language levels [i.e. to type (IIIb)-solutions we argue against below].[10]
The trick introducing the strengthened Liar is independent from the number of truth-values present. Thus (IIIa)-type solutions won‘t work!

No Levels

What is wrong with the hierarchy solution [ad (IIIb)]?
The main problem is not that at first sight we cannot find these levels in ordinary language. That is a problem, since the assumption of these levels would mean that there is some hidden syntactic structure with no corresponding surface structure, although it is decisive for truth! Such an analysis would be a major revision of our understanding of our language! Nonetheless there are even deeper problems in store:
The main problem is that if there were these levels and if the theory was true, the very statement of the theory and its given explanation (speaking *in*

[10] (Kripke 1975) has ultimately done that.

general about *all* language levels) would be impossible. The hierarchy conception says we are always talking from some level in the hierarchy, and *at the same time* makes a general statement to the effect that constructing the semantics of a language (level) we just go one level up.
Let's look at the details:
Suppose we had a hierarchy of truth-predicates. Each of them has an index *i*. Ascribing truth would be like:

(11) "p" is true-at-level-n (in L).

Now if indexes are numbers, we are able to talk about them in a sufficiently rich language, able to talk about its own *syntax*. So we can built for each sentence A the expression "the-level-of-A".
Consider then the supposedly semantic available sentence:

(12) (12) is not true-at-level-of-(12).

This sentence has to occur *somewhere* in the hierarchy on pains of the inexpressibility of some truths. Let us call this level "true-12"; then "true-at-level-of-(12)" is identical to "true-12". Convention (T) applies at every level of the hierarchy for sentences of that level:

(13) True-12(A) if and only if A.

Applying (13) to (12) as a sentence at level 12 we get:

(14) True-12(12) if and only if (12).

And this yields a new antinomy:

(15) True-12(12) if and only if not true-12(12).

Being able to talk about the indexes re-introduces antinomies in the context of semantic vocabulary. The only solution to resist the argument above is to give up the assumption that (12) occurs somewhere in the hierarchy, has a level. Given that (12) could not even be formulated.
Then, however, no sentence that talks in this general fashion about indexes is possible. The following sentence would be impossible too:

(16) The truth predicate of a level n is defined at level n+1.

This sentence, however, can be expressed in natural languages, which are said to be captured. And (16) better be expressible if the theory of language levels is to be expressed at all! – If sentences like (16) were impossible the whole theory of (IIIb) would be *inexpressible itself*!
Being unable to make statements about the hierarchy in general means that we are unable to understand the basic semantic concepts at all:

Either somebody who understands terms like "meaning", "denotation", "truth" etc. is able to express the building principles of definitions at some level, but this is impossible as we have just seen with sentence (16).
Or he has to have available the *whole completed hierarchy* in his mind, but this surely is not possible given that the human mind is a finite representational system and the hierarchy being infinite.
So the hierarchy conception leaves us hanging in the air concerning our ability to understand semantic concepts at all!
The hierarchy conception says we are always talking from some level in the hierarchy, and *at the same time* makes a general statement to the effect that constructing the semantics of a language (level) we just go one level up.
This is not just a contradiction. A contradiction one might suppose is what a dialetheist is to accept anyway. The situation is worse. If the theory is true – and, of course, as an adherent of the theory you believe it to be true – something is impossible *to do*, but you just do it! Given the theory the adherents are doing something impossible in the strict sense. It is not just a miracle. Suppose you believe in God: God in His glory might choose to perform miracles to authorise His revelations. Even He, however, cannot do what is logically impossible (as the Scholastics argued). He cannot make the square round. He cannot make the hierarchy solution work. What is done by the adherent of the hierarchy solution is completely mysterious.
I call this fact the MYSTERY.
Doing the impossible seems to me even more bizarre than claiming that some contradictions are true. Even if you don't think so, the failure of the hierarchy solution is obvious: Dialetheism provides semantic closure – so it claims – at the cost of true contradictions; the hierarchy model implies either the MYSTERY or a true contradiction *and* gets nothing for that, only the absence of semantic closure!
Tarski himself has not applied his hierarchy model to natural language, he even seems to concede that "truth" for natural languages is contradictory. One should, however, try if one is a Tarskian about formal languages to apply the construction to natural languages to have universal theories about language. The problem with the MYSTERY is that this *extended* Tarskian approach does not work.
The *particularist* Tarskian approach of only defining truth for some languages at least involves natural language statements like:

(17) We define the semantics of a language in its meta-language.

Now if natural language is ultimately considered inconsistent the last meta-language of this approach is inconsistent, and what then should these adherents of consistency think about the success of its workings?

Dialetheism avoids MYSTERY at the price of accepting some true contradictions. With respect to the general hypothesis concerning the failure of other solutions to the paradoxes one may refine the hypothesis by saying that either a linguistic framework will be rich enough to trade in new paradoxes for the old, or it will employ concepts ineffable within that framework or simply excludes linguistic resources obviously present in ordinary language.

One may introduce some methodological principles:

(MT) Whatever implies MYSTERY cannot be true.

This surely is somewhat vague, but the idea should be clear. If some argument leads us back to the hierarchy (i.e. MYSTERY), there has to be something wrong with it. This in a way is *ad hoc*, but one can consider corresponding discussions as a context of discovery which logical principles of some paraconsistent systems are still too strong. To restrict (MT) we need another methodological principle:

(MR) Avoid MYSTERY at minimal costs.

This is an extension of a more general idea in constructing paraconsistent logics. The revised logic should come as close as possible to classical logic to keep as many of the theorems we like as we can get.

Liars without Semantic Expressions

As a note to the foregoing it should be mentioned that semantic closure is a *sufficient* condition for antinomies, but that it isn't a necessary condition in that sense that one can have forms of the Liar which do not use semantic concepts like "truth", "satisfies", "denotes", but *propositional quantification* and negation.

Let's take "λ" to be another name for sentence (1):

(1) $(\forall p)((\lambda \equiv p) \supset \neg p)$

Then – by the definition of "λ" – we have:

(2) $\lambda \equiv (\forall p)((\lambda \equiv p) \supset \neg p)$

From this an antinomy ensues: Inserting (1) for "p" in (1) we can detach with (2) and have the negation of (1) as well as (1).

Propositional quantification is also antinomic if coupled with truth *operators* (not just a truth *predicate*).

Questions

(Q1) Why is First Order Logic not semantically closed?

(Q2) If truth is defined in a hierarchy, why does this also apply to the other semantic concepts like *denotation* or *meaning*?

(Q3) Suppose someone says that the Liar has no third truth-value, but is not eligible for truth-value-assignment. Does this move block the strengthened Liar strategy?

Exercises

(Ex1) Often the sentence given as the Liar example is "All Cretans are liars." said by a Cretan. Why does this not work as an antinomy if there is more than one Cretan?

(Ex2) Someone introduces not a three-valued, but a five-valued semantics. What is the strengthened Liar for that semantics? How does the argument proceed?

Further Reading

• On the failure of many-valued attempts to avoid the antinomies see, for example: Brendel, Elke. *Die Wahrheit über den Lügner*. Eine philosophisch-logische Analyse der Antinomie des Lügners. Berlin/New York, 1992.

• The problems of the hierarchy are explained, for example, in Priest's *In Contradiction* and his "Semantic Closure", *Studia Logica*, 1984; see also: Weir, Alan. "Naive Set Theory is Innocent!", *Mind*, 107 (1998); Weir, however, hints at a restriction of transitivity of deduction, which is neither acceptable even for a dialetheist nor worked out [cf. Chap. 3].

• The methods of arithmetization or Gödelization and results related to that are given in: Smullyan, Raymond. *Gödel's Incompleteness Theorems*. Oxford/New York, 1992; and in: Boolos, George/Jeffrey, Richard. *Computability and Logic*. Cambridge, 3rd Ed., 1989.

• The non-semantic antinomy is a version of a problem Tarski has with quotation functions, taken from (Haack 1978, Chap.8); for the problem with operators and propositional quantification see: (Grim1993).

3 | Methodological Considerations

The paraconsistent approach – for the moment – being justified in general we have to consider in which direction our reshaping of logic should proceed.
It will not be the case that any direction will do – in short, we need:

(a) *goals* that the logic we look for should satisfy;

(b) *criteria* that the logic has to meet on its way.

The goals in (a) have prominently to include:

• avoiding Explosion (i.e. invalidating at least some forms of *ex contradictione qoudlibet*)

• being able to model semantic closure [given the discussion in Chap. 2].

The criteria in (b) may contain features of a logical system that we are not ready to give up even when going paraconsistent. Any logical system not meeting these (necessary) conditions should be disregarded. If there were no paraconsistent systems satisfying these conditions, we would have either to reconsider the criteria – but this would be a desperate measure pointing to the insufficiency of paraconsistent logics – or we would have to turn to some alternative to paraconsistency if there is any.

Irrelevant Implications

ex contradictione qoudlibet in its several versions

(1) $A \supset (\neg A \supset B)$

(2) $A \wedge \neg A \supset B$

is one of the so-called "paradoxes of material implication": sentences that are logically true, although they are highly contra-intuitive. Other examples are:

(3) $A \supset (B \supset A)$

(4) $A \supset (\neg B \vee B)$

(3) and (4) are versions of *verum ex qoudlibet sequitur*. The truth (i.e. any true sentence) is said to follow from everything (since whatever the antecedents may be, the consequence is true).
In all these examples there is no connection between the content of the antecedent and the content of the consequent. Our intuitive notion of a conditional, on the other hand, is biased in favour of some causal or semantic connection between the parts of a true conditional. Relevant

Logics (in short: "RLs") try to model a conditional connective along these lines.[11]

For a paraconsistent logic this could be a goal as well. At least Explosion as a rule [$A, \neg A \vdash B$] has to go. If *ex contradictione qoudlibet* has to go that means that something involved in its derivation in **PC** has to go:

1.$\langle 1\rangle\ p$	PREM
2.$\langle 2\rangle\ \neg p$	PREM
3.$\langle 1\rangle\ p \vee q$	($\vee$I), 1
4.$\langle 1,2\rangle\ q$	($\vee$E), 2, 3
5.$\langle 1\rangle\ \neg p \supset q$	($\supset$E), $\underline{2}$, 4
6.$\langle\rangle\ p \supset (\neg p \supset q)$	($\supset$E), $\underline{1}$, 5 ■

The last two steps derive Explosion as a theorem by conditionalization, even without them we would have Explosion as a deductive rule.

Looking at the derivation, we see that there are not many options to choose from: We have to drop

-*either* Disjunction Introduction ($\vee$I)

-*or* Disjunction Elimination/Disjunctive Syllogism ($\vee$E)

-*or* we could modify some meta-logical properties of the relation of provability, namely its transitivity, such that $A \supset A \vee B$ and (given the standard definition of "$\supset$") $A \vee B \supset (\neg A \supset B)$ hold, but $A \supset (\neg A \supset B)$ does not!

Giving up the transitivity of provability seems to be a desperate measure and an unwanted result if it was to hold of some PLs, $\vdash$. Transitivity seems to be both a fundamental ingredient of our understanding of an implication and of joining two parts of a proof. Keeping the transitivity of the conditional connective or at least the transitivity of provable implication is a criterion [in the sense of (b) above] for our target logics. So I will not consider the third alternative here, although at least one author has in fact taken that route [cf. *Further Reading*].

---

11 The problem of Irrelevance, that antecedent and consequent share no content, cannot in a paraconsistent context simply be solved by requiring that they have to share some formula (in the propositional case). Since $B \wedge \neg B \supset B$ certainly holds [by ($\wedge$E)] and fulfils the requirement, we have $A \wedge \neg A \supset B$ once we admit that all contradictions are equivalent, which is supposedly *logically true*:

$$\vdash (A \wedge \neg A \equiv B \wedge \neg B)$$

and allow for the substitution of proven equivalents! Giving up the substitutivity of proven equivalents seems to be another severe revision of our intuitive understanding of logical matters, but may be unavoidable.

Or

Concerning the contra-intuitiveness of giving up transitivity the two other options do not seem to fare better. Consider the standard truth-table of disjunction:

A	B	A∨B
T	T	T
T	F	T
F	T	T
F	F	F

Given the truth of one disjunct it certainly holds that the whole disjunction is true [that corresponds to (∨I)] and given the falsity of one disjunct the truth of the disjunction has to depend on the truth of the other disjunct [that corresponds to (∨E)].

Giving up one of these rules, therefore, seems to be revisionist with respect to the meaning of "or", one of our most fundamental connectives! And that we should not allow too easily.

Giving up (∨I) seems impossible. Once we have the truth of a sentence it will not go away if that very sentence becomes part of a disjunction. And there are only a few logics that try to do this.

[One, **ANA**, is discussed in chapter 7, but we will see that it has a very deviant semantics for "∨". Weingartner's approach (cf. Weingartner 1999) is not a logic, but a filtering of given derivability relations, and so is no help in modelling actual reasoning (i.e the derivation of the to be filtered set). Another logic that invalidates (∨I) is Bochvar's 3-valued logic (Bochvar 1939): The third value is taken as "meaningless" and this feature is inherited from a part of a complex sentence to the complex sentence. Thus Bochvar arrives at the so called Weak Kleene Tables for a 3-valued logic, in which the value "meaningless" is infectious. One can have A but not A ∨ B, since if B is meaningless, the whole compound is meaningless, and meaninglessness is, of course, no designated truth value. Bochvar's logic, however, is not even weakly paraconsistent, since it validates Explosion!]

Giving up (∨E) is, therefore, the route taken in many paraconsistent logics. Here we can really think of a counterexample *without* having to modify the semantics of "∨":

If A is a true contradiction, then by it being true it makes A∨B true, but we should not employ Disjunctive Syllogism, because by A‘s being false, we could derive any B, even a B that is false, so we had a rule with true premises and a false conclusion!

In fact even though A is false, and so, hopefully, $\neg$A true, that does not fit our description of reasoning from the falsity of one disjunct to the truth of the other: Since A is a dialetheia, A is not false simpliciter, and so that *rationale* does not apply!

$\vee$ and $\supset$

There is another problem if we give up Disjunctive Syllogism: In standard semantics the conditional connective is defined by:

(5) $p \supset q \equiv \neg p \vee q$

or at least this holds as a theorem of duality.
If that is so then giving up Disjunctive Syllogism forces one to give up

$A \supset B, A \vdash B$ [being $\neg A \vee B, \neg\neg A \vdash B$]

that is, ($\supset$E) or *Modus Ponens*!
Detachment, *Modus Ponens*, however, is once again one of the most fundamental properties (if not *the* most fundamental property) we expect of a conditional connective. A connective not fulfilling *Modus Ponens* seems to be no *conditional* at all. How can it be a conditional if given the condition we are not allowed to reason to the consequent?
Keeping *Modus Ponens* for the conditional connective is a criterion for any logic.
For the PLs giving up ($\vee$E) this means that the semantics of the (main) conditional connective cannot be given by (5), but has to be worked out *independently* of "$\vee$". So their conditional is usually not the material conditional of **PC**.

Negation Again

Paraconsistency can also informally be defined by saying that it allows for some sentence and its negation to be true. Can the negation used such be our standard negation?
This depends on what "standard" or "intuitive" negation is. If standard negation means negation in standard logic, then being standard contains validating Explosion and thus precludes paraconsistency. Negation, however, is a controversial issue in the debate about logics, the question being which conditions on a negation symbol in some logic capture our intuitive understanding of negation most adequately. If Explosion is intuitively unacceptable, then it better be not valid in a logic (at least a logic for such everyday matters).
Two minimal conditions for negation in terms of semantics are:

(MN)(i) If A is false, then the negation of A is true.
(ii) If A is true, then the negation of A is false.

This may be too much for someone who rejects *Tertium Non Datur*, but since we are concerned there mainly with paraconsistency we assume this to be not the focus of discussion.
(MN) is easily fulfilled by standard logic, since in it "false" is the same as "not true" and *Tertium Non Datur* holds. (MN), however, may be equally satisfiable by non-standard negations and non-standard semantics, especially when "false" and "not true" come apart as in paraconsistency. So besides being extensional negation should satisfy (MN).
Arguing for other *necessary conditions* for something being a negation often beg the question against paraconsistency by *defining* standard properties like Explosion into negation [e.g. (Slater 1995)]. The justification for conditions on negation should also not presuppose the absence of true contradictions or the identity of non-truths with falsity.[12]

There Has to Be a Logic

The most basic of all conditions for a PL is that we still have a logic. This means that we really have a system of derivation. Although this sounds trivial, there are two ways to deal with the antinomies that do not fulfill this criterion:

(a) an approach focussing on semantics only,
(b) an approach focussing on the pragmatic usage of standard logic.

Approach (b) although it might be interesting severs the link between our ordinary concept of argumentation and the process of deriving conclusions in some prove system. We usually expect logic to be a formalization of our ordinary ways of reasoning and arguing. And given that linkage it seems implausible that we use logic to derive some conclusions *and then* revise this set of conclusions to retract all Irrelevant deductions. A goal of formalization is that the steps taken in the logical system mirror in some systematic way our steps of reasoning. [In this manner logic proceeds

[12] (Lenzen 1998) for example argues for Contraposition in the form

$$A \vdash B \Rightarrow \neg B \vdash (\neg A)$$

to be a *necessary* condition for a "real" negation – thus excluding many paraconsistent negations –, but his justification of this definition presupposes that we reason on a meta-level with a standard negation not accepting contradictions or that B being false means B being not true in the sense of excluding B being true as well (cf. ibid, p.219), presuppositions not acceptable for a dialetheist.

preferably as a natural deduction system.] (b), therefore, seems to be a desperate measure.[13]

Rescher/Brandom

The restriction to semantics [approach (a) above] we find in Rescher and Brandom's *The Logic of Inconsistency.* They assume *normal* possible worlds in which the status of A is independent of the status of ¬A, but ¬A∧A is never the case. This means *being the case* of states of affairs is not truth-functional in "∧"! It does not hold:

(1) $[A]_{w1}=1,[B]_{w1}=1 \Rightarrow [A \wedge B]_{w1}=1$

There are, however, non-standard worlds (derivable as the union or the cut of normal worlds) in which ¬A∧A occurs, and is true. Rescher and Brandom keep **PC** as logic, but they redefine the consequence relation: It no longer holds:

(2) If $A_1 \ldots A_n \vdash B$ then $[A_1]_{w1}=1 \ldots [A_n]_{w1}=1 \Rightarrow [B]_{w1}=1$

i.e. a syntactic conclusion of a premise set need not be true in a world although all the premises are true; instead of that we have only:

(3) If $A_1 \ldots A_n \vdash B$ then $[A_1 \wedge \ldots A_n]_{w1}=1 \Rightarrow [B]_{w1}=1$.

Now, in normal worlds (those worlds we may find ourselves in) the conjunction on the right hand side of (3) cannot be true if some A_j is the negation of A_i, so Explosion can be avoided.

The non-standard worlds, however, contain, every sentence of the language. They are trivial! The non triviality of standard worlds is only kept, since (1) fails. That means that (∧I) fails!

In their semantics even *Modus Ponens* is invalid. Take a world w_3 to be the union of the worlds w_1 and w_2 where we have:

(4) $[A]_{w1} = 1, [B]_{w1} = 0, [\neg A]_{w2} = 1, [B]_{w2} = 0$.

In w_3 we have that A and ¬A are true, and so is ¬A∨B (i.e. A⊃B), but B is false, since B is false both in w_1 and w_2. So we have a counterexample to *Modus Ponens*.

This approach, therefore, is unsatisfactory on several accounts:

- The truth-functionality of the basic connective "∧" is given up.
- The conditional connective does not obey *Modus Ponens*.
- We have no method to deal with the possibility that our world is an inconsistent world; all sentences would be *derivable* then, although we

[13] Schurz (1991) goes that way by stating that reasoning is not to be identified with logic, but with "logic + relevance", relevance being modelled as a filtering of **FOL**-inference, i.e. being introduced *after deriving conclusions.*

could – somehow – turn to semantics to see which of these are "really" derivable. Why use logic then at all?

• Furthermore – as Rescher and Brandom admit – the strengthened Liar can be introduced within their framework (cf. Rescher/Brandom 1980, p.34).

Criteria

As we said we need some goals and criteria to assess paraconsistent logics:
I. Avoiding Explosion and its relatives (otherwise the logic is not paraconsistent at all, unable to separate inconsistency from triviality). This we call the "Weak Anti-Triviality Condition".
II. Any logic needs a conditional connective which has *Modus Ponens* as a rule. This we call the "Modus Ponens Condition".
III. The other usual connectives (like negation, conjunction or disjunction) may not be redefined in a way which is at least as implausible as the paradoxes of material implication. This we call the "Extensionality Condition". Dualities like *DeMorgan* should hold true.
IV. Rules of deduction we commonly associate with the conditional connective (or the extensional connectives in [III]) are not be given up lightly (for example the transitivity of that connective). This we call the "Minimal Damage Condition". It allows of degrees of meeting it.
V. Naïve Semantics and Naïve Set Theory should be non-trivial given the logic in question. That is the main goal of dialetheism. This is called the "Strong Anti-Triviality Condition".

The "strong anti-triviality condition" is philosophically justified by the arguments concerning semantic closure. We can refine this condition by explicitly stating which formula or rules should be avoided. This refinement is due to Curry's Paradox.
Curry's Paradox comes in several versions. They show that given the validity of some formula Naïve Semantics and Naïve Set Theory are trivial.
Let us consider two versions. Both use the usual conditional and bi-conditional, but the paradox also holds for strict implication. "( ) is true" is used as a predicate, but the paradox also holds if "True( )" is taken as a sentential operator.
Define (A) as the sentence which states that if this sentence is true, then B is true:

$$(A) = True(A) \supset B$$

A semantically closed language has to contain a sentence like (A). By convention (T) we have

(1) $\text{True}(A) \equiv \text{True}(A) \supset B$

Now Curry's Paradox enfolds. A logical truth ("Absorption") for "$\supset$" is:

(2) $(A \supset (A \supset B)) \supset (A \supset B)$

Since (1) from left to right is an implication we get from (1) and (2):

(3) $\text{True}(A) \supset B$

Taking (1) from right to left this gives us:

(4) $\text{True}(A)$

and now with *Modus Ponens* we get with (3)

(5) B

where B is any sentence whatsoever! Since – given the *Modus Ponens* Condition – we won't give up *Modus Ponens*, we have to give up Absorption as a valid formula (that is: to fulfil the "strong anti-triviality condition" the logic we choose has to invalidate Absorption).
The second version also starts from sentence (A) and convention (T):

(1) $\text{True}(A) \equiv \text{True}(A) \supset B$

We have as a logical truths:

(2) $A \wedge (A \supset B) \supset B$

as an instance we have

(3) $\text{True}(A) \wedge (\text{True}(A) \supset B) \supset B$

We can now substitute equivalents, given (1), and get:

(4) $(\text{True}(A) \supset B) \wedge (\text{True}(A) \supset B) \supset B$

by simplification of a conjunction we get:

(5) $(\text{True}(A) \supset B) \supset B$

Now the left side of (5) just is A and by (1) and transitivity we get:

(6) $\text{True}(A) \supset B$

and with (1) again from right to left we get:

(7) $\text{True}(A)$

and with *Modus Ponens* (6), (7) finally:

(8) B

In the second version we derive any sentence B whatsoever by using some seemingly innocent means of deduction:

• transitivity of the conditional connective we won't give up (see the Minimal Damage Condition); the same holds for the substitution of provably equivalents (as the two formulas are given the definition);
• *Modus Ponens* as a rule we won't give up because of the corresponding condition;
• simplification of conjunction we cannot give up without violating the Extensionality Condition of keeping ordinary conjunction.
The only possible culprit here is, therefore, the *Modus Ponens Theorem*:

(MPT) $A \wedge (A \supset B) \supset B$

As with the first version this leads to a refinement of the "strong anti-triviality condition".[14]

In the light of the Curry Paradoxes we get into trouble if the four following conditions are met simultaneously:

1. Convention (T) and/or Naïve Comprehension hold.
2. Absorption as theorem: $(A\supset(A\supset B))\supset(A\supset B)$
   or Absorption as a rule: $A\supset(A\supset B)\vdash(A\supset B)$
   or the theorem version of *Modus Ponens* and furthermore *either* $\vdash(A\wedge A\equiv A)$ *or* $\vdash(A\wedge A\supset B)\Rightarrow\vdash(A\supset B)$
3. Closure under substitution of proven equivalents
   or $\vdash(B\equiv A), \vdash(B\supset C)\Rightarrow\vdash(A\supset C)$
   and $\vdash(B\equiv A), \vdash B\Rightarrow\vdash A$
   or $\vdash(C\wedge A)\Rightarrow\vdash A\ \&\ \vdash C$
   or $\vdash(B\equiv A), \vdash(C\wedge A\supset D)\Rightarrow\vdash(C\wedge B\supset D)$
4. Closure under *Modus Ponens*.

Property 4 cannot be given up because of the *Modus Ponens* condition. Property 1 cannot be given up in light of the aims of paraconsistency. Further on property 3 should not be given up lightly, since substitution of proven equivalents is a basic operation. Simplification of a conjunction is a basic property of conjunction. *Therefore* Absorption in both its forms and the *Modus Ponens* theorem have to go (blocking all three disjuncts in point 2).

[14] There might be more versions of Curry's Paradox; but – fortunately – no others are known. (Smiley 1993) tries to give another version, but he uses rules like contraposition that need not be paraconsistently valid, and uses a principle for the provability predicate that looks like Disjunctive Syllogism; and for a dialetheist it needn't be provable that not both A and ¬A are provable.

Some Failures

Judging from the list of criteria given some paraconsistent approaches are failures (whatever else their worth for pure logical investigations may be). One should stress here that there are at least two motivations to do logic: (a) the philosophical one, (b) the pure logical one.

(ad a)

We follow here both philosophical and logical aims, that is the whole point of having the set of criteria to be met; these criteria articulate philosophical goals (like semantic closure) and methodological aims (like keeping close to our ordinary intuitions).

(ad b)

Logics can be studied from a purely abstract point of view to see which systems are possible, tenable, and how they are related to each other. The systems may be smooth, but of no immediate use. There is nothing wrong about this, it just is not *philosophical* logic proper.

The approaches we look at are selected either because they are prominent, even if they do not comply with the criteria given, or because they are promising attempts to develop PLs fulfilling the criteria (some versions of them may still not satisfy the criteria).

Jaskowski Systems

Jaskowski was a pioneer of paraconsistency. His logic was thought to deal with drawing conclusions from a debate where several people have different opinions on a matter and so contradict each other. Although he did not see this system as a general PL, we will do him here some injustice – for methodological reasons only – to give an example of an approach that does not meet the criteria developed.

The logic is a modal logic. Each possible world represents a speaker and what she asserts (as true). Some sentence A is true in a model *M* if there is at least one speaker‘s world in which A is true:

(1) $M \vDash_d A \Leftrightarrow$ there is w in M, such that $w \vDash_d A$

Consequence and validity are defined accordingly:

(2) $\vDash_d A \Leftrightarrow (\forall M)(M \vDash_d A)$

(3) $\Gamma \vDash_d A \Leftrightarrow (\forall M)((\exists B \in \Gamma) \neg(M \vDash_d B) \vee (M \vDash_d A))$

A is a consequence of Γ iff either not all premises are true or A is true. Note that the premises are true iff they are true in *one* world of M.

The valid sentences of Jaskowski‘s system are the theses of the modal logic **S5** [cf. Jaskowski (1969)]:

$$\vdash_d A \Leftrightarrow \vdash_{S5} A$$

So *all* Irrelevant theses (like the paradoxes of strict implication) are valid! To avoid Explosion it must not be valid:

(*4) $\{A, \neg A\} \vDash_d B$

If two people contradict each other in a debate that doesn't mean that they now believe everything. That two contradictories are held true in a debate does neither imply that there is a single speaker who believes both nor that the debating group believes their conjunction. So it has to be invalid:

(*5) $\{A, B\} \vDash_d (A \wedge B)$

($\wedge$I) has to be rejected! Therefore this type of logic is called "non adjunctive". This is a severe violation of the Extensionality Condition.
In fact there is *no* recursive truth condition Ψ for "$\wedge$" such that

(*6) $M \vDash_d (A \wedge B) \Leftrightarrow \Psi(M \vDash_d A, M \vDash_d B)$

since in a real debate *some* sentences are joint and *some* are not, i.e. we can have in a model *M:*

$M \vDash_d A$, $M \vDash_d B$, $M \vDash_d C$, $M \vDash_d (A \wedge B)$, and *not* $M \vDash_d (A \wedge C)$.

Rejecting ($\wedge$I), however, does not make sense in modelling a debate either: Sometimes it is useful to assert which contradictions (between speakers) have arisen in a debate, and what follows from *that.*
Even though Explosion in the form of (*4) is blocked, Explosion in the form $\{A \wedge \neg A\} \vDash_d B$ is valid given that all S5-thesis and *Modus Ponens* hold. Jaskowski, therefore, introduced a discussive implication:

(7) $A \supset_d B \overset{\text{def}}{=} \Diamond A \supset B$

This implication fulfils the *Modus Ponens* Condition, since in system **S5** we have

(8) $A \supset \Diamond A$

But because of (8) the fact obtains that any sentence generated from a tautology of **PC** by substituting "$\supset_d$" for "$\supset$" is valid in Jaskowski's system (including Absorption). This brings with it the violation of the Strong Anti-Triviality Condition.
So it seems not to be too easy to develop some paraconsistent logic which satisfies all the criteria given.

Questions

(Q1) That $A \supset \Diamond A$ secures the obtaining of the usual detachment conditions in Jaskowski's system holds only if we keep another property of the conditional. Which one?

(Q2) The sentence "$p \wedge (p \supset q) \supset q$" is called *Modus Ponens Theorem*. Is that a good name?

(Q3) If one was to introduce a new intensional conjunction into Jaskowski's system, a conjunction which satisfies ($\wedge$I), why would this step still result in a system that violates the Extensionality Condition? (Think of the relation between the connectives.)

Further Reading

• On giving up transitivity of provable implication see: Tennant, Neil. *Anti-Realism and Logic*. Oxford, 1987. On Tennants work see (Bremer 1998, pp.59-66) and on the incompleteness of Tennant's system and the meta-logical validity of Explosion see (Milne 1996).

• The purely semantic approach is followed in Rescher, N./Brandom, R. *The Logic of Inconsistency*. Oxford, 1980.

• On Jaskowski see: Urchs, Max. "Discursive Logic: Towards a Logic of Rational Discourse", *Studia Logica*, 54 (1995), pp. 231-49, and Urchs, Max. "On the Role of Adjunction in Para(in)consistent Logic", in: (Carnielli/Coniglio/D'Ottavanio 2002), pp. 487-500. [Urchs defends the Jaskowski approach as one being unjustifiably "bashed" within the PL community. The present chapter might be considered one more instance of that bashing – the only question is, in the light of which criteria the system is rejected; in other contexts the criticism employed here may not apply.]

4 | LP and Relatives

Graham Priest is certainly the philosopher most widely known as a champion of paraconsistent logic and dialetheism. He has written several books and quite many papers on almost all aspects of paraconsistency.
In one of his earliest papers on the subject he introduces the "Logic of Paradox" (**LP**). This chapter is concerned with this system and some extensions and refinements of it.
Priest also has introduced other systems [Chap. 6 will deal with one version of one of them], but often talks in his work of "the" logic of paraconsistency, especially when arguing against critics, to claim that some theorems don't hold there. Often he refers to **LP** then. **LP**, however, fails on the *Modus Ponens* Condition! Priest sometimes then uses a "logic" that has no conditional connective at all! **LP** so needs – as Priest says as well – a supplementation by a Relevant conditional. The logic presented in this chapter should, therefore, be seen as to be extended by a Relevant conditional (both in its syntax as well as in its semantics, that then will no longer be extensional).
LP will be an ingredient in Chap. 7, Chap. 14 and Chap. 20 as well.

Quantification

The problems with standard-logic that we encountered arose on the level of propositional logic. The solutions offered in Relevant or other paraconsistent logics, therefore, are formulated foremost at this level. There is nothing wrong with standard quantificational logic, at least its problems have – usually – nothing to do with paraconsistency. The debate about non-referring proper *names*, for example, is independent from the debate on paraconsistency. To keep things simple, and not to engage in other debates, the paraconsistent propositional systems can be extended by a standard quantificational logic (as well, of course, as by your favourite non-standard quantificational logic). So we extend, e.g., **LP** to **QLP**.
One important exception to this general remark is the paraconsistent theory of impossible objects in the tradition of Meinong, taken up by Routley and others. Discussing a non-standard ontology will require a non-standard quantificational theory. [see Chap. 17; in the last chapter we consider also a combination of paraconsistency and Free Logic.]

Contradictions in LP

Contradictions in **LP** are sentences that are both true and false.
That means that the evaluation function v in **LP** semantics assigns to a sentence either $\{0\}$ (being false), or $\{1\}$ (being true), or $\{0,1\}$ (being true and false, i.e. a contradiction).[15]
The negation of a contradiction is true, since the contradiction is false (not only true). So in case of A being a contradiction A has the set of truth values $\{0,1\}$ and A and $\neg$A are both true.
Note: To avoid confusions from now on *simply true* sentences are sentences that are true and not false, whereas true sentences might be sentences that are true and false, i.e. contradictions. The same for *simply false*.

Negation in LP

Negation in **LP** has the semantic rule:

$$(\text{LP}\neg)\quad \text{(i)}\quad 1\in v(\neg A) \Leftrightarrow 0\in v(A)$$
$$\text{(ii)}\quad 0\in v(\neg A) \Leftrightarrow 1\in v(A)$$

Negation in LP not only fulfils the two conditions on an intuitive acceptable negation from Chapter 2, (i) is the standard clause for negation. (ii) supplements it for the case of contradictions: a contradiction A has $0\in v(A)$, so by (i) $1\in v(\neg A)$; but we also have to have that $\neg$A is a contradiction (any negation of a contradiction is a contradiction itself, since a contradiction is also true), i.e. $0\in v(\neg A)$, which we do not get by (i), since we cannot reason from the negation of the right hand side of (i) in case of a contradiction; thus we need (ii).
LP negation is an extension of standard negation. One can say:

(i') $\neg$A is at least true, if A is at least false.

(ii') $\neg$A is at least false, if A is at least true.

Not only negation, but all connectives are treated extensionally, thus meeting the Extensionality Condition.
With negation and conjunction the other connectives are definable. The LP conjunction has the rule:

$$(\text{LP}\wedge)\quad \text{(i)}\quad 1\in v(A\wedge B) \Leftrightarrow 1\in v(A) \text{ and } 1\in v(B)$$
$$\text{(ii)}\quad 0\in v(A\wedge B) \Leftrightarrow 0\in v(A) \text{ or } 0\in v(B)$$

---

[15] Later we shall see that we really need an evaluation *relation* instead of an evaluation function v to avoid hypercontradictions [see Chap. 16]. To keep things simple we avoid these complications here.

For a more concise overview we can give **LP** truth tables:

A	B	A ∧ B	A ∨ B	¬A	A ⊃ B	A ≡ B
1	1	1	1	0	1	1
1	0	0	1	0	0	0
1	0,1	0,1	1	0	0,1	0,1
0	1	0	1	1	1	0
0	0	0	0	1	1	1
0	0,1	0,1	0,1	1	1	0,1
0,1	1	0,1	1	0,1	1	0,1
0,1	0	0	0,1	0,1	0,1	0,1
0,1	0,1	0,1	0,1	0,1	0,1	0,1

For the connectives we get:
- The negation of a contradiction is a contradiction.
- A conjunction is simply true if both conjuncts are true only.
- A conjunction of true sentence with a contradiction is a contradiction.
- A disjunction is simply false if both disjuncts are simply false.
- One disjunct being simply true makes the disjunction simply true.
- The conditional is simply false only if a simply true antecedent has a simply false consequent [this corresponds to standard understanding].
- A conditional with a simply false antecedent is simply true.
- A conditional with a simply true consequent is simply true.

On first sight the **LP** truth tables look like the truth table of a 3-valued logic with "0,1" being the third value. Compare the truth tables of Lukasiewicz's 3-valued logic (with a 3rd value "indet(erminate)").[16]

Designated Values

The truth tables correspond to each other (take "indet" for "0,1").
But Lukasiewicz's logic is a restriction of standard logic in which, for example, Excluded Middle (A ∨ ¬A) fails, which **LP** will preserve.
How is that possible?
A tautology is a sentence which under any evaluation has a *designated* truth value. In standard logic the designated truth value is truth (designated

16 Lukasiewicz's work, incidently, started with his exploration of Aristotle's defense of (LNC) and the possibility of a non-Aristotelian logic; see (Raspa 1999).

by "1"), so that a tautology is a sentence the columns of which in a truth table has 1s only. A tautology is a sentence that is true always.

A	B	A ∧ B	A ∨ B	¬A	A ⊃ B	A ≡ B
1	1	1	1	0	1	1
1	0	0	1	0	0	0
1	indet	indet	1	0	indet	Indet
0	1	0	1	1	1	0
0	0	0	0	1	1	1
0	indet	indet	indet	1	1	indet
indet	1	indet	1	indet	1	indet
indet	0	0	indet	indet	indet	indet
indet	indet	indet	indet	indet	indet	indet

Lukasiewicz's Truth Tables

"indet" is no designated value in Lukasiewicz's semantics, since a sentence that is indeterminate need not be true. Therefore A ∨ ¬A fails: A being indeterminate makes ¬A indeterminate, and a disjunction of two indeterminate sentences is indeterminate, thus not true, thus the column of A ∨ ¬A has a line with a non-designated truth value.
In **LP** on the other hand we can point out that a tautology is a sentence that is always true. A contradictory sentence is *true* nevertheless, thus a sentence which has a line with "0,1" in its column still has a "1" in that very line. "0,1" is a designated truth value in **LP**. So A ∨ ¬A holds.

LP Validity

Taking the set of designated truth values to be {{1},{0,1}} we can define validity and consequence:

(LPV) $\vDash_{LP}A \Leftrightarrow (\forall v)(1 \in v(A))$

A sentence is LP-valid iff it is at least true in all evaluations.

(LPC) $\Gamma\vDash_{LP}A \Leftrightarrow (\forall v)(1 \in v(A) \vee (\exists B \in \Gamma)(\neg(1 \in v(B)))$

Sentence A is a LP-consequence of the premise set Γ iff it is either true or some sentence in Γ is simply false.
From this we get a simple meta-theorem:

(LPMT1) **LP** is an extension of **PC**.

Justification: By (LPV) at most more sentence may receive a designated truth value, all PC-tautologies are tautologies still.

Tautologies can be proven in **LP** by doing the truth table of a formula. As in **PC** truth table provide a decision procedure for (propositional) **LP**. The existence of the decision procedure proves (some kind of) completeness of **LP**, since any tautology can be found thus.

(LPMT2) **LP** is complete.

Universal Satisfiability

We should note a further peculiarity of taking both $\{1\}$ and $\{0,1\}$ as designated values:
We can no longer say – as we do in standard logic – that $A \vDash B$ just in case $\{A, \neg B\}$ is *unsatisfiable*, respectively that $A \nvDash B$ if $\{A, \neg B\}$ is *satisfiable*.
Indeed $\{A, \neg A\}$ is satisfiable, and we have $\vDash_{LP}(A \supset A)$.
Furthermore we can even have an LP-evaluation that interprets any atomic sentence as $\{0,1\}$ and thus evaluates every sentence as $\{0,1\}$.
This gives – since we can have such an interpretation for any set you like – the meta-theorem:

(LPMT3) There are no unsatisfiable sets of sentences in **LP.**

Truth Table Example

As an example of doing truth tables in **LP** we show that the usual dual of material implication and disjunction holds:

(LPT1) $\neg p \vee q \equiv p \supset q$We can do an evaluation in the usal manner:

p	q	¬p	∨	q	p	⊃	q
1	1	0	1			1	
1	0	0	0			0	
1	0,1	0	0,1			0,1	
0	1	1	1			1	
0	0	1	1			1	
0	0,1	1	1			1	
0,1	1	0,1	1			1	
0,1	0	0,1	0,1			0,1	
0,1	0,1	0,1	0,1			0,1	

Comparing the two columns beneath the main connective of "$\neg p \vee q$" and "$p \supset q$" we see that they coincide, so the two formula are logically equivalent.

Expressing Truth Values within LP

For later purposes [in this chapter and chapter 20] and as an interesting sideline we can express some of the semantic properties of LP-sentences with operators on object-language sentences.
Let ΔA be the sentence saying that A is simply true. Let ∇A be the sentence saying that A is simply false. TA says that A is true. FA says that A is false. °A says that A is not contradictory. •A says that A is contradictory. We can define these operators by truth tables:

A	TA	ΔA	FA	∇A	°A	•A
1	1	1	0	0	1	0
0	0	0	1	1	1	0
0,1	1	0	1	0	0	1

To these truth table definitions correspond obvious definitions of the operators in terms of each other, like:

$$\nabla A \overset{def}{\equiv} \Delta\neg A$$
$$°A \overset{def}{\equiv} \Delta A \vee \nabla A$$
$$\bullet A \overset{def}{\equiv} \neg °A$$

We could *extend* the language of **LP** to include these monadic operators.
In this chapter we only will use these operators in the decision procedure for **LP** and the semi-decision procedure for **LPQ**.
Note that all these operators are bivalent! In the light of our intended interpretation of them this means that making a statement about the truth value(s) of a sentence results never in a sentence that evaluates to {0,1}, i.e. is contradictory. If we added these operators to **LP** (to gain the extended language **LPe,** which also is an extension of **PC**) the metatheorem (LPMT3) would no longer be valid: Just consider {∇A, ΔA}.
Expressing semantic properties with these operators within a given PL will be the one major objective in the chapter on Da Costa-systems.

LP Standard Theorems and Rules

From (LPMT1) one might follow that **LP** is Irrelevant since it keeps all standard tautologies. **LP** keeps, for example:

(1) $p \wedge (p \supset q) \supset q$ [*Modus Ponens* Theorem]

(2) $(p \supset (p \supset q)) \supset (p \supset q)$ [Absorption Theorem]

The validity of (2) seems to endanger the Strong Anti-Triviality Condition. But the situation may be even worse, since LP has

(3) $p \wedge \neg p \supset q$

With sentence (3) even the Weak Anti-Triviality Condition seems to be violated.
One has to distinguish however, the validity of sentences, for which (LPMT1) holds, from the validity of a consequence relation. Many standard consequences do not hold in **LP**. "$\models_{LP}$" does not mirror the conditional or logical true conditionals.
Valid are the following consequence relations:

$A \models_{LP} A \vee B$

$A, B \models_{LP} A \wedge B$

$A \supset B \models_{LP} \neg B \supset \neg A$

$\neg\neg B \models_{LP} B$

$A \wedge B \models_{LP} A$

$(A \supset (C \supset B)) \models_{LP} (C \supset (A \supset B))$

So Contraposition, Negation-Elimination, Permutation, Addition, Conjunction-Introduction and -Elimination are all LP-consequences.
From chapter 3 we already know that there is a counterexample to Disjunctive Syllogism if one has true contradictions and standard negation. So:

$\neg A, A \vee B \not\models_{LP} B$

Other non-consequences of **LP** are:

$\neg A \wedge A \not\models_{LP} B$	[Explosion, *ex contradictione qoudlibet*]
$A \supset B, B \supset C \not\models_{LP} A \supset C$	[Transitivity of "$\supset$"]
$A, A \supset B \not\models_{LP} B$	[*Modus Ponens*]
$A \supset B, \neg B \not\models_{LP} \neg A$	[*Modus Tollens*]
$A \supset B \wedge \neg B \not\models_{LP} \neg A$	[Negation-Introduction]

The non-validity of Explosion ensures **LP** satisfying the Weak Anti-Triviality Condition, making **LP** paraconsistent. But this and the satisfaction of Strong Anti-Triviality depends on the non-validity of *Modus Ponens*. So **LP** fails on the Modus Ponens Condition, and – Transitivity also being not valid – with respect to "$\supset$" on the Minimal Damage Condition. **LP** has *no* acceptable conditional connective at all!
Taking **LP** as the logic of paraconsistency, therefore, requires that we supplement **LP** with a real conditional connective. [Keep this in mind for Chap. 5 where you might chose your favourite "$\rightarrow$" Relevant axioms.]

Testing for LP-Consequences

Using truth-tables we can establish all LP-theorems. Can we also establish all true LP-consequences? So far we have given no decision procedure to establish which consequence relationships hold in LP.
In **LP** the Deduction Theorem holds:

(LPMT4) $A_1 \ldots A_n \vDash_{LP} B \Rightarrow A_1 \ldots A_{n-1} \vDash_{LP} A_n \supset B$

Justification: If the antecedent of (LPMT4) is true (i.e. the consequence relationship holds), $A_1 \ldots A_n$ and B are each (at least) true; so by the truth table of "$\supset$" $A_n \supset B$ is (at least) true, so again the consequence relationship in the consequent of the theorem holds.
Formalizing an argument we can employ the Deduction Theorem to frame it as a conditional. We can test this conditional by the truth-table method. If the conditional is not logically true, the consequence relationship does not obtain: We have a *negative test* for consequences. We have no *positive test* for consequences. [Taking the validity of the built conditional as such a test would be affirming the consequent with respect to (LPMT4).]

LP-Trees

Using truth-tables can be tiresome. Using trees as a decision procedure leads quicker to results. Anthony Bloesch developed a tree procedure for **LP**, which can be extended to quantificational **LP**.
We use the statements expressing semantic properties in this procedure: TA, FA, ΔA, ∇A. We can say of these which are incompatible:

TA	∇A
FA	ΔA
∇A	ΔA

∇A and ΔA are not contradictories, but incompatible. The other two oppositions are contradictories.
Trees in general are objects that look like bottom up tress: the starting point is the *root*, points in general are called *nodes*, points which are connected are said to be on the same *branch*, nodes that are the last in a branch are called *leaves*. A branch extend as a series of nodes from the root to one leave. So a prototypical tree looks like that:

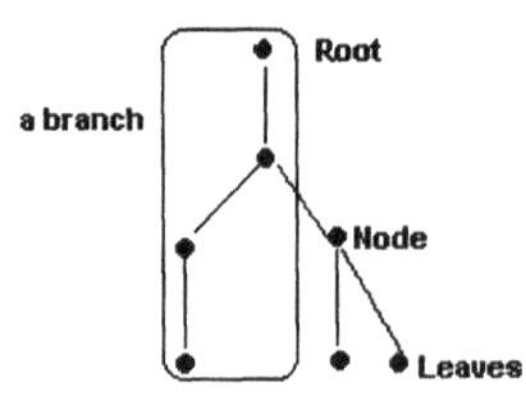

Trees provide a decisions procedure (in the propositional case) or a semi-decision procedure (giving the valid sentences in the quantificational case) by decorating the nodes with sentences and stepwise decreasing the syntactic complexity of a sentence. To do this we need (a) some general definitions of *closed* trees or branches relating to validity, and (b) specific rules for the logical vocabulary.

(LPB1) A branch of a tree is *satisfiable* iff all sentences on this branch can get a designated truth value in some interpretation v.

This could also be expressed in terms of incompatible truth values:

(LPB1') A branch of a tree is *satisfiable* iff no sentence on it has to be assigned incompatible truth values by the rules.

(LPB2) A branch that is not satisfiable is *closed.*

(LPB3) A tree is satisfiable if at least one branch is satisfiable.

(LPB4) A tree is closed iff all its branches are closed.

Trees are an indirect procedure: Given some supposed consequence relation $\Gamma \vDash A$ the root is decorated with TB for all $B \in \Gamma$ and ∇A; then the rules are employed. We get a tree for $\Gamma \vDash A$. In case of a supposed theorem Γ may be empty.

(LPB5) A is a logical truth ($\Gamma \vDash A$ holds) iff its tree is closed.

The decisive meta-theorem states the adequacy of the tree procedure:

(LPMT5) $\Gamma \vDash_{LP} A \Leftrightarrow$ the tree $TB_1 \ldots TB_n$ $(B \in \Gamma)$, ∇A is closed.

To use trees we need rules to decrease syntactic complexity for every connective and for all four basic truth operators.
The formulas written beneath the complex formula are the next node(s) in a given tree with the formula above occurring in it. A "|" indicates that a branching occurs at this node in the tree.

$T(A \wedge B)$ TA TB	$F(A \wedge B)$ $FA \mid FB$	$\Delta(A \wedge B)$ ΔA ΔB	$\nabla(A \wedge B)$ $\nabla A \mid \nabla B$
$T(\neg A)$ FA	$F(\neg A)$ TA	$\Delta(\neg A)$ ∇A	$\nabla(\neg A)$ ΔA
$T(A \vee B)$ $TA \mid TB$	$F(A \vee B)$ FA FB	$\Delta(A \vee B)$ $\Delta A \mid \Delta B$	$\nabla(A \vee B)$ ∇A ∇B

$T(A \supset B)$ $FA \mid TB$	$F(A \supset B)$ TA FB	$\Delta(A \supset B)$ $\nabla A \mid \nabla B$	$\nabla(A \supset B)$ ΔA ∇B
$T(A \equiv B)$ $TA \mid FA$ $TB \mid FB$	$F(A \equiv B)$ $TA \mid FA$ $FB \mid TB$	$\Delta(A \equiv B)$ $\Delta A \mid \nabla A$ $\Delta B \mid \nabla B$	$\nabla(A \equiv B)$ $\Delta A \mid \nabla A$ $\nabla B \mid \Delta B$

To give an example of a LP-tree we show that *Modus Ponens* does not hold as a consequence relationship:

```
        T(p)
        T(p ⊃ q)
        ∇(q)
       /    \
   F(p)      T(q)
```

There is only one rule applicable here, the truth-rule for "⊃". The right branch is *closed*, since T(q) and ∇(q) are incompatible, so there is no interpretation that can make both these sentences (at least) true. The left branch, however, is *satisfiable*, since T(p) and F(p) are not incompatible in case "p" was a contradictory sentence.

Since one of its branches is satisfiable, the tree is satisfiable, so it is not closed, so the tree for *Modus Ponens* is not closed, so by (LPMT5) *Modus Ponens* is not LP-valid.

Let us look at another example. Absorption as a theorem is valid in **LP**. So we get a closed tree for it:

```
∇((p ⊃ (p ⊃ q)) ⊃ (p ⊃ q))
     |                    (rule ∇(A ⊃ B))
Δ(p ⊃ (p ⊃ q))
∇(p ⊃ q)
     |                    (rule ∇ (A ⊃ B))
    Δ(p)
    ∇(q)
   /    \                 (rule Δ(A ⊃ B))
 ∇(p)    Δ(p ⊃ q)
```

One can stop here, although we could apply a rule once more on the right branch, since both branches are closed: The left branch is closed, since Δ(p) and ∇(p) are incompatible; the right branch is closed, since

$\Delta(p \supset q)$ and $\nabla(p \supset q)$ are incompatible. Since all branches of the tree for Absorption are closed, the tree for Absorption is closed, therefore Absorption is LP-valid.
[Remember: A closed tree means that there is no interpretation *v* that gives a coherent assignment of truth values in the supposed *counterexample* to the sentence's validity.]

Quantificational LP

LP like most PLs can be extended by standard quantificational logic as said before. As said we consider only the basic construction with a fixed domain of individuals. All extensions (like a theory of – possibly non-referring – names and descriptions, and an existence predicate) pose questions not directly related to paraconsistency, at least most of the time [see (Priest 1999) and Chap. 20].
The interesting point is how in the semantics of predicates true contradictions can arise.
Quantificational **LP**, **LPQ**, is a language that results from **LP** (and its syntax) by introducing n-ary predicates like "$F_1(,)^n$", individual constants like "a", individual variables like "x", and quantifiers, $(\forall x)$, $(\exists x)$, in the usual way. Only formulas where all variables are bound are called "sentence", otherwise "open formula".
We use the same expressions in the meta-language as translations when talking about individual LPQ-sentences ("homophonetic translation"). As schematic expressions we use "$P_1(,)^n$" etc. for n-ary predicates/relations, "á" etc. for individual constants and variables for variables.[17]

Quantificational Semantics

An **LPQ** model *M'* is a tuple <D, *v*, *G*>, where D is the domain of individuals we quantify over, *v* some interpretation function and *G* the set of all variable assignments. Two Models *M'* and *M''* differ either in their domain or in the interpretation used.

(LPQS1) $v(\acute{a}) = d \in D$

(LPQS2) For $g \in G$ $g(x) = d \in D$

So individual constants are interpreted over the domain, individual variables get assigned some member of the domain.
For predicates P we assign them not only an extension (as usually done by taking some set of individuals of the domain), but also an *anti- extension.* Both are subsets of the domain D. We write: P^+ and P^-.

---

[17] This convention is from now on applied in all chapters!

(LPQS3) $v(P^n)=<P^+, P^->, P^+ \subseteq D^n, P^- \subseteq D^n$.

D^n is the nth Cartesian product of D, the set of all n-tuples in D.
The idea is that there might be criteria the application of which may result in grouping an object within the extension of the predicate in question. There may also be other criteria the application of which may result in grouping an object within the anti-extension of the predicate in question.
Inasmuch as these criteria need not be the exact complements of each other it might be that some object is grouped in the extension *as well as* in the anti-extension of the predicate. This objects thus has the property/feature corresponding to the predicate, and it lacks the property (or has a complementary property).
Let a^n be a n-tuple of individual constants. Thus we get for elementary sentences:

(LPQS4) $d^n = v(a^n)$, $v(<P^n, a^n>)=\{1\}$ iff $d^n \in P^{n+}$ and $d^n \notin P^{n-}$,
$v(<P^n, a^n>)=\{0\}$ iff $d^n \in P^{n-}$ and $d^n \notin P^{n+}$,
$v(<P^n, a^n>)=\{0,1\}$ iff $d^n \in P^{n+}$ and $d^n \in P^{n-}$.

If $P(x_1...x_n)$ is an open formula, the interpretation of P does its work with respect to $< P(x_1...x_n),<g(x_1)...g(x_n)>>$, i.e. with a variable assignment. We write $v(A, g)$ to say that interpretation v evaluates formula A relative to variable assignment g.
A universal sentence is simply false if there is an object for which the open formula in question is simply false. A universal sentence is contradictory if it is not simply false and at least one object is in the extension as well as the anti-extension of the open formula.
As a semantic rule:

(LPQS5) Let A be a sentence of the form $(\forall x)P(x)$, then:
$v(A, g)=\{1\}$ iff for all $g'\in G$: g' is different from g at most with respect to x, and $g'(x)\in P^+$ and $g'(x)\notin P^-$.

$v(A, g)=\{0\}$ iff for some $g'\in G$: g' is different from g at most with respect to x, and $g'(x)\in P^-$ and $g'(x)\notin P^+$.

$v(A, g)=\{0,1\}$ iff for all $g'\in G$: g' is different from g at most with respect to x, and $g'(x)\in P^+$, and for some $g''\in G$: g'' is different from g at most with respect to x, and $g''(x)\in P^-$.

For existential quantification the dual holds in **LPQ**:

(LPQT1) $(\exists x)P(x) \equiv \neg (\forall x) \neg P(x)$

so one gets a dual semantic rule for $(\exists x)P(x)$.
We define LPQ-validity and consequence, *M* being the set of models:

(LPQV) $\vDash_{LPQ}A \overset{\text{def}}{=} (\forall M' \in M)(1 \in v'(A))$

(LPQC) $\Gamma\vDash_{LPQ}A \overset{\text{def}}{=} (\forall M' \in M)(\exists B \in \Gamma)(v'(B)=\{0\} \vee (1 \in v'(A))$

LPQ-Trees

We won't characterise **LPQ** axiomatically here, but derive some theorems by LPQ-trees as a semi-decision procedure.
To do this we need rules for the two quantifiers with cases for the four semantic operators. Everything else we take over from LP-trees.
As in standard instantiations of the quantifiers we have to take care that some formulas are instantiated to a new constant, some rules can be employed more than once.

$T((\forall x)P(x))$ $T(P(á))$ +	$F((\forall x)P(x))$ $F(P(á))$ *	$\Delta((\forall x)P(x))$ $\Delta(P(á))$ +	$\nabla((\forall x)P(x))$ $\nabla(P(á))$ *
$T((\exists x)P(x))$ $T(P(á))$ *	$F((\exists x)P(x))$ $F(P(á))$ +	$\Delta((\exists x)P(x))$ $\Delta(P(á))$ *	$\nabla((\exists x)P(x))$ $\nabla(P(á))$ +
+ this rule can be employed more than once * á has to be a constant that did not occur in the tree before			

Let us then look at LPQ-Trees examples:

(LPQT2) $(\forall x)F(x),(\forall x)G(x)\vDash_{LPQ}(\forall x)(F(x) \wedge G(x))$

Proof:

$T(\forall x)F(x)$
$T(\forall x)G(x)$
$\nabla(\forall x)(F(x) \wedge G(x))$
| (rule $\nabla\forall$ with "a" new)
$\nabla(F(a) \wedge G(a))$
/ \ (rule $\nabla\wedge$)
$\nabla(F(a))$ $\nabla(G(a))$
| | (rule $T\forall$)
$TF(a)$ $TG(a)$

Both branches of this tree are closed, since TF(a) is incompatible with $\nabla(F(a))$ and TG(a) with $\nabla(G(a)$. So the consequence relationship holds. Rules with an "*" are better employed at the beginning of a tree, since so one can later instantiate "+" rules on these constants. Beginning this tree with a usage of (T∀) would have been a waste, since the constants used then would have to be different from constants used with (∇∀).

(LPQT3) $\vDash_{LPQ}(\forall x)F(x) \supset (\exists x)F(x)$

Proof:

$\nabla((\forall x)F(x) \supset (\exists x)F(x))$

| (∇⊃)

$\Delta(\forall x)F(x)$

$\nabla(\exists x)F(x)$

| (∇∃)

$\nabla F(a)$

| (Δ∀)

$\Delta F(a)$

The incompatibility of the last two sentences closes this tree.
Also valid are the following:

(LPQT4) $(\forall x)(F(x) \supset G(x)) \vDash_{LPQ}(\forall x)(\neg G(x) \supset \neg F(x))$

a quantified version of Contraposition.

(LPQT5) $(\forall x)(F(x) \supset G(x)) \vDash_{LPQ}(\exists x)F(x) \supset (\exists x)G(x)$

(LPQT6) $(\forall x)(P(x) \supset A) \vDash_{LPQ}(\exists x)P(x) \supset A$
where x does not occur in A

(LPQT7) $(\forall x)(F(x) \supset G(x))\vDash_{LPQ}(\forall x)F(x) \supset (\forall x)G(x)$

Proof:

$T(\forall x)(F(x) \supset G(x))$

$\nabla((\forall x)F(x) \supset (\forall x)G(x))$

| (∇⊃)

$\Delta(\forall x)F(x)$

$\nabla(\forall x)G(x)$

| (∇∀)

$\nabla G(a)$

| (T∀)

$T(F(a) \supset G(a))$

/ \ (T⊃)

$F(F(a))$ $T(G(a))$

| (Δ∀)

$\Delta F(a)$

LPQ Adequacy

We have seen that trees are mirroring **LP**-validity. Trees are also sound and complete for **LPQ**.
Soundness is given by considering an invalid A. Since A is not valid there is an interpretation in some model that makes A simply false. The assumption that A is simply false at the root of the tree for A develops this interpretation in detail. The existence of this interpretation is mirrored by an open branch, so the tree is not closed. So A is not derivable by an **LPQ**-tree. Contrapositive: If A is derivable, A is valid.
Completeness is given by considering a satisfiable tree. A sentence with its tree satisfiable is not derivable. A satisfiable tree determines by one of its branches an interpretation in some model. This interpretation includes the root of the branch, i.e. makes the sentence A simply false, so A is not valid. Contrapositive: If A is valid, A is derivable.

(LPQMT1) $\Gamma \models_{LPQ} A \Leftrightarrow$ the tree $TB_1 ... TB_n$ $(B \in \Gamma)$, ∇A is closed.[18]

LPQ with Identity

Once we have **LPQ** we might want to extend **LPQ** with an identity relation (designated by "="). Let's call this language **LPQ**$^{=}$.
How could we define identity?
Does for any object, *inconsistent* objects included, $(\forall x)(x=x)$ hold?
Often identity is defined by *Leibniz' Law*: *a* and *b* are identical if all properties that *a* has *b* has as well. In second order logic we can say:

(LL) $(\forall x,y)(x = y \equiv (\forall F)(F(x) \equiv F(y)))$

Since **LPQ** is first order, we cannot express (LL) in it.[19]
Even if we cannot define identity within **LPQ**, we may ask ourselves which rules/theorems should hold with respect to "=". The two obvious candidates for natural deduction rules are:

(=I) $\ldots \Rightarrow á = á$
(=E) $á = é, P(á) \Rightarrow P(é)$

(=E) is an expression of substitution of identicals.

---

[18] For the details in the propositional case see (Bloesch 1993), for the necessary refinement in an adequacy proof for trees in the quantificational case in general see (Ben-Ari 1993, pp.112-27).

[19] A schematic representation of (LL) would hold only for some predicate P, or for too many constants, or requires infinite premises/knowledge for right to left detachment.

Interestingly enough substitution of identicals does *not* hold! Given (LL) substitution of identicals comes down to detachment with respect to "≡". But like the conditional "≡" is not detachable in **LP**.
The same failure of detachment blocks the validity of

(*) $a = b, b = c \Rightarrow a = c$

Given (LL) and "≡" in **LP** (*) comes down to transitivity of "≡", which does not hold in **LP**. So supervenient on that failure the transitivity of identity does not hold in **LPQ**$^{=}$. This seems to be a major shortcoming for a definition along (LL) in second order **LPQ**. It may turn out, however, to be a merit [see Chap. 16]!

Summary

LP provides a paraconsistent logic with an easily understood semantics keeping the Extensionality Condition.
LP can be easily employed, also in its quantificational extension **LPQ**, using trees.
LP, however, fails on the Modus Ponens Condition and so contains no acceptable conditional. **LP**, therefore, can only be regarded as a possible ingredient for the real paraconsistent logic (e.g. one extending **LP** with a Relevant conditional). **LP** certainly *is not* "the logic of paradox".
Keep in mind as assets for other PLs:
• the standard treatment of negation,
• the usage of {0,1} as a designated truth value,
• the expressibility of bivalent "semantic" connectives with respect to the paraconsistent distribution of truth values,
• the idea of the pair of extension and anti-extension in the interpretation of a predicate/relation.

Questions

(Q1) What is the philosophical justification to take {0,1} as a designated truth value? Isn't it in conflict with our ordinary concept of logical truth?

(Q2) Consider **LPQ**. The criteria for the anti-extension of some P apply to all objects. Does this make $(\exists x)P(x)$ false?

(Q3) Consider the difference between a "true contradiction" and a (merely) "false contradiction" – what is that difference?

(Q4) Given a sentence A such that $A \equiv B \wedge \neg B$, what are the truth values of TA and FA? What is the intuitive reading of these sentences?

(Q5) Given a paraconsistent quantificational logic and its semantics should we allow for objects such that $a \neq a$?

Exercises

(Ex1) Give counter-examples for the consequence relations that do not hold in **LP** [*Modus Tollens* etc.].

(Ex2) Show by truth tables that $\models_{LP}(p \supset q) \supset (\neg q \supset \neg p)$

(Ex3) Show by a satisfiable **LP**-tree that transitivity of "$\supset$" does not hold as a consequence relationship. Do the same for standard Negation-Introduction.

(Ex4) Show the validity of (LPQT4)-(LPQT6) by trees.

(Ex5) Show by trees that the following are not **LPQ**-valid:

$(\forall x)(F(x) \supset G(x)), (\forall x)F(x) \models (\forall x)G(x)$
$(\forall x)(F(x) \supset G(x)), (\forall x)\neg G(x) \models (\forall x)\neg F(x)$
$(\forall x)(F(x) \supset G(x)), (\forall x)(G(x) \supset H(x)) \models (\forall x)(F(x) \supset H(x))$

(Ex6) Suppose we extended **LPQ** with the consistency/inconsistency operators "$^{\circ}$"/"$^{\bullet}$". We would need a further quantificational axiom (tree decomposition clause) to replace occurrences of " $^{\bullet}(\forall x)P(x)$ " (starting with "$^{\bullet}$", defining "$^{\circ}$"). Read off the axiom from the semantics of "$\forall$".

Further Reading

• The classic paper on **LP** is: Priest, Graham. "The Logic of Paradox", *Journal of Philosophical Logic*, 8 (1979), pp. 219-41.
• The propositional tableau method you find in: Bloesch, Anthony. "A Tableau Style Proof System for Two Paraconsistent Logics", *Notre Dame Journal of Symbolic Logic*, (1993), pp. 295-301.
• On Priest's dialectic use of **LP** see (Priest 1982, 1991, 1993, 1994, 1995, 1997, 1999 ...).

5 | Relevant Logics

Relevant Logics (in short "RLs", in America also called "Relevance Logics") are one of the major groups of paraconsistent logics. Relevant logics are a subset of the paraconsistent logics (i.e. the requirements to be Relevant are stronger than only avoiding Explosion).
The essential aim of Relevant Logic is to capture a natural and intuitive appropriate concept of entailment, one for which the paradoxes of implication (or similar ones) do not appear.
The very earliest axiomatization of a paraconsistent logic by Orlov was in fact a Relevant logic. The development known today as Relevance Logic started in the USA in the 1960s with work done by Anderson, Belnap, Dunn, Meyer and their students and collaborators, and resulted in two volumes entitled *Entailment*. In the 1970s Routley, Meyer, Brady and others developed in Australia their version of Relevant Logic and semantics. This issued in two volumes *Relevant Logics and their Rivals*.
We are interested in Relevant Logic here as a means to define a conditional that keeps *Modus Ponens* and its other essential properties, but does not fail on the conditions we proposed for paraconsistent logics (e.g. the Curry Conditions).
The defining properties of Relevant Logics concern the propositional level, so we will focus on propositional systems here. [At the end of this chapter we introduce the quantificational logic $\mathbf{DJ^dQ}$, since we will need it as a quantificational logic in the chapter on set theory.]

Defining Relevant Logics

Relevant logics not just avoid Explosion, all Irrelevant theorems and consequence relationships of **PC** (and standard modal logics with an Irrelevant strict implication) should be avoided.
These include all versions of Explosion like

(1) $A \supset (\neg A \supset B)$
(2) $A \wedge \neg A \supset B$

and all versions of *verum ex qoudlibet sequitur* like

(3) $A \supset (B \supset B)$ or
(4) $B \supset (A \supset B)$ [resp. $B \vdash (A \supset B)$]

What have all these sentences in common? If there is one such property, excluding it will yield only Relevant implications.

The diagnosis of proponents of Relevant Logics is that in all these sentences the consequent ultimately to be detached is a sentence that has no connection in content to the antecedent sentences. That there is no connection in content can be seen in the propositional case by the fact that given the full logical structure at the propositional level the consequent and the antecedent share no propositional letters.
This observation led to the *variable sharing requirement* (speaking of a letter for a basic sentence as a "propositional variable"), which in turn leads to the following definitions:

(R1) Only those conditional theorems are Relevant in which the antecedent and the consequent share a propositional variable.

(R2) Only those consequence relationships are Relevant in which the premises and the conclusion share a propositional variable.

(R3) Just those logics are Relevant which have only Relevant theorems and Relevant consequence relationships.

Requirement (R1) is necessary, since given the validity of *Modus Ponens* any Irrelevant theorem would spread its Irrelevance.
Seen in the light of these definitions **LP** is not a Relevant logic if we consider "$\supset$" as its conditional.
We will not discuss the adequacy and philosophical background of these definitions in detail here. We will see what sticking to these properties requires, and whether we are willing to go this way.

First Degree Entailment

Relevant Logics aim at a concept of entailment that is stronger than the material conditional.
The first approach could be to keep the material conditional as the usual abbreviation of $\neg A \vee B$ and consider $\vdash$ as formalising entailment. $\vdash$, of course, is a stronger relation than "$\supset$". Alternatively once could require entailments $A \rightarrow B$ to be of first degree only (i.e. there are no nested arrows $\rightarrow$). This approach was taken in the late 1950s by Anderson and Belnap. Their system is called First Degree Entailment (**FDE**).
One can give a tree-characterisation of this system by rules similar to the rules we used in chapter 4 for **LP**. This system also allows for truth value gaps. The resulting logic is in fact a sub-logic of **LP** (since **LP** allows for some Irrelevant deductions). **FDE** has no *theorems* at all! Its logic resides completely in the consequences that hold in it.[20]

[20] For a brief tree-based introduction to **FDE** see (Priest 2000, Chap.8).

The fundamental shortcoming of this system – besides being even weaker than **LP** – is that it does not allow to model nested entailments, whereas many intuitive logical truths for the conditional (Permutation, Transitivity etc.) are just that.

Example Relevant Logic

Let us rather look at a system with a nestable conditional connective "→". The system **DL** ("dialectical logic") is used by (Routley/Meyer 1976) in a paraconsistent context. Its axiom schemata are:

(A1) $A \rightarrow A$
(A2) $(A \rightarrow B) \wedge (B \rightarrow C) \rightarrow (A \rightarrow C)$
(A3) $A \wedge B \rightarrow A$
(A4) $A \wedge B \rightarrow B$
(A5) $(A \rightarrow B) \wedge (A \rightarrow C) \rightarrow (A \rightarrow B \wedge C)$
(A6) $A \wedge (B \vee C) \rightarrow (A \wedge B) \vee (A \wedge C)$
(A7) $\neg\neg A \rightarrow A$
(A8) $(A \rightarrow \neg B) \rightarrow (B \rightarrow \neg A)$
(A9) $A \rightarrow A \vee B$
(A10) $B \rightarrow A \vee B$
(A11) $(A \rightarrow C) \wedge (B \rightarrow C) \rightarrow ((A \vee B) \rightarrow C)$
(A12) $\neg A \wedge \neg B \rightarrow \neg(A \vee B)$
(A13) $\neg(A \wedge B) \rightarrow \neg A \vee \neg B$

Rules:

(R1) $A, A \rightarrow B \Rightarrow B$
(R2) $A \rightarrow B \Rightarrow \neg B \rightarrow \neg A$

In logics like **DL** the consequence relation only inherits truth from the premises to the conclusion (and so it's done in a derivation). The conditional "→" expresses a stronger relation. It expresses the obtaining of some connection between the antecedent and the consequent. Because of this it is not valid that

(*) $\vdash A \rightarrow B$ if $A \vdash B$

The *Deduction Theorem* generally does not hold for entailment.[21]

[21] To have a *Deduction Theorem* the reading of $A_1,\dots A_n \vdash B$ has to be changed (taking the left hand side as a so called "multiset", which in distinction to a set can have several identical elements although their order is irrelevant), and further connectives are introduced like an intensional conjunction (called "fusion") and disjunction (called "fission"), but all this is beyond our current interests [cf. (Mares 2004, pp. 164-70)].

As you see, these logics need quite more axioms than standard logics, since a lot of proofs are no longer available. For example distribution needs a special axiom (A6). We need two axioms, (A12) and (A13), to establish the DeMorgan dualities. With respect to negation (A7) shows its standard character. Note also that contraposition has to be taken as a rule of its own right.

No Binary Accessibility

The greatest challenge for Relevant logicians is to give a semantics that makes exactly the consequence of the axioms given true.
Usually modal logics (i.e. logics that model a stronger conditional) use a possible worlds semantics. A typical truth conditional for a strict conditional (with the set of possible worlds W) is:

$$(*S\to)\quad v(A \to B,w) = 1 \text{ iff } (\forall w' \in W)(Rww' \Rightarrow (v(A,w') \Rightarrow v(B,w'))$$

This rule makes A → A a logical truth. This is O.K., since (A1) says so, but it also makes B → (A → A) a logical truth, and this sentence is Irrelevant, since B and A → A share no propositional variables.
The problem is combining the supposedly obvious truth of sentences like A → A with avoiding Irrelevance. A binary accessible relation seems to be unable to keep them apart. Therefore many Relevant logics have a *ternary* accessibility relation!
To model inconsistency not only consistent, but also inconsistent worlds are considered, even worlds in which the laws of logic are thought to be out of force. [This is modelled by not applying the usual rules of the connectives to these worlds.]
A model is a tuple M=<@, N, W, R, *, D, G, v> consisting of the actual world @, the set of *normal worlds* (those worlds in which logic holds), the set of all worlds (normal or not), the accessibility relation, the monadic *-operation, a domain of objects and a set of variable assignments (in the quantificational case [we are not considering here at the moment]), and an interpretation v.
We require:

1. $@ \in N \subseteq W$
2. $D \neq \varnothing$ (in the quantificational case)
3. A is true in some Model M' iff $v'(A,@)=1$.

This last requirement states that we assess the truth of a sentence relative to the actual world only. All other worlds are only operative in determining the truth conditions of a sentence. This may be justified by considering that we want to know which sentences are true, and a sentence is true (in

distinction to its being logically true) if it is true in the obtaining world (i.e. the actual world).
The semantic rules are the usual ones for the connectives with the exception of the intensional negation rule [see below] and the rule for the truth of entailments in terms of ternary accessibility:

$$(R\rightarrow) \quad v(A\rightarrow B,w)=1 \Leftrightarrow$$
$$(\forall w',w'')(R(w,w',w'') \wedge v(A,w')=1 \Rightarrow v(B,w'')=1)$$

An entailment is true at some world if this world sees an accessibility between *two other worlds* such that if A is true at the first of these worlds B is true at the other.
For normal worlds a further requirement is stated:

$$(NC) \quad (\forall w,w',w'')(w\in N \wedge R(w,w',w'') \Rightarrow w' = w'')$$

This serves to recover the idea that under normal conditions an entailment just is true if in all accessible worlds the truth of the antecedent guarantees the truth of the consequent. The *normality condition* is important in its application to @ and in regaining a model of intuitive entailment as *normal implication.*
As an example let us see why $A\rightarrow(B\rightarrow B)$ is no longer a logical truth: Since we are free to interpret atomic formula at worlds and the truth condition ($R\rightarrow$) refers to 3 worlds of evaluation, we can have $v(B,w')=1$ and $v(B,w'')=0$, being accessible from w''', thus $B\rightarrow B$ being false at w''', thus with @ being the actual world of some model accessing a world w'''' where A is true and w'''' accessing w''', R(@,w'''',w'''), we have according to ($R\rightarrow$) made $A\rightarrow(B\rightarrow B)$ false! That $B\rightarrow B$ is false at w''' does not matter, since only @ matters for assessing truth in a model. $B\rightarrow B$ cannot be made false at @, since the normality condition (NC) has it that for a normal world the seen accessing and accessed world are identical.

Some Binary Accessibility

Further requirements re-introduce a *binary* accessibility relation $\leq$ for two worlds w and w':

4. $w \leq w'$ iff $(\exists w''\in N)(R(w'',w,w')$

That is worlds are binary accessible only if some *normal* world "sees" the accessing.
Given this definition in 4.

5. $w \leq w$

6. $w \leq w' \wedge R(w',w'',w''') \Rightarrow R(w,w'',w''')$

This preserves the seeing of accessibility from an accessed world to the accessing world. The next requirement ensures double negation:

7. $w = w^{**}$

8. $w \leq w' \Rightarrow w'^{*} \leq w^{*}$

This last supports contraposition.
"≤" defines a *binary* accessibility relation in terms of R and normal worlds. One can uses *this* relation to model a concept of entailment that expresses that the truth of the antecedent necessitates the truth of the consequent. Thus we define a common notion of entailment:

(DE) A *entails* B $\Leftrightarrow (\forall w \in W)(v(A,w)=1 \Rightarrow v(B,w)=1)$

To achieve expressing this within Relevant semantics using the ternary R and the binary ≤ we add a further heredity requirement:

9. $v(A,w)=1 \wedge w \leq w' \Rightarrow v(A,w')=1$

and we define *normal implication* as:

(DNI) A *normally implies* B $\Leftrightarrow (\forall w \in N)(v(A \rightarrow B,w)=1)$

Normal implication thus is Relevant implication in the normal worlds only. Interestingly enough now one can prove an important meta-logical theorem:

(MT1) A entails B iff A normally implies B.

The non-normal worlds, however, are *essential* to Relevant semantics (to invalidate Irrelevant theorems for "→"). We forbid that the actual world of a model is a non-normal world, but maybe we should not!
So the set of normal implications need not match the set of *true* conditionals A→B of a model (and, of course, of the logic as a whole).
(MT1) expresses that given normality the Relevant entailments coincide with our "usual" entailments (of binary accessibility modal logics). Relevant entailment itself, however, is different.
What does (R→) tell us?
This seems quite unclear. No intuitive reading is obvious. But if the semantics is not justifiable with respect to our intuitive concept of entailment, the whole approach using a ternary accessibility relation seems questionable. Even Relevant Logicians [cf. Anderson/Belnap/Dunn 1992, pp. 163-64] summarize that (R→) *has no intuitive basis* and no connection to our ordinary understanding of the conditional! Even the definition of the binary accessibility relation ≤ [cf. requirement 4] has no intuitively obvious justification.

There is, however, a new promising reading of the ternary accessibility relation in terms of the theory of information (flow).
But before we look at this we look at the Routley semantics of negation.

The Routley Star

To give a semantics for negation that allows for true contradictions Richard Routley introduced his (in)famous star operator. Negation becomes an intensional connective.
Each world w is accompanied by a *witness* world w*. The rule for negation is:

(*¬) $v(\neg A,w)=1$ iff $v(A,w^*)=0$

Once again the evaluation of a sentence is spread across worlds. Note that nothing is said whether the behaviour of A (i.e. not negated) depends on what is the case at w*.
Example:
We can have $v(A,w)=1$, $v(A,w^*) = v(B,w) = 0$ giving us that $A \wedge \neg A \rightarrow B$ turns out false, since w is a world where A and ¬A are true (i.e. being non-normal) and B isn't. Explosion fails.
It is hard to see any intuitive sense in the witness world and the rule for negation. The construction validates the theorems, but it has been considered by many logicians as a formal trick only [for example, cf. (van Bentham 1979)].
As in the case of the ternary accessibility relation there is also a new reading of the Routley star in terms of information theory based on situation semantics.

Information Flow Semantics

A more justifiable semantics for negation and the relevant conditional can be given in the framework of information flow (the theory of distributed systems and information channels) based on the framework of situation semantics.[22]
Information flows in *distributed systems* (like a circuit that connects a switch with a bulb). These systems can be considered *channels* along which we reason. The laws and rules operative in such a system are *constraints* that define a proper working system and allow to reason along these constraints (like knowing that the switch was pressed if the bulb is burning).

---

[22] It is not possible to throw in quickly an introduction to that field as well, we make use here only of some of the basic ideas of situation semantics; see the *Further Readings* section. An overview is provided by (Bremer/Cohnitz 2004).

Talking in situation semantics language we can say that information about one *situation* is derived from another situation by some channel. The basic building blocks of information are *infons*, which resemble Russellian propositions (i.e. they contain objects, their relations, and truth values).
Situations are parts of reality. The channel is also a part of reality (trivially so if we see the distributed system as a channel). Therefore there is a situation that comprises exactly the channel. The infons made factual by that situation are the infons that describe the structure of the channel. The important thing is: The channel as well as the parts (be it two or more) are situations and can be relata of a ternary relation connecting entities of some type. The channel and two sites *connected by a channel* can be seen *as the relata of the ternary accessibility relation* R. Look again at the truth condition of "→": The relation that is said to hold between w' and w" is established or observed from w. Let w be the channel and w' and w" be the sites connected by the channel. We can say that the channel establishes the connection between the sites, and from the perspective of the distributed system the sites are relata of information flow.
A→B receives the following interpretation: A→B is true at w if all the sites/situations w' and w" connected by that channel are such that if the information A is available at the one end w the information B is available in situation w". The more constraints hold for a distributed system *the less* situations can be derived from it, since the derived situations have to meet all the constraints. Having more constraints operative in a channel means zooming in on a very specific part/situation.
This amounts to an interpretation of a ternary accessibility relation in terms of information flow. And it allows us to introduce a second reading of "→" (besides the usual one).

(R→2) A→B is true with respect to a channel *c* iff

$\{A\} \vdash_C \{B\}$ is a constraint for that channel *c*.

To spell out this reading there should be infomorphisms mapping what is said in A and B at the system level to statements/infons of the part classifications. An interpretation also has to be developed for the equivalent of the occurrence of nested arrows "→". It seems that one has to allow constraints that constrain lower level constraints.
Edwin Mares gives a further interpretation of "→" in terms of situations and information flow exploiting the fact that an infon (made true by some situation) can contain information about situations (i.e. contain parameters or constants for situations). An infon can contain information about relations between infons and situations. Infons of this kind are

informational links. They tells us that some infon being factual *involves* a second infon being factual.
An informational link has the form: <<*involves*, Φ, Ψ, 1>> where Φ and Ψ are situation types. One can take R to represent these informational links. If some informational link is said to hold in situation w saying that an infon ϕ (of type Ψ) carries the information that the infon φ (of type Φ) also has to hold (somewhere), then if R(w,w',w") and w' contains/supports the infon ϕ, then w" contains/supports the infon φ. The ternary relation models an informational link of one situation/infon constraining another. Thus (taking $\rightarrow$ here for a moment as connecting infons):

(R$\rightarrow$3) $\phi \rightarrow \varphi$ is true w.r.t. situations w, w', w" with R(w,w',w") if in case w$\models$<<*involves*, Φ, Ψ, 1>> and w'$\models \phi$, then w"$\models\varphi$.

If we take R to be about or related to informational links some features of information linkage should be mirrored by the relation R. Every situation is closed under informational linkage, since information is factual. This means for relation R that one should require it to be reflexive: R(w,w,w)
The set of statements made true by w is closed under *Modus Ponens* then.
Note that reflexivity does not make obvious sense, however, in the second reading of "$\rightarrow$": Not every channel carries information from itself to itself! On the other hand it seems vacuously true, since the information present in the system is present in the system (as its own improper part) if it is present in the system (as its own part).
What about negation?
If the situation framework could deal with the *-operator as well it might well become the preferred reading of Relevant truth conditions!
A piece of information can be incompatible with another piece of information. This may be due to the polarities within the infons supported by the situation or due to constraints yielding implied information of the one infon incompatible with the other. Suppose we had made this intuition more precise and given a formal account of compatibility, say by using infon logic or by considering meta-logical properties of the theories of distributed systems (i.e. their set of supported constraints).
We could introduce then a relation C(w,w') of *compatibility* between situations or the sets of infons supported by these situations. The statement $\neg$A is true at w, then, if the truth of A is incompatible with the other information contained in a related situation w'. The closure of a situation can be taken as what the situation says. The set of compatible situations can be taken as that which is not excluded by what the situation says.
If the negation of some state of affairs A is a fact in all w compatible situation, the state of affairs is not compatible with w, so presumably its

negation is contained within what w says. w* (the witness world) can be taken as the *maximal* situation such that the information given in w is compatible with it. We arrive at:

(R*2) $v(\neg A,w)=1 \Leftrightarrow (\forall w')(C(w,w') \Rightarrow v(A,w')=0)$

That is a negation is true in a situation w if in all other situations compatible with the information given in w the statement under consideration is false. w* just is the most informative (since most comprehensive) of these situations. *Not* every situation is compatible with itself, since we assumed that there are inconsistent situations.
So a situation framework may also give us a more intuitive understanding of the *. Note, however, that this requires spelling out the relation C in an acceptable way. Sometimes this relation is just taken as basic [e.g. (Mares 2004, p. 77)]!

Worlds and Situations

The information (flow) semantics outlined was developed in terms of situations.
Situations – in contrast to possible worlds – are *partial*. They do not contain A or ¬A for every sentence A of the language. They are not – in case we don't require this otherwise – closed under some rules.
Especially situations (in contrast to situation *types*) can be taken as parts of the universe. Taken thus it makes sense to say that some situations are connected or parts of a greater distributed systems.
The same cannot be said for worlds. Worlds are not only total, only one of them is actual. Different possible worlds stand in no causal or part-whole relation whatsoever.
Therefore it might be crucial to rephrase the whole semantics into talk about situations and situation types.
This change to partiality might, however, conflict with the information semantics for *, since assessments of compatibility may require closure of the situations under consideration.
So more work has to be done here. We have seen so far the idea of such a semantics. [More complications arise when the partiality of the situation framework is combined with quantificational semantics in an intensional framework of supposedly world relative domains.]

Systematisation

The typical systems of Relevant Logic can be systematized as being extension of a basal Relevant logic **B**.
B is defined by the following axiom schemes and rules:

(A1) $A \to A$
(A2) $A \to A \vee B$
(A3) $B \to A \vee B$
(A4) $A \wedge B \to A$
(A5) $A \wedge B \to B$
(A6) $A \wedge (B \vee C) \to (A \wedge B) \vee (A \wedge C)$
(A7) $(A \to B) \wedge (A \to C) \to (A \to B \wedge C)$
(A8) $(A \to C) \wedge (B \to C) \to ((A \vee B) \to C)$
(A9) $\neg\neg A \to A$

(R1) $A, A \to B \Rightarrow B$ [*Modus Ponens*]
(R2) $A, B \Rightarrow A \wedge B$ [$\wedge$I]
(R3) $A \to B \Rightarrow (C \to A) \to (C \to B)$ [Prefixing]
(R4) $A \to B \Rightarrow (B \to C) \to (A \to C)$ [Suffixing]
(R5) $A \to \neg B \Rightarrow B \to \neg A$ [Contraposition]

The systems that extend **B** are called *affixing* systems, since they all share the pre- and suffixing rules. Candidates for further axiom schemes are:

(A10) $(A \to \neg B) \to (B \to \neg A)$
(A11) $(A \to B) \to ((C \to A) \to (C \to B))$
(A12) $(A \to B) \to ((B \to C) \to (A \to C))$
(A13) $(A \to ((A \to B) \to B)$
(A14) $(A \to (A \to B)) \to (A \to B)$

(A10) – (A12) are the theorem versions of the rules (R3)-(R5). (A13) is a version of the *Modus Ponens* theorem, (A14) Absorption (or "Contraction").
All of these are not valid in **B**. One can define the systems:

DW = **B** + (A10) [(R5) can be dropped then]
TW = **DW** + (A11) + (A12) [drop (R3) and (R4)]
RW = **TW** + (A13) [drop (A11) *or* (A12)]
R = **RW** + (A14)
T = **R** – (A11) + $((A \to \neg A) \to \neg A)$
E = **T** + $((A \to C) \to (((A \to C) \to B) \to B)$
+ $((A \to A) \wedge (B \to B)) \to ((A \wedge B) \to (A \wedge B))$

R being the strongest of these systems contains all PC-theorems! That does not make **R** Irrelevant. The interesting question is which theorems hold for "$\rightarrow$" (not "$\supset$").

The systems that extend **B** validate more sentences by excluding more counter models by requiring further properties of the relation R (as stronger modal logics in general work by restricting accessibility).

For example:

- making Prefixing as an axiom true corresponds to:

$$(\forall w',w'',w''',w'''')((\exists w \in W)(R(w',w'',w) \wedge R(w,w''',w'''')) \Rightarrow (\exists w''''' \in W)(R(w',w''',w''''') \wedge R(w'',w''''',w''''))).$$

- making Contraction as an axiom true corresponds to:

$$(\forall w',w'',w''')(R(w',w'',w''') \Rightarrow (\exists w \in W)(R(w',w'',w) \wedge R(w,w'',w''')))$$

Both this requirement on R have no intuitive sense and can hardly be rephrased to make them obvious. The affixing theorems, however, look pretty natural. Why do they demand such strange restrictions?

These conditions on R also have most unfortunate consequences. They employ nested existential quantification. If one uses them in a tree like decision procedure this results in branches of *infinite* length. In fact in can be proven that even Relevant propositional logic is, therefore, *undecidable*! It can be really hard to ascertain what holds in system **R**.

The systems that extend **B** up to **R** are indeed Relevant in the sense that in a logically true conditional the *variable sharing requirement* is met.

This can be shown (using some strange 8-valued semantics) for **R**. Given that it holds for the strongest of these systems, it has to hold for all of them.[23]

Brady's Logic of Entailment

Ross Brady proposes the following system as a Relevant logic that captures the intuitive notion of entailment. Its semantics is modelled on the idea of *containment of content*. The basic idea is that a content is connected to each sentence and the relation of entailment is that of containment of content.

---

[23] Cf. (Priest 2001), pp.197-98, and p.209 for a much simpler proof for logic **B**. Note that taking some strange semantics – that is not the intended semantics of our system – to prove this fact is admissible: First one proves that **R** is sound with respect to the strange semantics; then one shows that given some such semantics Irrelevant conditionals are not logically true; so, given the soundness of **R**, they cannot be proven; if they cannot be proven (a *syntactic* meta-property), they cannot be proven in the intended semantics either! This method of using arbitrary (non-intended) semantics to prove meta-theorems is often employed in paraconsistent meta-logic.

Brady's logic is important, since he considers it to be a universal logic that can be employed in any context [see Chap. 20]. He uses it for his version of paraconsistent set theory [see Chap. 11].
Brady's logic, called **DJ^{d}Q,** is very weak and has to assume axioms for relations derivable otherwise. Brady's logic does *neither* use the ternary accessibility relation *nor* the Routley star *. That, too, makes it worth looking at.
DJ^{d}Q – Axiom schemes:

(A1) $A \to A$
(A2) $A \wedge B \to A$
(A3) $A \wedge B \to B$
(A4) $(A \to B) \wedge (A \to C) \to (A \to B \wedge C)$
(A5) $A \to A \vee B$
(A6) $B \to A \vee B$
(A7) $(A \to B) \wedge (C \to B) \to (A \vee C \to B)$
(A8) $A \wedge (B \vee C) \to A \wedge B \vee A \wedge C$
(A9) $\neg\neg A \to A$
(A10) $(A \to \neg B) \to (B \to \neg A)$
(A11) $(A \to B) \wedge (B \to C) \to (A \to C)$
(A12) $(\forall x)P(x) \to P(á)$
(A13) $(\forall x)(A \to P(x)) \to (A \to (\forall x)P(x))$ *
(A14) $(\forall x)(A \vee P(x)) \to (A \vee (\forall x)P(x))$ *
(A16) $P(á) \to (\exists x)P(x)$
(A17) $(\forall x)(P(x) \to A) \to ((\exists x)P(x) \to A)$ *
(A18) $A \wedge (\exists x)P(x) \to (\exists x)(P(x) \wedge A)$ * * [x not free in A]

DJ^{d}Q – Rules:

(R1) $A \to B, A \Rightarrow B$
(R2) $A, B \Rightarrow A \wedge B$
(R3) $A \to B, C \to D \Rightarrow (B \to C) \to (A \to D)$
(R4) $A \Rightarrow (\forall x)A$

Meta-Rules:

(MR1) If $A \Rightarrow B$ then also $A \vee C \Rightarrow B \vee C$
(MR2) If $A \Rightarrow B$ then $(\exists x)A \Rightarrow (\exists x)B$

where in both meta-rules in the derivation $A \Rightarrow B$ (R4) does not generalize on a free variable in A.
For **DJ^{d}Q**–semantics we start with contents:
The *content* of a set of sentences Γ are all the sentences that can be *analytically established* from the terms occuring in the sentences in Γ.

Often we take Γ to be a singleton {A}. The *range* of Γ is the set of all sentences that analytically ensure that at least one sentence in Γ is true.
Each sentence A corresponds a set of sentences c(A), which is its content (the analytic closure of A). The content set of A can be taken as a great conjunction. $A \models B$ for $B \in c(A)$ is analytic.
Each sentence corresponds a set of sentences r(A), which is its range. The range set of A can be taken as a great disjunction.
The logical operations can be semantically modelled by algebraic operations on these (content) sets. Every basic sentence is assigned some content. The content of $A \wedge B$ is the set of analytic consequences of the union of c(A) and c(B). The content of $A \vee B$ is $c(A) \cap c(B)$.
Entailment is now semantical defined as *containment of content*:

$$v(A \rightarrow B) = 1 \text{ iff } c(B) \subseteq c(A).$$

To ensure a Relevant logic postulates for content relations are laid down, e.g. $c(A \vee B) = c(A) \cap c(B) \subseteq c(A)$.
An exception to this algebra is negation, since taking negation as set complement would give $A \wedge \neg A$ universal content, and would validate Explosion and *verum ex qoudlibet* for entailment. The negation of a sentence can be better understood as all those sentences that represent alternative situations, i.e. the content of $\neg A$ are all facts the absence of which made A possible: $c(\neg A) \stackrel{\text{def}}{=} \{B \mid \neg B \in r(A)\}$. This set is $c(A)^*$. The interpretation v assigns $c(A)^*$ to $\neg A$.
The semantics of entailment – taking it as content containment – seems to be close to our natural understanding of entailment. Nothing about accessing the accessibility of worlds is involved.
This semantics – obviously – *presupposes* a theory of establishing the analytic consequences of a given sentence, i.e. a theory of analyticity! This may require meaning postulates, which in turn may contain expressions (like "$\rightarrow$") the semantics of which operates on contents! A meaning postulate – usually a conditional – may look like the prototypical entailment. Basic content assignment (at the beginning of the interpretation semantics) therefore may not be so basic at all.
Notwithstanding this, Brady's logic seems to have some nice meta-logical properties:
$\mathbf{DJ^d}$ is sound and complete relative to the semantics of contents [cf. (Brady 1996)]. Sentences with identical contents can always be *substituted* for each other. [For contained meaning semi-substitutivity in a context holds.]
Several typical theorems do not hold in $\mathbf{DJ^dQ}$:
Contraction, the Law of Excluded Middle $[A \vee \neg A]$, Disjunctive Syllogism, neither the *Modus Ponens* Theorem, nor $(A \rightarrow \neg A) \rightarrow \neg A$.
Therefore $\mathbf{DJ^dQ}$ satisfies the Strong Anti-Triviality Condition.

Assessment

The established systems of Relevant logic capture at least parts of our concepts of relevance and entailment.

The most pressing problem is to give an intuitively convincing semantics for entailment and negation within the RL context. The Routley star is a cross violation of the Extensionality condition. Semantic work seems to be still going on; the focus on information theory may prove to be useful.

We cannot take some RL to be our target logic for paraconsistency if it fails on the Strong Anti-Triviality Condition. Neither can be take a logic that validates Contraposition in general (as we will see in Chap. 16). The typical systems **B**, **R**, **E** are, therefore, not available to us.

For an assessment of the information (flow) semantics consider questions (Q1), (Q2), and remember the note on situations vs. worlds.

One of the most promising of the logics presented here is $\mathbf{DJ^dQ}$. It satisfies the Strong Anti-Triviality condition. It has Contraposition, but this depends on a corresponding *postulate* on content semantics, that might be dropped.

Questions

(Q1) Consider the information flow characterization of the ternary accessibility relation. Given that it is an appropriate characterization of accessibility relations within distributed systems (information channels) does it *by this* provide an analysis/model for our concept of *semantic* entailment?

(Q2) Consider the characterization of the Routley star in terms of compatible (completed) situations. Given that this is a good characterization of negation, is it truth-functional or intensional or neither of them? How to we ascertain the truth of $\neg A$? If every situation was compatible with itself, what would this imply for Explosion?

(Q3) Why is the content of $A \vee B$ less than the content of the single sentences: $c(A) \cap c(B)$ (i.e. the cut and not the union $c(A) \cup c(B)$)?

Exercises

(Ex1) Using the truth condition (R→) show that *verum ex qoudlibet sequitur*, $A \rightarrow (B \rightarrow A)$, is not a logical truth.

(Ex2) Show that given the restriction on R associated with Contraction (A14) cannot be invalidated.

(Ex3) Why is the *Modus Ponens* theorem not valid in the content semantics of **DJ^{d}Q**? Consider the *closure* conditions of contents (what do they involve and what do they not involve), and the *content* of the conjunction A ∧ (A → B).

Further Reading

• On Relevant Logics in general you may look in the two volumes of *Entailment* (ed. by A. Anderson et al.) or the two volumes of *Relevant Logics and their Rivals* (ed. by R. Routley, R. Brady et al.), but for a introduction to these logics you better use: Read, Stephen. *Relevant Logic*. Oxford, 1994. A short introduction you find in (Priest 2000). A philosophical introduction and discussion you find in: Mares, Edwin. *Relevant Logic*. A Philosophical Interpretation. Cambridge, 2004.

• The idea of a information (flow) semantics for Relevant logics you can find in: Mares, Edwin. "Relevant Logic and the Theory of Information", *Synthese*, 109 (1996), pp. 345-60; and: Restall, Greg. "Information Flow and Relevant Logics", in: Seligmann, Jerry/ Westerstahl, Dag (Eds). *Logic, Language and Computation*. Stanford, 1996, pp. 463-77. On the theory of information flow see (Barwise/ Seligman 1997), (Bremer/Cohnitz 2004); on situation semantics in general see: (Devlin 1991).

• Brady's logic is presented in: "Entailment, Negation and Paradox Solution", in: (Batens et al. 2000), pp.113-36.

• An approch similar to Relevant logic in requiring the sharing of content is the relatedness logic in (Epstein 1995), but it is explosive.

6 | A Sequential Calculus

In this chapter we look at another calculus that fits the criteria of Chapter 3, including the Strong Anti-Triviality Condition. This calculus contains a conditional connective that is stronger than the material conditional and satisfies *Modus Ponens* and *Transitivity*. The logic is not, however, a Relevant Logic in the sense of Chapter 5. The semantics of the entailment connective does not employ the ternary accessibility relation or some variant of it.
The logic **SKP** is based on (Priest 1980), supplemented with standard quantificational theory; the revisions (like dropping Contraposition and restricting Substitution of Identicals) will be motivated in Chapter 16.

Sequential Calculi

A sequential calculus gives a logic of sequences (of well-formed formula). The formulas in the sequence are separated by the symbol "⊩" which means that the formulas on the right of it, taken conjunctively make true the formulas to the left of it, taken disjunctively. Formulas on the right and left of "⊩" are separated by commas.
The original approach (Gentzen 1934/35) employed rules for the introduction/elimination of connectives and quantifiers on the right and the left side. In our calculus we have only single formulas on the right side (the case of a disjunction of one disjunct only). The calculus is not developed in the systematic fashion of introduction and elimination rules (like in Natural Deduction systems descending from sequential systems), but by giving axioms and rules according to our needs and in the not so systematic fashion that results from restricting standard logic.
A sequence is a formula with exactly one "⊩" occurring in it. On the left of "⊩" are nil, one or more than one formula separated by commas, taken conjunctively. On the right of "⊩" stands a single formula.
These lines like

A, B⊩C

are *sentences of the language*, not the meta-language. "⊩" expresses within the language the inheritance of truth from the formulas on the left to the formula on the right. In fact it works thus like "⊃". One may introduce "⊃" into the language of **SKP** using its usual definition, but, of course, many of its theorems and consequences are missing.
SKP works with the distinction between inheritance of truth, symbolized by "⊩" and entailment, symbolized by " →".

There are no rules for "$\Vdash$" itself. Rules of a sequential calculus tell us how to derive a new *sequence* given other sequences. Derivation *only* contain lines with sequences. In the example A, C and B do not contain occurrences of "$\Vdash$".
How "$\Vdash$" works can also be seen in its semantics. Since it is part of our language we need semantic clauses for "$\Vdash$"; especially in evaluating lines in deductions.
The only case in which inheritance of truth is false is that in case of a true left hand side the right side is false *only*. In case the right hand side is antinomic truths is – trivially – inherited. Since *simply false* is binary [see Chap. 4], a sequence can be only true or false, never both!
Writing thus $(A_1...A_n)\Vdash B$ for $v((A_1...A_n)\Vdash B, 1)$ and $\neg((A_1...A_n)\Vdash B)$ for $v((A_1...A_n)\Vdash B, 0)$ we state the truth conditions:

(S$\Vdash$) (i) $(A_1...A_n)\Vdash B \Rightarrow \neg(\exists v)(v(A_1,1) \wedge ... \; v(A_n,1) \wedge \neg\, v(B,1))$
(ii) $\neg(\exists v)(v(A_1,1) \wedge ... \; v(A_n,1) \wedge \neg\, v(B,1)) \Rightarrow (A_1...A_n)\Vdash B$
(iii) $(\exists v)(v(A_1,1) \wedge ... \; v(A_n,1) \wedge \neg\, v(B,1)) \Rightarrow \neg((A_1...A_n)\Vdash B)$
(iv) $\neg((A_1...A_n)\Vdash B) \Rightarrow (\exists v)(v(A_1,1) \wedge ... \; v(A_n,1) \wedge \neg\, v(B,1))$

(iii) and (iv) give the contrapositives of (i) and (ii).

We have used some natural deduction systems already and later will introduce some of them more systematically. Sequent systems are the historic ancestors of these systems. For a better understanding of "$\Vdash$" it might help you to see the line

$(A_1...A_n)\Vdash B$

in a deduction in this sequent calculus as another representation of what in our natural deduction format would look like:

n.$\langle A_1...A_n\rangle$ B

"$\Vdash$" would thus express the presence of premises in the object language itself, what is *shown* only by the way of rendering natural deduction proofs.

Syntax

The language of **SKP** is the same as that of the Relevant Logics, supplemented by the symbol "$\Vdash$". The formation rules are adapted accordingly for sequences and the definition of a derivation.
We take conjunction, negation, and entailment "$\rightarrow$" as the basic connectives and define in the usual way:

(D1) $A \leftrightarrow B \overset{\text{def}}{=} (A \rightarrow B) \wedge (B \rightarrow A)$

(D2) $A \vee B \overset{\text{def}}{=} \neg(\neg A \wedge \neg B)$

One may add the definitions:

(D3) $A \supset B \overset{\text{def}}{=} \neg A \vee B$
(D4) $A \equiv B \overset{\text{def}}{=} (A \supset B) \wedge (B \supset A)$
(D5) $\top \overset{\text{def}}{=} \neg A \vee A$

The quantifies are both introduced in the quantificational rules.
$\Vdash B$ says that the premise set from which B inherits truth is empty, i.e. B is considered to be logically true. [A, B are again schematic letters of the meta-language for object-language formulas "p", "p $\rightarrow$ q" etc. (cf. Chap. 1).] In stating rules, executing set theoretical operations on the premise sets we use "Γ", "Π" and "Θ" for premise *sets*. These sets may be empty or may be identical.

The axiom schemes of **SKP** are:

(A1) $\{A\} \Vdash A$
(A2) $\Vdash A \wedge B \rightarrow A$
$\Vdash A \wedge B \rightarrow B$
(A3) $\Vdash A \rightarrow A \vee B$
$\Vdash B \rightarrow A \vee B$
(A4) $\Vdash A \rightarrow \neg\neg A$
(A5) $\Vdash \neg\neg A \rightarrow A$
(A6) $\Vdash A \wedge (B \vee C) \rightarrow (A \wedge B) \vee (A \wedge C)$
(A7) $\Vdash A \vee \neg A$
(A8) $\Vdash (\forall x)x=x$

Everything makes itself true (Axiom 1). Corresponding to the Extensionality Condition conjunction and disjunction are duals and have their usual properties, including distribution (Axioms 2, 3, 6). Negation is treated classically, not intuitionistically, validating *Tertium Non Datur* (Axioms 4, 5, 7). The last axiom is the basic axiom for **SKP** being a quantificational logic with identity.
The real power of **SKP** resides with the rules. The rules of **SKP** are:

(R1) $\Gamma \cup \{A\} \Vdash B \;\&\; \Pi \cup \{C\} \Vdash B \Rightarrow \Pi \cup \Gamma \cup \{A \vee C\} \Vdash B$
(R2) $\Gamma \Vdash (B \rightarrow A) \;\&\; \Pi \Vdash (B \rightarrow C) \Rightarrow \Pi \cup \Gamma \Vdash (B \rightarrow A \wedge C)$
(R3) $\Gamma \Vdash (A \rightarrow B) \;\&\; \Pi \Vdash (C \rightarrow B) \Rightarrow \Pi \cup \Gamma \Vdash (A \vee C \rightarrow B)$
(R4) $\Gamma \Vdash (A \rightarrow B) \;\&\; \Pi \Vdash A \Rightarrow \Pi \cup \Gamma \Vdash B$
(R5) $\Gamma \Vdash (A \rightarrow B) \;\&\; \Pi \Vdash (B \rightarrow C) \Rightarrow \Pi \cup \Gamma \Vdash (A \rightarrow C)$
(R6) $\Gamma \Vdash A \;\&\; \Pi \Vdash C \Rightarrow \Pi \cup \Gamma \Vdash (A \wedge C)$

Rules (R1) and (R3) corresponds to prefixing, (R2) to postfixing. (R6) states conjunction introduction. (R4) is *Modus Ponens* for entailment. (R5) is transitivity for entailment. **SKP**, thus, meets the *Modus Ponens* Condition, and seems to meet the Minimal Damage Condition with respect to the conditional connective. Substitution of (semantic) equivalents holds by

(R7) $\Gamma \Vdash (A \leftrightarrow B) \Rightarrow \Gamma \Vdash (C \leftrightarrow C(A/B))$
where C(A/B) is built by replacing all tokens of A in C by B.

SKP contains also – in addition to transitivity of entailment, and like other sequential calculi – a Cut rule for "$\Vdash$":

(R8) $\Gamma \cup \{A\} \Vdash B$ & $\Pi \Vdash A \Rightarrow \Pi \cup \Gamma \Vdash B$

Contraposition can be *added* (to give us **SKP**$^+$):

(R14) $\Gamma \Vdash (A \rightarrow B) \Rightarrow \Gamma \Vdash (\neg B \rightarrow \neg A)$

SKP contains standard quantificational rules. [Remember: "P( )", "á" ... are schemata for predicates and constants.]

(R9) $\Pi \Vdash P(é) \Rightarrow \Pi \Vdash (\exists x)P(x)$

(R10) $\Pi \Vdash (\exists x)P(x)$ & $\{P(á)\} \cup \Gamma \Vdash B \Rightarrow \Pi \cup \Gamma \Vdash B$
where á doesn't occur in B, $(\exists x)P(x)$ or in a formula in $\Pi \cup \Gamma$.

(R11) $\Pi \Vdash P(é) \Rightarrow \Pi \Vdash (\forall x)P(x)$
where é does not occur in any premise in Π.

(R12) $\Pi \Vdash (\forall x)P(x) \Rightarrow \Pi \Vdash P(á)$

In case of Substitution of Identicals we introduce the set Ξ of inconsistent objects (i.e. objects such that: $P_i(á) \wedge \neg P_i(á)$ for some P_i). Let δ be the denotation function of quantificational semantics. Then:

(R13) $\delta(á) \notin \Xi$ & $\Gamma \Vdash á=é$ & $\Pi \Vdash P(é) \Rightarrow \Pi \cup \Gamma \Vdash P(á)$

If á does not denote an inconsistent object then substitution applies.
Applying (R13) is problematic, since to apply it we have to know whether $\delta(á) \notin \Xi$. If we want to express the consistency of an object *in* our language we needed set theoretical expressions. For the purposes of chapter 16 the restriction $\delta(á) \neq m$ suffices with m being the least inconsistent number. Nevertheless this would be needed as additional premise. [Remember that in **LPQ**$^=$ substitution of identicals fails *in general*.]
(R13) without the restriction concerning inconsistent objects can – with (R14) – be taken as rule of **SKP**$^+$.

Derivations

A derivation is a list of numbered lines, each containing a sequence. On the right we note how the line was generated.
For better readability we number the premises and refer to them in a sequence by writing down the number, for example:

$\vdash_{SKP}((\forall x)F(x) \Vdash F(a))$

Proof:

(1) $(\forall x)F(x)$

1. 1 $\Vdash(\forall x)F(x)$	A1
2. 1 $\Vdash F(a)$	R12, 1 ■

Do not confuse "$\vdash_{SKP}$" with "$\Vdash$"!
Numbers on the right of course refer to lines of the derivation to which the rule in question has been applied (*not* to formulas to the left of the "$\Vdash$").

SKP Theorems

(SKPT2) $(\forall x)(F(x)\rightarrow G(x)), (\forall x)F(x) \Vdash (\forall x)G(x)$

Proof (1) $(\forall x)(F(x)\rightarrow G(x))$
(2) $(\forall x)F(x)$

1. 1 $\Vdash(\forall x)(F(x)\rightarrow G(x))$	A1
2. 2 $\Vdash(\forall x)F(x)$	A1
3. 1 $\Vdash(F(a)\rightarrow G(a))$	R12, 1
4. 2 $\Vdash F(a)$	R12, 2
5. 1,2 $\Vdash G(a)$	R4, 3, 4
6. 1, 2 $\Vdash(\forall x)G(x)$	R11, 6 ■

Note that the corresponding consequence relation was invalid in **LPQ**.

(SKPT3) $(\forall x)(F(x) \wedge G(x)) \Vdash (\forall x)F(x) \wedge (\forall x)G(x)$

Proof (1) $(\forall x)(F(x) \wedge G(x))$

1. 1 $\Vdash(\forall x)(F(x) \wedge G(x))$	A1
2. 1 $\Vdash F(a) \wedge G(a)$	R12, 1
3. $\Vdash F(a) \wedge G(a) \rightarrow F(a)$	A2
4. 1 $\Vdash F(a)$	R4, 3, 4
5. 1 $\Vdash(\forall x)(F(x)$	R11, 4
6. $\Vdash F(a) \wedge G(a) \rightarrow G(a)$	A2

7. 1 $\Vdash G(a)$ R4, 2, 6
8. 1 $\Vdash (\forall x)G(x)$ R11, 7
9. 1 $\Vdash (\forall x)F(x) \wedge (\forall x)G(x)$ R6, 5, 7 ■

(SKPT4) $\Vdash p \leftrightarrow \neg\neg p$

Proof
by (A4), (A5), (D1), (R6) ■

(SKPT5) ||- $p \wedge p \leftrightarrow p$

Proof
1. $\Vdash p \wedge p \rightarrow p$ A2
2. $\Vdash p \rightarrow \neg\neg p$ A4
3. $\Vdash p \leftrightarrow \neg\neg p$ Theorem 3
4. $\Vdash p \rightarrow p$ R7, 2, 3 [=(SKPT6)]
5. $\Vdash p \rightarrow p$ R7, 2, 3
6. $\Vdash p \rightarrow p \wedge p$ R2, 4, 5
7. $\Vdash p \wedge p \leftrightarrow p$ D1, 1, 6 ■

(SKPT7) $\Vdash p \vee p \leftrightarrow p$

Proof
by (A3), (SKPT6), (R3), (D1) ■

(SKPT8) $\Vdash (p \wedge q) \vee (p \wedge r) \rightarrow p \wedge (q \vee r)$

Proof
1. $\Vdash (p \wedge q) \rightarrow q$ A2
2. $\Vdash q \rightarrow q \vee r$ A3
3. $\Vdash (p \wedge q) \rightarrow (q \vee r)$ R5, 1, 2 (Transitivity)
4. $\Vdash (p \wedge q) \rightarrow p$ A2
5. $\Vdash (p \wedge q) \rightarrow p \wedge (q \vee r)$ R2, 3, 4
6. $\Vdash (p \wedge r) \rightarrow p \wedge (q \vee r)$ (similar to lines 1-5)
7. $\Vdash (p \wedge q) \vee (p \wedge r) \rightarrow p \wedge (q \vee r)$ R3, 5, 6 ■

Interestingly enough the Law of Non-Contradiction holds in **SKP**:

(SKPT9) $\Vdash \neg(p \wedge \neg p)$

Proof
1. $\Vdash (p \vee \neg p)$ A7
2. $\Vdash \neg(\neg p \wedge \neg\neg p)$ D2, 1

3. $\Vdash p \leftrightarrow \neg\neg p$ Theorem 3
4. $\Vdash \neg(p \wedge \neg p)$ R7, 2, 3 ■

(SKPT10) $(p \rightarrow (q \rightarrow r), p \wedge q \Vdash r$ [like Importation]

Proof

by (A1), (A2), (R4) ■

Disjunctive and Conjunctive Syllogism are not derivable in **SKP**. Indirect methods of proofs are, because of the absence of Contraposition, not available in **SKP**, but in **SKP**$^+$ (see Exercises).
There are two modest ways of something like indirect argumentation in **SKP**, namely:

(DR1) $A \Vdash (\neg A) \Rightarrow \Vdash (\neg A)$

Proof

1. $A \Vdash (\neg A)$ Assumption (using schematic A)
2. $\neg A \Vdash (\neg A)$ A1
3. $A \vee \neg A \Vdash (\neg A)$ R1, 1, 2
4. $\varnothing \Vdash A \vee \neg A$ A7
5. $\varnothing \Vdash \neg A$ R8, 3, 4 ■

(DR2) $\Vdash (A \rightarrow \neg A) \Rightarrow \Vdash (\neg A)$

Proof

by (SKPT6), (R3), (A7), (R4) ■

The dualities of the extensional "$\supset$" have, of course, no corresponding dualities involving entailment, "$\rightarrow$". Nevertheless there are some theorems [see (SKPT10) and Exercise (2)] with similar content. Nested entailments might be problematic with respect to our natural understanding of entailment (a nested entailment would say something like that the content of the antecedent contains that some other content containment obtains). The rules of **SKP** do not allow to introduce some sentence into the antecedent of "$\rightarrow$" crossing "$\Vdash$".

SKP Semantics

SKP can be given a semantics that combines elements of a possible worlds semantics (for entailment) with a special role for the actual world @, elements of extensional truth conditions for the extensional connectives, and the quantificational semantics we introduced in Chap. 4, extended to the modal case.

A **SKP** model *M* is a tuple <W, R, @, D_i, *v*, G> where W is a set of possible worlds, R is the accessibility relation as it obtains in the model (there may be some general requirements on R), @ is the actual world, D_i is the set of domains (one domain for each possible world), *v* is the interpretation relation, G is the set of variable assignments.
The interpretation relation *v* has a further argument place now for a possible world: each sentence is evaluated relative to a world; each basic predicate gets its extension and anti-extension relative to a world. We take individual constants to be *rigid designators*.
We require for accessibility that all worlds are accessible from the actual world – one may say, because there are alternatives *for us*:

(SKPSR1) $(\forall w \in W)R(@,w)$

We already have seen how to evaluate the "⊩" in a sentence.
To deal with identity we require any interpretation to treat the identity symbol as a constant referring to the identity relation on the domain:

(SKP=) $(\forall v)(v("=")=id(D_i))$

One might allow an anti-extension for "=", but these would be objects that aren't identical to themselves! We don't do this and keep (A8).
The standard truth conditions for the extensional connectives and the quantifiers can be used [see Chap. 4], the only intensional connective is entailment. Intuitively an entailment is true in a world iff in all worlds which are accessible the truth of the antecedent brings with it the truth of the consequent; an entailment is false in a world iff a world is accessible in which the antecedent is true, but the consequent isn't.
[Note that we don't have in **SKP** the contrapositive condition.]
To give a formal statement of the intuitive truth condition one has to state *all cases* of the equivalence relation, and keep an eye to the distinction between false and *simply* false entailments. Furthermore we don't use a conditional " ⇒ " in the meta-language that allows for Contraposition, since the object- *vs.* meta-language distinction is ultimately to be dropped. This leads to the complex condition:

(SKPS→)
(i) $v(w, A\to B, 1) \Rightarrow (\forall w'\in W)(R(w,w') \wedge v(w',A,1) \Rightarrow v(w',B,1))$
(ii) $\neg\, v(w, A\to B, 1) \Rightarrow \neg(\forall w'\in W)(R(w,w') \wedge v(w',A,1) \Rightarrow v(w',B,1))$
(iii) $(\forall w'\in W)(R(w,w') \wedge v(w',A,1) \Rightarrow v(w',B,1)) \Rightarrow v(w, A\to B, 1)$
(iv) $\neg(\forall w'\in W)(R(w,w') \wedge v(w',A,1) \Rightarrow v(w',B,1)) \Rightarrow \neg v(w, A\to B, 1)$
(v) $v(w, A\to B, 0) \Rightarrow (\exists w'\in W)(R(w,w') \wedge v(w',A,1) \wedge v(w',B,0))$
(vi) $\neg\, v(w, A\to B, 0) \Rightarrow \neg(\exists w'\in W)(R(w,w') \wedge v(w',A,1) \wedge v(w',B,0))$

(vii) $(\exists w'\in W)(R(w,w') \wedge v(w',A,1) \wedge v(w',B,0)\ ) \Rightarrow v(w,\ A\rightarrow B,\ 0)$
(viii) $\neg(\exists w'\in W)(R(w,w') \wedge v(w',A,1) \wedge v(w',B,0)\ ) \Rightarrow \neg v(w,\ A\rightarrow B,\ 0)$

Truth *in a model* is bound to being true *in the actual world* (of the model). All others worlds are only tools of evaluating formula.
Validity is truth in all models (i.e. in all of their *actual* worlds):

(SKPV) $\Gamma\vDash A \Leftrightarrow (\forall M'\in M)((\forall B\in\Gamma)\ v'(@,B,1) \Rightarrow v'(@,A,1))$

A consequence being valid in case that for all models the conclusion is (at least) true at the actual world of the model if the premises are (at least) true at the actual world of that model. A valid sentence is one that follows from the empty set of premises.[Do not confuse "$\vDash$" with "$\Vdash$"!]
On the one hand this definition of validity is non-standard in as much as standard modal logic require a logical truth to be true in all worlds of all models. On the other hand *we* are in the actual world (or the thing corresponding to that description) and all other possible worlds are only tools in our reasoning what sentences are true. Thinking of some of *them* that they might be actual is thinking of *another model*. So it is not clear that the notion of validity of **SKP** fares worse than the standard notion.
All worlds being accessible from the actual world makes the actual world accessible from itself, otherwise R need not be reflexive.
We depict accessibility by arrows "→ "and write true sentences beneath a given world letter.
Given this semantics we can show that **SKP** fulfils the Strong Anti-Triviality Condition. We show that Contraction/Absorption is not valid in this semantics, neither is the *Modus Ponens* Theorem.

(SKPNT1) $\varnothing\Vdash p\rightarrow(p\rightarrow q)\nvDash_{\mathbf{SKP}}\varnothing\Vdash(p\rightarrow q)$

Proof
Let @ and w" be reflexive. w only sees w". w" only sees w".

	@		w		w"
1.			p		p
2.					q
3.			p→q		p→q
4.	p→(p→q)				

(arrows in header row: @ → w → w")

The third line occurs, since w only sees w", and w" only sees itself, but @ sees w, so that p→q does not hold at @. p→(p→q) does however hold at

@, since @ sees w and w". So the premise of Contraction is true at the actual world, but the consequent is not. So Contraction fails.

(SKPNT2) $\varnothing \nvDash_{SKP} p \wedge (p \rightarrow q) \rightarrow q$

Proof

	@	←→	w
1.	p		p
2.	q		
3.			p→q
4.			p ∧ (p→q)

Line 3 occurs, since w sees @ only (not itself). Line 4 is truth functional from other sentences in w. @, however, does not have "p→q", since @ sees w, and so does not have "p ∧ (p→q)". @ sees a world in which the antecedent of the *Modus Ponens* Theorem is true, but the consequent is not, so the supposed theorem fails.

SKP does further on invalidate *verum ex qoudlibet sequitur*.

Entailment in **SKP** is *weaker* than meaning containment (by meaning postulates) in **S5** modal logics, where accessibility is an equivalence relation, since R is *not that restricted* in **SKP** semantics – otherwise Contraction and *verum ex qoudlibet sequitur* would be valid!

SKP Meta-Logic

SKP can be shown to be *sound and non-trivial* (i.e. from true sequents we are never let to sequences that are simply false by the rules of inference, and there is at least one well-formed formula that cannot be derived with that logic). Simple consistency is, of course, not to be had in a system that is (later) extended by principles that give rise to antinomies.

(SKPMT1) $\Gamma \vdash_{SKP} A \Rightarrow \Gamma \vDash_{SKP} A$ (*Soundness*)

Proof (Outline)

(A1) is trivially true. (A2)-(A7) hold, since in the worlds the truth functional dependencies hold [e.g. in the case of (A2) the truth of A ∧ B contains the truth of A and of B]. All rules refer only to inheritance of truth (i.e. they do not *cross* worlds). (R1), (R6), (R8) are truth functionally truth preserving. (R4) is valid, since @ is reflexive. (R6) holds, since if in every A world B holds, and in very B world C holds, then in every A world C holds. In similar vain (R2) and (R3) hold. Substitution of proven equivalents, (R7), trivially preserves truth. The quantificational rules can be justified in the same way as in case of **LPQ**. (A8) is true by (SKP=). (R13) is weaker than the usual rule. ■

The theorems of **SKP** are – as we have just seen – correct with respect to its modal semantics. And we have proven – in (SKPNT1) and (SKPNT2) – that some sentences are *not valid*, and that some standard consequence relationships are *not valid.* If these theorems could be proven nevertheless, **SKP** would not be correct, but it is, so these sentences are *not provable* as well. This gives us *non-triviality*:

(SKPMT2) $(\exists A) \nVdash_{SKP} A$

A completeness proof of **SKP** has not been given so far.

SKP Trees

The trees for LPQ [see Chap. 4] may be extended to SKP trees. The rules for the extensional connectives and the quantifiers remain the same, we need rules for "⊩" and "→". Since "→" is a modal connective, these rules will "create" accessible worlds. So the trees have to be marked at which world a sentence is evaluated thus.
We change the trees to the following procedure:

1. Evaluate the sentence A to be checked with ∇A in @.
2. If a sentence contains "⊩", then:
   (2a) $T(A_i \Vdash B)$ or $\Delta(A_i \Vdash B)$ resolves to ∇A_i *or* T(B).
   (2b) $F(A_i \Vdash B)$ or $\nabla(A_i \Vdash B)$ resolves to ΔA_i *and* ∇B.
3. If "→" is the main connective to be resolved, then:
   (3a) If w has T(A → B), then in all accessible worlds w' T(B) is the case if either T(A) or ΔA is.
   (3b) If w has ∇(A → B), then add an accessible w' where we have TA and ∇B.
   (3c) If w has F(A → B), then add an accessible w' where we have TA and FB.
   (3d) If w has Δ(A → B), then in all accessible worlds w' ΔB is the case if either T(A) or ΔA is.
4. Within a world w employ the other **(LPQ)** rules.
5. All worlds have to be accessible from @.
6. If in one world an incompatible evaluation of a sentence occurs the sentence checked is *valid.*

Points (2) and (3) can be read of the semantic clauses for "⊩" and "→", as you may check.
These trees provide *not* a decision procedure, but we can say:

(SKPMT3) (i) $\nvDash_{SKP} A \Rightarrow$ A's tree is not closed.

(ii) A's tree closes $\Rightarrow\ \vDash_{SKP} A$

Proof (Outline)
In case the tree closes, the tableau, the rules of which correspond to the **SKP** semantic rules, contains incompatible evaluations; so there is not a *single* evaluation which makes A false only, so A has a designated truth value in all interpretations. If A is not valid, there will be an evaluation of the subformulas of A – following the decomposition of A like the semantic rules do – which makes A false only, so that the tree does not close. ■

As an example let us see why Contraposition fails in **SKP**:

@	$\nabla(p \rightarrow q \Vdash \neg q \rightarrow \neg p)$	
	↓	(rule for "$\Vdash$" (ii))
@	$T(p \rightarrow q), \nabla(\neg q \rightarrow \neg p)$	
	↓	(added world after "$\rightarrow$" (ii))
w	$T(\neg q), \nabla\neg p$	
	↓	(negation rules in w)
w	$Fq, \Delta p$	
	↓	(rule "$\rightarrow$" (i), @ sees w)
w	Tq	

The tree is not closed. Tq and Fq are compatible.

Summary

SKP provides us with a calculus that fits the mark in several respects:

- it is extensional with respect to the standard connectives,
- it contains an entailment connective satisfying many conditions we basically associate with a conditional,
- its semantics is only minimally deviant, given the standard possible worlds approach.
- given this semantics the logic is correct, so in light of the dialetheist's case stated in chapter 2, we have – besides **LPQ** – a second logic that can serve in sound derivations (and even one fitting the criteria better).

On the other hand, using a sequential calculus like that is not usual and one needs to accustom to it a bit. That, of course, is only a pragmatic concern.
A more interesting question is what the intuitive reading of the SKP-conditional is, since it is not semantic entailment in the usual sense of alethic modal logic, nor is it Relevant entailment as in **R**. The accessibility relation used in **SKP** cannot be used for necessity, since the failure of reflexivity makes $\Box A \supset A$ false!

Questions

(Q1) In the truth conditions for "$\Vdash$" we use an evaluation relation *v* and write $\neg\, v(B,1)$ and not $v(B,0)$ – why? And why can we *then* write just $\neg((A_1...A_n) \Vdash B)$ for $v((A_1...A_n) \Vdash B, 0)$?

(Q2) Given (SKP$\rightarrow$) explain the cases that an entailment is true, simply true, false, simply false, antinomic! The entailment being antinomic derives from which sentence being antinomic?

(Q3) What clauses had to be added in (SKP$\rightarrow$) and the tree rules for "$\rightarrow$" to make Contraposition valid?

Exercises

(Ex1) Give the definitions of a well-formed formula and a derivation for **SKP**.

(Ex2) Proof in **SKP** the following theorems:

$p \vee \neg p \rightarrow q \Vdash q$
$\neg p \rightarrow q, p \rightarrow q \Vdash q$
$p, q \Vdash p$ [a theorem similar to "Weakening"]
$p \wedge q \Vdash p \vee q$
$p \wedge q \Vdash q \wedge p$
$(\forall x)F(x) \Vdash (\exists x)F(x)$
$(\exists x)(\forall y)R(x,y) \Vdash (\forall y)(\exists x)R(x,y)$
$(\exists x)(P(x) \rightarrow B), (\forall x)P(x) \Vdash B$ ["x" not in B]
$(\exists x)(F(x) \rightarrow G(x)), (\forall x)F(x) \Vdash (\exists x)G(x)$

(Ex3) Proof in **SKP**$^+$ the following rules:

$\Gamma \Vdash A \rightarrow (\neg B \wedge B) \Rightarrow \Gamma \Vdash (\neg A)$
$\Gamma \Vdash A \rightarrow B \ \&\ \Pi \Vdash (\neg B) \Rightarrow \Gamma \cup \Pi \Vdash (\neg A)$

So indirect proofs and *Modus Tollens* are valid in **SKP**$^+$ but not in **SKP** itself.

Further Reading

- The basic paper on **SKP** is Priest, Graham. "Sense, Entailment and *Modus Ponens*", *Journal of Philosophical Logic*, 9 (1980), pp.415-35. The paper contains a second (algebraic) semantics, which, however, has less if any intuitive force compared to the possible worlds approach [see also (Bremer 1998, pp.100-110)].
- The classic paper on sequential calculi is (Gentzen 1934/35).
- On Natural Deduction as descendant of sequential calculi, and a brief presentation of the Gentzen approach, see (Essler/Martinez 1991).

7 | Adaptive Logics

The Adaptive Logics program is the third major group in current paraconsistent logic research. Its centre is the group of Diderik Batens at the university of Ghent (forming the "Ghent Centre for Logic and Philosophy of Science"). It was there that in 1997 the First World Congress of Paraconsistency took place. Batens and his group (including Joke Meheus, Guido Vanackere, Kristof De Clercq and others) deal not only with paraconsistent logics, but one main inspiration to develop adaptive logics (ALs) was to develop inconsistency adaptive logics. Meanwhile the research on adaptive logics involves logics for explanation and induction, partial revision, logics for ambiguities ...

General Idea

Modelling actual reasoning requires a dynamic modelling: Depending on what information is *available at some time* inferences are drawn and may be *retracted.* Common sense reasoning often is non-monotonic, i.e. $\Gamma \cup \{A\} \nvDash B$ where as $\Gamma \vDash B$

This non-monotonicity appears with respect to exceptions to some rule (default logic) or with respect to discovering inconsistencies in a given premise set Γ (inconsistency adaptive logic).

In case of the usual non-monotonic logics the dynamics in reasoning can be called an "external" dynamics since it ensues by adding further premises/information to the premise set.

External dynamics corresponds to the non-monotonicity of the inference (respectively consequence) relation.

In distinction to this adaptive logics are concerned with so called "internal" dynamics: Within the reasoning on a conclusively given premise set the insight on logical relations within the premise set and its consequences increases.

Internal dynamics are concerned with the reasoning process itself.

Internal dynamic need not be mirrored in the (final) consequence set of a premise set Γ. Extensions and retractions may cancel out in the end.

Modelling internal dynamics is closer to modelling real reasoning in discovering the power of a premise set. To do this we have to refer to the *stages* of a proof, and what has been established *so far* (without this "so far" being dependent on new information extending the premises available at that stage).

Modelling internal dynamics is an extension of the Natural Deduction approach.
Retracting in the process of reasoning from a premise set cannot be completely avoided, since there is no general algorithmic procedure (for any logic) to test whether Γ or $\Gamma \cup \{A\}$ is consistent.
So we often extend our premise set Γ by a new assumption on the supposition that this extension is consistent, although it sometimes turns out not to be.
Especially if $\Gamma \vdash A$ *depends* on $\Gamma \nvdash C$ and no negative test (say in **FOL**) is available for $\Gamma \nvdash C$, then we have even no positive test for $\Gamma \vdash A$. [The derivability of A may depend on the absence of C if say C states some exceptional condition on employing some rule to derive A.]
Retraction is of most interest with respect to internal dynamics, since given one and the same premise set the sentence A may be derivable at some stage and retracted later. A then might not belong to the final consequence set, but it appeared to during some stages of the reasoning process.

Lower and Upper Limit Logic

An adaptive logic is characterized by:

- an Upper Limit Logic (ULL)
- a Lower Limit Logic (LLL)
- an adaptive strategy.

The *Upper Limit Logic* (ULL) allows for the unrestricted application of logical rules to derive the most consequences possible. Typically ULL is (standard) **FOL**. Since the set of consequences of this logic is larger, it is the *upper* limit logic.
The *Lower Limit Logic* (LLL) is chosen to model some type of restricted reasoning. In our case it is a paraconsistent logic, i.e. a logic that blocks the application of some rules of standard logic. Since the set of consequences is correspondingly smaller, it is the *lower* limit logic.

$$Con_{LLL}(\Gamma) \subseteq Con_{ULL}(\Gamma),$$

The *adaptive strategy* is the way to handle the management of restrictions and the corresponding retractions.
An adaptive logic such defined with a paraconsistent logic (PL) as LLL could behave like a flip-flop: It behaves like ULL if the premise set Δ is consistent and behaves like the LLL (PL) if Δ is inconsistent. But such a behaviour (and such a logic) is not interesting, since it simply means to revert to LLL in case of inconsistency.Adaptive logics do not do that in general: An AL generates a set of consequences of an inconsistent Δ that can lay between $Con_{LLL}(\Delta)$ and $Con_{ULL}(\Delta)$. That is, the interesting case is:

$Con_{LLL}(\Delta) \subset Con_{AL}(\Delta) \subset Con_{ULL}(\Delta)$.

Some rules (e.g. Disjunctive Syllogism [$\neg A, A \vee B \vdash B$] and *ex contradictione qoudlibet* [$\neg A, A \vdash B$]) are not valid in many paraconsistent logics. Given their non-validity one cannot employ them to derive consequences.

But this is too restrictive: These rules fail only if A is a true contradiction. They could be applied to consistently behaving sentences. The idea of adaptation is therefore: Think of these rules as applicable and make exceptions *only* if one of the premises is known to be inconsistent. Since we do not know beforehand which premises *are* consistent, we may employ these rules incorrectly. That is why there is retraction. Retraction occurs (in the case of a paraconsistent LLL) if some sentence to which one of the restricted rules was applied turns out to be inconsistent. The application of that rule is retracted then. All consequences of that application are retracted as well.

Examples:

Some rules like Disjunctive Syllogism [$\neg A, A \vee B \vdash B$] and *ex contradictione qoudlibet* [$\neg A, A \vdash B$], and all derived rules depending on them, have to be restricted.

Restriction means here that they are only used if on the left hand side of the application no contradiction is involved.

1. Disjunctive Syllogism leads to triviality if A in
   $\neg A, A \vee B \vdash B$ is a contradiction.
2. *ex contradictione qoudlibet* leads to triviality if A in:
   $\neg A, A \vdash B$ is a contradiction.
3. *Modus Ponens* (in some PLs like **LP**) leads to triviality if A in
   $A, A \supset B \vdash B$ is a contradiction.
4. *Modus Tollens* (in some PLs like **LP**) leads to triviality if B in
   $A \supset B, \neg B \vdash (\neg A)$ is a contradiction.

[Note: Negation Introduction [$A \supset (B \wedge \neg B) \vdash (\neg A)$] is not valid at all in a paraconsistent context. One may take: $A \supset \neg A \vdash (\neg A)$ instead.]

Without adaptivity we had to reason using some PL in all contexts which we suppose to contain contradictions. Given that quite a lot of standard logic is missing [including contraposition, transitivity (of identity) etc.] that is a severe restriction. We cannot capture a lot of (harmless) consequences in that field then.

Philosophy as that area of universal talk about semantics and epistemology would have to use such a restricted logic. It is questionable how many of

its theses and arguments could really (i.e. without hidden recourse to standard logic) be expressed.
Adaptivity, on the other hand, makes clear that reasoning from the present contradictions is rather the exception than the rule. Concerning some inconsistent theory T one can say, "We keep T – except for the pernicious consequences of its inconsistency".

Types of Adaptive Approaches

Most ALs are *corrective*, i.e. LLL $\subseteq$ ULL = FOL, but some are *ampliative*, i.e. they extend the set of standard consequences of a premise set (e.g. in adaptive inductive reasoning).
Flat adaptive logics are such that all premises are of equal importance. Otherwise an AL is *prioritised*. Prioritisation can occur in a proof by giving premises indexes to show their different importance. Prioritisation means that in case we have a choice in retraction we retract on that premise which has the lowest priority.
An AL needs an *adaptive strategy* to deal both with inconsistencies (exceptions) *and* the problem that an inconsistent premise set need not tell us which premise is to blame (for example take $\{\neg p, \neg q, p \vee q\}$). The most common strategies are the *Reliability* strategy and the *Minimal Abnormality* strategy. Depending on the chosen strategy the consequence set of an AL is greater or smaller.

Dab(Δ)-Formulas

Given a premise set Γ one likes to know which of them may be abnormalities. *Abnormalities* here are formulas of the form $A \wedge \neg A$ (we also say in this case that A is an abnormality, a contradiction).
Some premise sets might be such that we know:

(1) $(p \wedge \neg p) \vee (q \wedge \neg q)$

whereas neither disjunct is a consequence (so far). So maybe each of them or either "p" or "q" behaves abnormally.
"Dab(Δ)" abbreviates the disjunction of $(A \wedge \neg A)$ for all $A \in \Delta$. "Dab(Δ)" then expresses that at least one of the premises in Δ is abnormal. "Dab" means "disjunction of abnormalities". We are looking for *minimal* Dab-formulas (since the less disjuncts a Dab-formula has the more premises we have excluded as suspects).
Besides the formulas occuring in a Dab-formula there might be formulas which are *already* known as being abnormal. In general:

$\Gamma \vdash_{LLL} (A \vee Dab(\Delta))$ iff $\Gamma \vdash_{ULL} A$

Here Δ contains the formulas on the consistency of which the application of some rules used in deriving A depends. Note:

1. Δ typically is taken as the set of formulas in Γ that are or may be unreliable.
2. Hopefully $\Delta \neq \Gamma$, but, of course, $\Delta \subseteq \Gamma$.
3. Even if some formulas have been established as abnormal, there may be further formulas that are suspected as possibly abnormal; i.e. there may be a set of inconsistencies $\Lambda \subseteq \Gamma$ with $\Lambda \cap \Delta = \varnothing$. Dab($\Delta$) then expresses that there is at least one more member of Λ but we do not know which disjunct it is.
4. Formulas A for which $A \wedge \neg A$ has been proven are *unreliable per se.* Which A contained in Δ for which we have Dab(Δ) are taken as *unreliable* depends on the adaptive strategy.

Adaptive Strategies

One can follow the *Reliability* strategy that considers all $A \in \Delta$ as unreliable, or the *Minimal Abnormality* strategy, which with respect to (1), for example, assumes that once we consider the one abnormal we can take the other as normal (i.e., we can derive more consequences, since less exceptions are now operative).
A logic following the Minimal Abnormality strategy does not coincide in its consequence set with a logic that employs the reliabilist strategy thus allowing for more counterexamples in the models.
In cases like (1) one can get indeterministic proofs following the Minimal Abnormality strategy: One chooses either "p" or "q" as being abnormal.
If at some later stage in a proof one can derive one of the disjuncts in (1) [in general in: Dab(Δ)], then (1) [or Dab(Δ)] is no longer *minimal.* So this Dab-formula is replaced – even using the reliabilist strategy – by one stating that derived inconsistency. Retractions based on the supposed inconsistency of one of the other disjuncts are taken back then [by *marking/unmarking* lines in the proof, see below].

Proof Theory

Proofs look like Natural Deduction Proofs with a further column:

n.<k,...>A   Rule, m, l   {B}

We number the lines and include in "< >" the premises a line depends on, then follows the formula, then a column naming the rule applied to get this line and the lines used in that application. The 5th column contains the set

of formulas (possibly empty) on the consistency of which the derivability of the formula depends. These sets are called "conditions".
Conditions obey the following abstract rules:

(RU) If $A_1 \ldots A_n \vdash_{LLL} B$, then from $A_1 \ldots A_n$ on the conditions $\Delta_1 \ldots \Delta_n$ derive B on the condition $\Delta_1 \cup \ldots \cup \Delta_n$.

The rule (RU) concerns rules of Natural Deduction which do not require in LLL the consistency of the ingredient formulas. B just inherits the conditional dependencies.
Rules requiring such consistency operate on

(RC) If $A_1 \ldots A_n \vdash_{LLL}(B \vee Dab(\Delta_m)$, then from $A_1 \ldots A_n$ on the conditions $\Delta_1 \ldots \Delta_n$ derive B on the condition $\Delta_m \cup \Delta_1 \cup \ldots \cup \Delta_n$

In this case consistency assumptions for the formulas in Δ_m are added.
The last line of a proof is the stage that the proof has arrived at.
Now, if one of the formulas in the condition gets to be known as non fulfilling the essential criterion (here: consistency) the line is *marked.*
This is the reliabilist *Marking Rule*:

If $Dab(\Delta)$ has been established, take as unreliable all $A \in \Delta$, and given the set U_s of formulas that turned out to be unreliable at stage s of the proof: If for $A \in \Delta_i$, $A \in U_s$, then line *i* is marked.

The marking rule of the Minimal Abnormality strategy is more complex, but says roughly:

If for $A \in \Delta_i$, A occurs in some Dab-formula, then line *i* is *not* marked because of that Dab-formula if there is another disjunct of that Dab-formula which is taken as unreliable.

Lines that depend on a marked line have inherited the condition by either (RU) or (RC) and are, therefore, marked as well.
Depending on the strategy – or the premise set – a line can get *unmarked* later, even in case of the reliabilist strategy.
Proof Example:
Instead of simply writing "(RU)", "(RC)" the detailed rules are given.[24]

1.<1>	$\neg p \wedge r$	PREM	$\emptyset$
2.<2>	$q \supset p$	PREM	$\emptyset$
3.<3>	$s \vee \neg r$	PREM	$\emptyset$
4.<4>	$r \supset p$	PREM	$\emptyset$

[24] This proof uses **LP** as LLL, see below.

5.<5>	$p \vee \neg r$	PREM	$\varnothing$		
6.<1>	$\neg p$	$\wedge$E, 1	$\varnothing$	(RU)	
7.<1>	r	$\wedge$E, 1	$\varnothing$	(RU)	
8.<1,2>	$\neg q$	Contrap., 6, 2	{p}	(RC)	marked at 10
9.<1,3>	s	$\vee$E, 3, 7	{r}	(RC)	marked at 10 unmarked at 11
10.<1,5>	$(\neg p \wedge p) \vee (\neg r \wedge r)$	Dilemma, $\wedge$I, 5, 6, 7	$\varnothing$	(RU)	
11.<1,4>	$\neg p \wedge p$	$\supset$E, 4, 7	{r}	(RC)	

In line 10 we get to know that at least one of "r" and "p" is inconsistent, so lines depending on them get marked.

Given a Minimal Abnormality strategy *or* seeing in line 11 that "p" is inconsistent we can blame "p" for line 10 and unmark the lines depending on the consistency of "r". The Dab-formula in 10 is no longer *minimal* after 11 (so a reliabilist would agree with blaming "p").

Let's look at derivability:

...

8.<1,2>	$\neg q$	Contrap., 6, 2	{p}	(RC)	marked at 10
9.<1,3>	s	$\vee$E, 3, 7	{r}	(RC)	marked at 10 unmarked at 11
10.<1,5>	$(\neg p \wedge p) \vee (\neg r \wedge r)$	Dilemma, $\wedge$I, 5, 6, 7	$\varnothing$	(RU)	
11.<1,4>	$\neg p \wedge p$	$\supset$E, 4, 7	{r}	(RC)	

At stage 9 "s" is derived, but no longer so at stage 10 because of the marking. At stage 11 "s" is once again derived. "$\neg$ q" is not derived from stage 10 on.

Given the dynamic character of the proofs one has to distinguish:

- derivability at some stage
- final derivability.

The latter can be defined:

> A is *finally derived* at line *i* of a proof at a stage *s* iff line *i* is unmarked at *s*, and whenever line *i* is marked in an extension of the proof, then there is a further extension in which line *i* is not marked.

Of course this property is (in most cases) not recursive (nor r.e.). One would like to have criteria to make an assessment.

Even if final derivability is not recursive (i.e. we have to *guess* whether some formula derivable now is finally derivable) this resembles our actual reasoning where we (mostly) lack similar assurance against revision.

Note also: There is *nothing* dynamic about final derivability.

LP as LLL

Being concerned with inconsistency, and since adaptive logicss are said to use paraconsistent logicss as LLLs one can use quantified **LP** (**LPQ**) as a paradigmatic paraconsistent logic with an intuitive semantics, and enrichable by a detachable conditional junctor besides "$\supset$", as LLL and FOL as ULL. [The example above used **LP** as LLL.]
Using **LP** as LLL combined with an adaptive strategy that relies on minimalizing the number of abnormalities leads to the effect that inconsistencies once present are spread (i.e. further inconsistencies can be derived). That is because some rules of spreading, which are blocked in **LP**, are no longer generally blocked when **LP** is used as LLL in an AL [see the example below].
Nonetheless this spreading of inconsistencies does *not* lead to triviality. The important meta-theorem is:

$$(\exists A)\,\Gamma \nvdash_{LP} A \;\rightarrow\; (\exists A)\,\Gamma \nvdash_{ALP} A$$

That is: Given that **LP** can avoid triviality, so can the AL that is based on **LP** as LLL (here called "**ALP**"). This fact is called *Reassurance* [cf. (Priest 1991)].
The following example shows that:

$$Con_{LP}(\Gamma) \subset Con_{ALP}(\Gamma) \subset Con_{PC}(\Gamma)$$

with $\Gamma=\{p \wedge \neg p,\ (q \wedge \neg q) \vee r\}$ [i.e., $Con_{PC}(\Gamma)$ is universal]. We follow again the conventions given above:

1.$\langle 1\rangle$	$p \wedge \neg p$	PREM	$\varnothing$	
2.$\langle 2\rangle$	$(q \wedge \neg q) \vee r$	PREM	$\varnothing$	
3.$\langle\ \rangle$	$\neg(q \wedge \neg q)$	LP-Theorem	$\varnothing$	RU
4.$\langle 2\rangle$	r	$\vee$E, 2, 3	$\{q \wedge \neg q\}$	RC
5.$\langle 1,2\rangle$	$r \wedge \neg p$	$\wedge$E, $\wedge$I, 1, 4	$\{q \wedge \neg q\}$	RU
6.$\langle 1,2\rangle$	$r \wedge p$	$\wedge$E, $\wedge$I, 1, 4	$\{q \wedge \neg q\}$	RU
7.$\langle 1,2\rangle$	$\neg(r \wedge p)$	DeMorgan, 5	$\{q \wedge \neg q\}$	RU
8.$\langle 1,2\rangle$	$\neg(r \wedge p) \wedge (r \wedge p)$	$\wedge$E, 6, 7	$\{q \wedge \neg q\}$	RU

The contradiction in line 8 is *not* derivable in **LP**, since ($\vee$E) is not valid in **LP**. "$q \wedge \neg q$" is not taken as abnormal here, since there is no need to do so: "$(p \wedge \neg p) \vee (q \wedge \neg q)$" is no minimal Dab-formula given premise (1). [Remember: The Law of Non-Contradiction in line (3) is a LP-Theorem (as any PC-Theorem is)].

CLuN

CLuN is the LLL prominently used by Batens et. al. **CLuN** is a very weak PL. It is defined by the *positive* fragment of standard PC [all rules/axioms not containing "$\neg$"]:

(A1)	$p \supset (q \supset p)$
(A2)	$(p \supset (q \supset r)) \supset ((p \supset q) \supset (p \supset r))$
(A3)	$p \wedge q \supset p$
(A4)	$p \wedge q \supset q$
(A5)	$p \supset (q \supset p \wedge q)$
(A6)	$p \supset p \vee q$
(A7)	$q \supset p \vee q$
(A8)	$(p \supset r) \supset ((q \supset r) \supset ((p \vee q) \supset r))$
(A9)	$(p \equiv q) \supset (p \supset q)$
(A10)	$(p \equiv q) \supset (q \supset p)$
(A11)	$(p \supset q) \supset ((q \supset p) \supset (p \equiv q))$

added to positive PC is the axiom

(A12) $p \vee \neg p$

Rules: (MP) and *Uniform Substitution*

Since the negation in **CLuN** is very poor (by the absence of most negation rules/theorems) inconsistencies are isolated from each other. The above example of spreading inconsistencies does not go through in **CLuN**, since DeMorgan and LNC are not valid in **CLuN**. Notice that (MP) for "$\supset$" is valid in **CLuN**, in contrast to **LP**.

Negation in **CLuN** is peculiar since $v(\neg A)$ does *not* depend on the subformulas in A [see "$\neg$" semantics]! It complies only with a minimal condition on paraconsistent negation: Paraconsistency does not require $v(A) = 1 \rightarrow v(\neg A) = 0$, but only $v(A) = 0 \rightarrow v(\neg A) = 1$ in case that gaps are to be avoided. This is also true in **CLuN**.

Replacement of proven equivalents is not valid in **CLuN**, nor is unrestricted replacement of identicals in quantificational **CLuN** with identity:

$$\vdash_{CLuN}[((\neg P(a) \wedge a{=}b) \supset \neg P(b)) \vee (\neg P(a) \wedge P(a))]$$

That is: Substitution of identicals fails for inconsistent objects. [The other rules/axioms for quantifiers and "=" are standard.]

Let us look at a CLuN-Example:

$\Gamma=\{(p \wedge q) \wedge t, \neg p \vee r, \neg q \vee s, \neg p \vee \neg q, t \supset \neg p\}$

1.<1>	$(p \wedge q) \wedge t$	PREM	$\emptyset$	
2.<2>	$\neg p \vee r$	PREM	$\emptyset$	
3.<3>	$\neg q \vee s$	PREM	$\emptyset$	
4.<4>	$\neg p \vee \neg q$	PREM	$\emptyset$	
5.<5>	$t \supset \neg p$	PREM	$\emptyset$	
6.<1,2>	r	$\wedge$E, $\vee$E, 1, 2	$\{p\}$ (RC)	marked at stage 8
7.<1,3>	s	$\wedge$E, $\vee$E, 1, 3	$\{q\}$ (RC)	marked at stage 8 unmarked at stage 9
8.<1,4>	$(p \wedge \neg p) \vee (q \wedge \neg q)$	$\wedge$E, Dilemma, 1, 4	$\emptyset$ (RU)	
9.<1,5>	$p \wedge \neg p$	$\wedge$E, $\supset$E, 1, 5	$\emptyset$ (RU)	

At stage 8 lines (6) and (7) are marked using the Reliabilist strategy, since $U_8(\Gamma)=\{p,q\}$, but at stage 9 we have $U_9(\Gamma)=\{p\}$. Line (7) becomes unmarked, since "$(p \wedge \neg p) \vee (q \wedge \neg q)$" is then no longer a *minimal* Dab-formula. So "s" is derivable, but "r" is not.

AN

Paraconsistent logics typically give up Disjunctive Syllogism to avoid Explosion. An alternative would be to give up Addition ($\vee$I: $A \vdash A \vee B$), which looks much more like the entrance point of arbitrary sentences B.

AN in distinction to **CLuN** validates all negation reducing rules and Disjunctive Syllogism, but does *not* validate Addition and Irrelevance ($A \vdash B \supset A$) in general.

AN is said to be closer to actual reasoning.

AN semantics is 3-valued; 0 is the only non-designated value.

Decisive is the third value "X" ("contradictory"), where a disjunction with a contradictory disjunct is false only! At the same time a conjunction with a contradictory conjunct is true only! Because of the former Disjunctive Syllogism is valid (if A and $\neg$A were contradictory and B false, $A \vee B$ wouldn't be true). Addition has exceptions: If $v(A)=X$ (i.e. designated) combining with $v(B)=0$ gives $v(A \vee B)=0$.

[Compare the truth tables in **LP**: If A is contradictory (i.e. *both* true and false) a disjunction involving it cannot be false *only*!]

Let us look at an example including Addition:

1.<1>	p	PREM	$\emptyset$		
2.<2>	$p \supset q$	PREM	$\emptyset$		
3.<3>	$r \supset s$	PREM	$\emptyset$		
4.<1>	$p \vee r$	$\vee$I, 1	$\{p\}$	RC	marked at stage (7)
5.<1,3>	$q \vee s$	Dilemma, 2, 3, 4	$\{p\}$	RU	marked at stage (7)

6.<6> $\neg p$	PREM	$\varnothing$	
7.<1,6> $p \wedge \neg p$	$\wedge$I, 1, 6	$\varnothing$	RU
8.<1,2> q	$\supset$E, 1, 2	$\varnothing$	RU
9.<1,2> $q \vee s$	$\vee$I, 8	$\{q\}$	RC

Using Addition in line (4) requires "p" to be consistent. Seeing that "p" is inconsistent lines (4) and (5) get marked. The content of (5), however, is derivable in (9) given the consistency of "q". ($\supset$E) being a variant of Disjunctive Syllogism holds unrestrictedly in **ANA**, i.e. is a (RU)-rule not requiring the consistency of the antecedent.[25]

Semantics

Semantics for ALs can be considered in terms of the models of the LLL and the ULL involved.

Since these logics are (usually) given beforehand, *their* semantics is given beforehand, and the semantics of adaptive logic "only" concerns the relationship between their models.

$Con_{AL}(\Gamma)=Con_{ULL}(\Gamma)$ if Γ has ULL-models.

Γ has ULL-models if ULL is **FOL** just in case Γ is consistent. In general:

$$Con_{LLL}(\Gamma) \subseteq Con_{AL}(\Gamma) \subseteq Con_{ULL}(\Gamma)$$

In case of inconsistency the AL-models are *just those* LLL-models that behave standardly on the consistent part of the premises.

Adaptive logics are sometimes said to deny inconsistency "in the world" (i.e. dialetheism) and only handle reasoning "in the face of" inconsistency; but to make the premises true (in the adaptive logic, i.e. in the LLL), there are *true* contradictions as far as the reasoning is concerned: The semantics of an according adaptive logic (i.e. its LLL) has to allow for assigning *true* both to a sentence and its negation.

In as much as some LLLs are introduced with their applicability within an AL in mind we will need some semantics for them (e.g., the deviant semantics of **CLuN** and **G** where the evaluation function of a model v_M can inherit *non-compositional* assignments from a model independent evaluation function *v)*.

The crucial deviant part of **CLuN** semantics looks like this:

- the set S of sentences is mapped by v to $\{0,1\}$, v_M agrees with v here.
- every object in the domain has a (pseudo-)name.

---

[25] In fact the AL **ANA** based on **AN** is not presented with any proof theory or examples at all in Meheus' paper introducing **ANA**, although it is often referred to.

• the set of wffs of *the form* ¬A is independently (i.e., not withstanding their composition) mapped to {0,1} by *v*.
• $v_M(\neg A)=1$ iff $v_M(A)=0$ or $v(\neg A)=1$ (i.e. v_M can inherit evaluations of negations from *v*).
Because of the last clause there are **CLuN** models that make "¬ (p ∧ q)" true, but make "¬p" and "¬q" false only! [Batens appropriately calls these thrown in negated formulas "skyhooks", but gives no reason for giving up the compositionality of negation, a step not included in the general rationale for a PL.]

Meta-Logic

The meta-theory is phrased in a standard logic/language.
Since a *theorem* does not depend on any premise (so no inconsistency can be exploited) the *set of theorems* of an adaptive logic comprises all the A such that $\varnothing\vdash_{ULL}A$. That is: The AL-theorems are just the ULL-theorems (as LP-theorems are just the PC-theorems).
If one considers formula A that are derivable from *any* premise set, then the set of these formula is the set of A such that $\Gamma\vdash_{LLL}A$ for any Γ (since Γ may be inconsistent).
Adaptive logics so to speak have no theorems "of their own". Looking at the *consequence relation* only one sees the selective character of applying certain rules.
Adaptive logics are adequate with respect to final derivability.
A general meta-theorem about derivability:

> $\Gamma\vdash_{AL}A$ iff there is a finite set of abnormalities Δ such that $\Gamma\vdash_{LLL}(A \vee Dab(\Delta))$ and $\Delta \cap U(\Gamma)=\varnothing$.

[Remember: U(Γ) being the set of disjuncts of the minimal Dab-consequences of Γ in LLL, plus all the proven single contradictions.]

An Application

Batens and Meheus have developed ALs to handle topics like reasoning from an *explanandum* to the *explanans* (esp. the initial conditions) given some theory. In these approaches the usual natural deductive approach of reasoning from premises to conclusions is put on the head: Some goal formula is the starting point and the dynamics aims at deriving that goal stepwise from the premises by some rules (of thumb) of reasoning "backwards".[26]
A more straight forward application to problems of DN-explanation was

26 Explicating that work would require to go into the elaboration of these variants, what will not be done here; cf. the sources in *Further Reading*.

offered by Weber and van Dyck. Consider an inconsistent set like: {Birds fly, Penguins don't fly, Tweety is a bird and a penguin, Billy is a bird but not a penguin}. These premises *can* explain that Billy flies, *although* being inconsistent. In **FOL** the premises explain nothing. An AL can model the case, since in the derivation of "Billy flies" the inconsistency involving Tweety is not used.
Demanding from any explanation that E and ¬ E are not explainable *at the same time*, the premises do not explain that Tweety does not fly.

Assessment

Adaptive logics take the ideas of dynamics and reasoning with **FOL** as default seriously. That is their greatest merit.
The AL program contains several approaches more closely linked to investigating proof dynamics than paraconsistency, and thus a judgement on the AL program does neither depend on a judgement of paraconsistency nor on the AL program's treatment of paraconsistency.
The paraconsistent logics **CLuN**, **G** and their variants used by the Ghent team seem to be more deviant than other PLs (e.g., Relevant Logics, **SKP** or **LP**).

Questions

(Q1) Why do ALs not have theorems of their own?

(Q2) If an AL was to be employed to naive semantics and the Liar was derived, would the Liar be part of a Dab-formula?

(Q3) Why is it problematic that an AL involves the notion of final derivability which is not algorithmic? Compare the problem with the problem of a derivation that is "not finished" in some natural deductive versions of **FOL** (because of *flagged* singular terms)!

Exercises

(Ex1) What can be derived using **LP** as LLL from the following premise set: $\Gamma=\{\neg r,\ r \vee t,\ p \wedge v,\ p \supset \neg q,\ r \vee \neg p,\ \neg t \vee s\}$? Where does marking occur? What can be said about "s" and "q"?

(Ex2) What can be derived using **LPQ**$^{=}$ as LLL from the following premise set: $\Gamma=\{(\forall x)(\neg Q(x) \supset \neg F(x)),\ F(b),\ \neg Q(a),\ R(a),$

b=a, F(b) ∨ R(b), Q(a) ∨ S(a), (∀x)(S(x) ≡ ¬ R(x))}? Where does marking occur? Is "R(b)" derivable? At which stage has an application of substitution of identicals to be checked? [see Chap.4 on the definition of identity in **LPQ**$^=$ with a non-detachable "≡" , that has to be modelled into an (RC) type adaptive rule!]

(Ex3) Give a formal presentation and an account of the "Billy flies" case (application of AL to DN-explanations)!

Further Reading

- An updated overview of adaptive logics can be found at:
  http://logica.rug.ac.be/adlog/al.html
- A list of writings of the Ghent team (with some downloads available) can be found at:
  http://logica.UGhent.be/centrum/writings
- One survey of ALs is: Batens, Diderik, "A Survey of Inconsistency-Adaptive Logics", in: Batens, Diderik et. al. (Eds.) *Frontiers of Paraconsistent Logic*. Baldock, 2000. (In this volume you also find Joke Meheus' paper introducing **ANA**.)

8 | LFI and da Costa Systems

Newton da Costa was one of the first to invent paraconsistent logics. He developed a hierarchy of so called *C-Systems*, logics which are inconsistency tolerant, but may have explosion with respect to some sentences. Working together with a couple of visiting researchers he applied these systems to problems of science and mathematics.
Starting from da Costa's work the Brazilian approach to paraconsistency was established, and is today one of the main pillars of the paraconsistent world. Several researchers use C-Systems as their preferred paraconsistent logic.
In the honour of Newton da Costa the 2nd World Congress on Paraconsistency was held in Brazil in 2000. Da Costa's work and the Brazilian approach has been extended and systematized by Walter Carnielli and his co-workers. They developed the more general framework of *Logics of Formal Inconsistency* (LFI), into which the C-Systems can be integrated as one variant. This chapter follows the LFI approach and thereby introduces da Costa-Systems on the way.

LFI-Systems Defined

Logics of Formal Inconsistency (LFI) are paraconsistent logics that contain within themselves ways to express consistency and inconsistency (i.e. within the object language), introducing operators. Consistency is taken as a *primitive* notion and expressed by "°", "°A" says that A is consistent, i.e. we do *not* have A and ¬A [cf. Chap. 4 on expressing truth values in **LP**, and on "°A" and "•A"].
C-Systems are those LFIs that are extensions of the positive part of some consistent logic (like **PC**). The behaviour of negation and in which ways one wants to have Explosion, Contraposition, Excluded Middle etc. distinguishes different C-Systems.
Da Costa in introducing his systems wanted to combine paraconsistent reasoning with the strength of standard logic in restricted contexts. Although paraconsistent reasoning is non-explosive, explosion should, according to da Costa, be valid in contexts considered consistent. So some formula was taken to *express the consistency* of a formula A: $\neg(A \wedge \neg A)$. A formula considered consistent in this way should exhibit explosive behaviour in case one had A and ¬A! Da Costa-systems in the narrow sense are systems *in which* "°" is *definabl*e thus.

Principles

The LFI-approach distinguishes inconsistency from contradiction. A logic respects the *Principle of Non-Contradiction* (PNC) if it has non-contradictory theories (i.e. sets of sentences closed under that logic that do either not contain A or not ¬A). This requires that the logic itself has not contradictions as *theses* (as some version of naive semantics may have). A logic is contradictory if all of its theories are.
A logic respects the *Principle of Non-Triviality* (PNT) if it is not trivial:

$$(\exists\Gamma)\ (\exists B)(\Gamma \nvdash B)$$

A logic respects the *Principle of Explosion/Pseudo Scotus* (PPS) if it is explosive. All paraconsistent logics disrespect (PPS).
A logic respects the *Principle of Ex Falso Qoudlibet Sequitur* (ExF) if it has some formula that can trivialize the logic by itself:

$$(\exists C)\ (\forall\Gamma, B)(\Gamma, C \vdash B)$$

A logic respects the *Supplementing Principle of Explosion* if it (also) has a strong negation "~" for which Explosion holds.

Being Gently Explosive

LFIs are "gently explosive" in the vain of da Costa's idea:

> (gPPS) A theory Γ is *gently explosive* when there is a way of expressing the consistency of a formula A by way of formulas which depend only on A and which cannot be added to Γ together with {A, ¬A} without yielding triviality.

So LFIs distinguish between fulfilling (PPS) and being explosive in some way, i.e. fulfilling (gPPS).
In this context one may investigate whether a logic allows to define or to add a bottom particle "⊥" that allows to conclude everything.
Further on one may introduce different negations. A paraconsistent negation " ¬ " disrespecting (PPS) and a "strong" negation "~" respecting (PPS).

" ∘ " and " • "

The consistency and the inconsistency operator can either be introduced into a system as primitive or as being defined by some formula.
If "∘A" is taken as defined by ¬(A ∧ ¬A) it says that only one of these obtains, so is a hidden *disjunction*. It does *not* say that A obtains!
If " •A" is taken as defined by (A ∧ ¬A) it is a hidden *conjunction*.
In case the operators are syntactic primitives their semantics may be given by a truth table:

A	°A	•A
1	1	0
0	1	0
1,0	0	1

LFI 1

There is a plenty of LFI systems. [In fact because of combinatorial reasons related to the choice of inheriting consistency "°" over connectives like "∧" or "∨" there are *thousands* of different systems.]
The LFI-approach tries to incorporate into the field of LFIs also systems like **Pac** or **J_3** that were independently developed.
Before we look at the syntactic generation of successively stronger LFI systems let us take a look at a basic truth functional semantic presentation.
LFI 1 (also called "**Pac**" in case "°" is missing, also called "**J3**" if additionally a strong negation and a bottom particle are present) is given by the following truth tables[27]:

A	B	A ∧ B	A ∨ B	¬A	A ⊃ B	°A
1	1	1	1	0	1	1
1	0	0	1	0	0	1
1	0,1	0,1	1	0	0,1	1
0	1	0	1	1	1	1
0	0	0	0	1	1	1
0	0,1	0,1	0,1	1	1	1
0,1	1	0,1	1	0,1	1	0
0,1	0	0	0,1	0,1	0	0
0,1	0,1	0,1	0,1	0,1	0,1	0

A strong negation is not *definable* within **LFI 1**, but can be added. **LFI 1** is not the weakest of the systems. The systems can be generated systematically from the axiomatic basis of the weakest system **bC**.

27 To keep a more or the less coherent formalization the conditional connective is here represented as "⊃" to distinguish it from that of the Relevant Logics and from **SKP**. The truth value of inconsistent formulas is again given as "0, 1" and not as "½".

The Axiomatic Basis of LFI Systems

The Axiomatization of LFI systems can start from this basis:

(A1) $p \supset (q \supset p)$
(A2) $(p \supset q) \supset ((p \supset (q \supset r)) \supset (p \supset r))$
(A3) $p \supset (q \supset p \wedge q)$
(A4) $p \wedge q \supset p$
(A5) $p \wedge q \supset q$
(A6) $p \supset p \vee q$
(A7) $q \supset p \vee q$
(A8) $(p \supset r) \supset ((q \supset r) \supset ((p \vee q) \supset r))$
(A9) $p \vee (p \supset q)$
(A10) $p \vee \neg p$
(A11) $\neg\neg p \supset p$

Rules: (MP) and *Uniform Substitution.*

Notice that by (A1) these systems are not Relevant, by (A10) they are anti-intuitionistic; (A1) – (A8) is usually called "positive logic". (A9) is a positive formula, but not provable from (A1) – (A8) [cf. Batens' **CLuN** in Chap. 7].
Given (A1) and (A2) the *Deduction Theorem* holds here:

$\Gamma, C \vdash B \Rightarrow \Gamma \vdash (C \supset B)$

This is indeed a basis of paraconsistent logics. Adding

$\neg p \supset (p \supset q)$

would yield standard PC, but this formula is not valid, as can be seen by the **LFI 1** truth tables.
This basis does neither have a strong negation nor a bottom particle.
This system has not a negated theorem:

$\neg\, (\exists A) \vdash (\neg A)$

Thus:

$\nvdash (\neg\, (p \wedge \neg p))$

The *Law of Non-Contradiction* is no theorem here!

The System bC

Adding to the basis the following rule gives the system **bC**:

(bc1) $°A, A, \neg A \vdash_{\mathbf{bC}} B$

bC contains a primitive connective "°" and this rule of gentle explosion. This leads to a conservative extension of the basis logic.
Given "°" a strong negation and a bottom particle can be defined:

(D~) $\sim A \overset{\text{def}}{=} \neg A \wedge {}^{\circ}A$

(D⊥) $\bot \overset{\text{def}}{=} \sim A \wedge A$

since Explosion is valid for strong negation:

$A, \sim A \vdash_{\mathbf{bC}} B$

In contrast to be basis **bC** does have negated theorems:

$\vdash_{\mathbf{bC}}(\neg \bot)$

and equivalent negated formulas, but no theorems of the form °A, i.e. even:

$\nvdash_{\mathbf{bC}} {}^{\circ}(p \vee \neg p)$

The following rules but *not their converses* hold in **bC**:

(i) $A, \neg A \vdash_{\mathbf{bC}} \neg{}^{\circ}A$

(ii) $A \wedge \neg A \vdash_{\mathbf{bC}} \neg{}^{\circ}A$

(iii) ${}^{\circ}A \vdash_{\mathbf{bC}} \neg(A \wedge \neg A)$

(iv) ${}^{\circ}A \vdash_{\mathbf{bC}} \neg(\neg A \wedge A)$

[This can be shown by changed **LFI 1** truth tables that take "¬" from "0,1" to "0", " ∨" from "0" and "0,1" to "1", and " ⊃" from "1" and "0,1" to "1". Since these tables are sound for **bC**, but invalidate the converses of (i) – (iv), these cannot be provable; this procedure is used for all results of this type; the deviant tables may not have an intuitive reading, their sole purpose is to prove the deductive weakness of the system in question.]
The dualities for the connectives usually do *not hold* in **bC**, e.g.:

$\neg(p \wedge q) \nvdash_{\mathbf{bC}} \neg p \vee \neg q$ [neither the converse]

$\neg(\neg p \vee \neg q) \nvdash_{\mathbf{bC}} (p \wedge q)$ [neither the converse]

$p \vee q \nvdash_{\mathbf{bC}} \neg p \supset q$ [converse holds]

$p \supset q \nvdash_{\mathbf{bC}} \neg(p \wedge \neg q)$ [neither the converse]

$\neg (p \supset q) \nvdash_{\mathbf{bC}} (p \wedge \neg q)$ [neither the converse]

Contraposition does not hold:

$(p \supset q) \nvdash_{\mathbf{bC}} \neg q \supset \neg p$

otherwise by (A1) and (MP) **bC** would turn out to be explosive! In fact, adding this form of Contraposition would yield **PC**.

The System bbbC

In **bC** we have "$\circ$", but no corresponding axioms or theorems concerning its dual "$\bullet$". There are four rules of duality:

(bc2) $\neg{}^{\bullet}A \vdash {}^{\circ}A$

(bc3) $\neg{}^{\circ}A \vdash {}^{\bullet}A$

(bc4) ${}^{\bullet}A \vdash \neg{}^{\circ}A$

(c5) ${}^{\circ}A \vdash \neg{}^{\bullet}A$

In **bC** neither (bc2) nor (bc3) hold. The addition of (bc2) does, by the absence of Contraposition, not yield (bc3). Adding (bc2) and (bc3) to **bC** gives the system **bbC**. In this again neither (bc4) nor (bc5) are provable, which again are independent of each other. Adding (bc4) and (bc5) to **bbC** yields **bbbC**.

In **bbbC** the relation between $^{\circ}A$ and $\neg{}^{\bullet}A$ *cannot* be characterised by the intuitive definition:

(D$^{\bullet}$) ${}^{\bullet}A \overset{\text{def}}{=} \neg{}^{\circ}A$

since then by (bc5) and straightforward substitution we would have

$\vdash({}^{\circ}p \supset \neg\neg{}^{\circ}p)$

which is not valid in **bbbC**! The converse of (A11) does not hold.

The System Ci

In **bbbC** we have for "$\bullet$" not its intuitive definition. One should expect that ${}^{\bullet}A$, meaning that A is contradictory, has a corresponding syntactic characterization. This is given in the system **Ci**.

Ci is **bbbC** supplemented by the rule:

(ci) ${}^{\bullet}A \vdash (A \wedge \neg A)$

So in **Ci** we have the inconsistency operator "$\bullet$" being characterized by formulas, but we do not have:

$\neg(A \wedge \neg A) \vdash {}^{\circ}A.$

One could reach **Ci** also by using one of the intuitive definitions:

(D$^{\bullet}$) ${}^{\bullet}A \overset{\text{def}}{=} \neg{}^{\circ}A$

or

(D$^{\circ}$) ${}^{\circ}A \overset{\text{def}}{=} \neg{}^{\bullet}A$

and add this to **bC** and (ci). We get then (bc2) – (bc5). In **Ci** we have:

(DR1) ${}^{\circ}A, {}^{\bullet}A \vdash B$

(DR2) $^\circ A, \neg^\circ A \vdash B$

(DR3) $^\bullet A, \neg{}^\bullet A \vdash B$

(DR4) $^\circ A \vdash {}^\circ\neg A$

(DR5) $^\bullet\neg A \vdash {}^\bullet A$

(T1) $\vdash {}^\circ{}^\circ p$

(T2) $\vdash {}^\circ{}^\bullet p$

(T3) $\vdash (p \vee {}^\circ p)$

A particular schema in **Ci** is consistent if and only if we have controlled explosion with that schema in **Ci**:

$$\Gamma \vdash_{Ci} {}^\circ A \Rightarrow \Gamma, A, \neg A \vdash_{Ci} B$$

If one added Contraposition as a rule to **Ci** one would regain **PC**. Axiom (A9) is redundant in **Ci**.

The System Cil

In **Ci** we could identify inconsistency (expressed by "$^\bullet$") with contradictoriness by

(ci) $^\bullet A \vdash (A \wedge \neg A)$

We could not derive consistency (expressed by "$^\circ$") from the negation of contradictoriness, since we have:

(*) $\neg (A \wedge \neg A) \nvdash_{Ci} {}^\circ A.$

If we add to **Ci** the scheme

(cil) $\neg (A \wedge \neg A) \vdash {}^\circ A.$

we get the logic **Cil** which identifies contradictoriness with inconsistency, da Costa's original approach. ($D^\bullet$) and (D°) can be used.
From (cil) it is obvious – since otherwise simple Explosion would be back – that from **Cil** on no LFI-system can have $\neg(A \wedge \neg A)$ as a theorem, *except* substitution of provable equivalents fails in these systems.
The consistency of A can be expressed in **Cil** by $\neg(A \wedge \neg A)$, but *not* by $\neg(\neg A \wedge A)$! The latter can even be added to **Cil** without it loosing its paraconsistent character:

$$\neg(\neg A \wedge A) \nvdash_{Cil} \neg(A \wedge \neg A) .$$

In **Cil** we could propagate consistency to negation by

$$^\circ A \vdash_{Cil} {}^\circ \neg A$$

How then can consistency be propagated from subformula to complex formula? A natural assumption seems to be that the consistency of each subformula is sufficient for the consistency of the complex formula, thus

(ca1) $(^\circ A \wedge {^\circ B}) \vdash {^\circ(A \wedge B)}$

(ca2) $(^\circ A \wedge {^\circ B}) \vdash {^\circ(A \vee B)}$

(ca3) $(^\circ A \wedge {^\circ B}) \vdash {^\circ(A \supset B)}$

The logic obtained by adding (ca1) – (ca3) to **Cil** is **Cila**.[28]
We have by (T1) of subsystem **Ci**, (D°), (ca1) and (cil):

$\vdash_{Cila} {^\circ\bot}$

whatever that is supposed to mean! [Remember: $\bot \equiv {^\circ p} \wedge (p \wedge {\sim p})$]
In **Cila/C1** we could propagate from the subformulas to the formula. What about the other direction? One might have it that the consistency of the formula requires the consistency of all its subformulas – thus having the converses of (ca1) to (ca3) – or one may be satisfied with one of the subformulas being consistent, i.e. $^\circ(A \wedge B) \vdash {^\circ A} \vee {^\circ B}$ etc.
There is a plenty of options, and *thus* of LFI-systems.
One may also start not with **Cila**, but with the weaker assumptions that the consistency of *one* subformula is sufficient for the consistency of the complex formula, i.e. $(^\circ A \vee {^\circ B}) \vdash {^\circ(A \supset B)}$ etc. The corresponding system is **Cilo**.
If supplementary to these options one toys with the options how the value (0,1) in a complex formula is related to the values of its subformula, keeping the compositionality of consistent formulas as in **PC**, one has a choice of about 8000 (in words: *eight thousand*) different LFI-systems! All these systems extend **Ci** and are subsystems of **ePC**.

LFI 1 Proof Theory

LFI 1 characterized by truth tables before can now be characterized syntactically. It is the system extending **Ci** with the rules:

(ce) $A \vdash \neg\neg A$

(cj1) $^\bullet(A \wedge B) \vdash ({^\bullet A} \wedge B) \vee ({^\bullet B} \wedge A)$

(cj2) $^\bullet(A \vee B) \vdash ({^\bullet A} \wedge \neg B) \vee ({^\bullet B} \wedge \neg A)$

(cj3) $^\bullet(A \supset B) \vdash (A \wedge {^\bullet B})$

---

28 Da Costa's hierarchy of systems is based on **Cila** (his C_1); each system in the hierarchy of ever weaker systems modifies the definition of consistency of the previous one with nested occurrences of "°"; cf. (da Costa 1974).

So in **LFI 1** the propagating concerns inconsistency instead of consistency. (cj1) – (cj3) can be read off the truth tables.
Remember that (D°) is not part of **LFI 1,** since (LNC) holds as a theorem in both forms (i.e. with a commuted conjunction); otherwise the order of conjuncts in **LFI 1** may have importance [see (cj1)].

LFI 2

LFI 2 is the system extending **Ci** with the rules:

(ce) $A \vdash \neg\neg A$

(co1) $(°A \vee °B) \vdash °(A \wedge B)$

(co2) $(°A \vee °B) \vdash °(A \vee B)$

(co3) $(°A \vee °B) \vdash °(A \supset B)$

(cr1) $°(A \wedge B) \vdash °A \vee °B$

(co2) $°(A \vee B) \vdash °A \vee °B$

(co3) $°(A \supset B) \vdash °A \vee °B$

Note that in **LFI 2** (cil) is missing, i.e. the consistency operator is not defined by some formula; thus **LFI 2** is not a da Costa-system. The **LFI 2** truth tables are:

A	**B**	**A ∧ B**	**A ∨ B**	**¬A**	**A ⊃ B**	**°A**
1	1	1	1	0	1	1
1	0	0	1	0	0	1
1	0,1	1	1	0	1	1
0	1	0	1	1	1	1
0	0	0	0	1	1	1
0	0,1	0	1	1	1	1
0,1	1	1	1	0,1	1	0
0,1	0	0	1	0,1	0	0
0,1	0,1	0,1	0,1	0,1	0,1	0

Restrictions on Equivalence

Typically (proven) equivalents can be substituted for each other. There is a long list of equivalencies coming with **PC**. Many of these do not hold paraconsistently. [Famously "$A \wedge \neg A \equiv B \wedge \neg B$" cannot hold for a paraconsistent logic avoiding triviality: Every contradiction is different, so to say.]

In LFI systems, however, there is *massive* failure of equivalencies and substitution of equivalencies:

(i) in the basis no different negated formula are provably equivalent; e.g. $\neg(A \wedge B) \Leftarrow\!/\!\Rightarrow \neg(\neg(\neg A \vee \neg B))$

(ii) in **bC** intersubstitutivity of provable equivalents *fails*: $(A \wedge B) \Leftrightarrow_{bC} (B \wedge A)$, but $\neg(A \wedge B) \Leftarrow\!/\!\Rightarrow_{bC} \neg(B \wedge A)$ $(A \vee B) \Leftrightarrow_{bC} (B \vee A)$, but $\neg(A \vee B) \Leftarrow\!/\!\Rightarrow_{bC} \neg(B \vee A)$

(iii) intersubstitutivity of provable equivalents fails also in **Ci** and *all logics* based on it, like **Cil** (on pains – as we have seen – on making these systems fall back into standard logic)!

Expressing Standard Logic

Typically LFI systems are *linguistic extensions* of **PC**, the set of well formed formula of **PC** being a proper subset of the well formed formula of some LFI.
Given the – syntactic – expressive power of a language with a consistency operator "°" and an inconsistency operator " • ", possibly supplemented by a bottom particle "⊥" and a strong negation "~" it will be possible to *express the standard tautologies* in such a system.
This is done by having a *translation* of standard formulas into the corresponding formulas of a LFI system.
Those standard theorems and rules that are not paraconsistently valid have counterparts in the LFI system that are valid and which really express what the standard formula is thought to say. For example

(1) $\neg p \wedge p \supset q$

is not valid paraconsistently, but a gently explosive LFI may have:

(1') $^{\circ}p \wedge (\neg p \wedge p) \supset q$

One can uses an *extended* **PC** with °A having always value 1, and •A having always value 0. In **PC** proof theory one adds (D•) and the scheme:

$\vdash {}^{\circ}A.$

Relative to *extended* **PC** [**ePC**] systems like **Ci** can be seen as subsystems of **ePC**. By translating PC-negation into the strong negation "~" of **Ci** one can have *all* the classical theorems expressed in **Ci**. The translation proceeds by a mapping:

(i) t(A) = A, for atomic A (e.g. t(p)=p)

(ii) t(A#B) = t(A) # t(B) for any binary connective #

(iii) $t(\neg A) = \sim t(A)$

As a result of the mapping this meta-theorem is true:

$$\Gamma \vdash_{ePC} A \Leftrightarrow t(\Gamma) \vdash_{Ci} t(A)$$

where $t(\Gamma)$ is the application of the translation to the formulas in Γ.

Assessment

The thousands of LFI systems are a topic worth to be explored within pure logic of its own right.

The philosophical motivation, however, to prefer some such system over another seems to be mostly missing. Especially the comparison to Relevant Logics, **LP** and **SKP** is not that favourable as it seems given the methodological constraints like the Extensionality Condition and the Minimal Damage Condition [in Chap. 3] – facing the failures of substitution and dualities of extensional connectives.

The main criticism of **LP** that it is "an extremist position" in having no inconsistency being explosive, and commenting "that *consistency* is exactly what a contradiction might be lacking to become explosive", thus introducing "consistent contradictions" (Carnielli/Marcos 2002, pp. 26-28) awaits epistemic elucidation: If we have A and ¬A, then we should take °A as false, shouldn't we? And how can we *take* A to be consistent and have A and ¬A at the same time?

The LFI-approach is, therefore, not the approach favoured here.

Despite these criticisms the LFI-approach is one of the liveliest in the paraconsistent world, and turning to the literature surely requires knowing it. The idea of having primitive operators to express consistency and inconsistency is a useful idea that may lead to extensions of other systems [cf. Chap. 4 on the (possible) usage in **LP**].

Questions

(Q1) Which logic does not respect (PNT)?

(Q2) Why does any non-trivial logic with a bottom particle and a conditional obeying the Deduction Theorem have a strong negation?

(Q3) What distinguishes **LFI 1** from **LP** truth tables? And what consequences does this have?

(Q4) Why isn't it contradictory to claim that **Ci** is a subsystem of **ePC** and nevertheless claim that *all* standard tautologies have *valid* translations in **Ci**?

(Q5) What does: $\vdash_{\text{Cila}} \circ\bot$ say? Is it disastrous to have "$\circ\bot$"?

(Q6) The **LFI 2** truth table for disjunction seems strange, doesn't it?

Exercises

(Ex1) Why can "$A \wedge \neg A \equiv B \wedge \neg B$" not hold in a typical PL with Conjunction Elimination? Show that it is not valid for some LFIs. In **LP** the formula is valid. Why is that not problematic? [Note that in **SKP** the rule (R7) of substitution requires provable mutual *entailment*; and: $\nvdash_{\mathbf{SKP}} (A \wedge \neg A \leftrightarrow B \wedge \neg B)$.]

(Ex2) Show by **LFI 1** truth tables that $\neg A \supset (A \supset B)$ is not valid. (Is this different from **LP**?)

(Ex3) Show by – deviant – truth tables:

$$\neg(A \wedge B) \nvdash_{\mathbf{bC}} \neg A \vee \neg B$$

$$\neg(\neg A \vee \neg B) \nvdash_{\mathbf{bC}} (A \wedge B)$$

$$A \vee B \nvdash_{\mathbf{bC}} \neg A \supset B$$

$$A \supset B \nvdash_{\mathbf{bC}} \neg(A \wedge \neg B)$$

$$\neg(A \supset B) \nvdash_{\mathbf{bC}} (A \wedge \neg B)$$

(Ex4) In **bbC** map " $\bullet$ " to truth value 1, and "$\circ$" to 0 in case of 0 and 1 and to (0,1) in case of (0,1). Show that (bc4) and (bc5) are not provable in **bbC**.

Further Reading

The chapter is based on two comprehensive surveys of LFI-Systems:

- Carnielli, Walter/Marcos, Joao. "A Taxonomy of C-Systems", in: (Carnielli/Coniglio/Ottaviano 2002), pp. 1-94.
- Carnielli, Walter/Coniglio, Marcelo/Marcos, Joao. "Logics of Formal Inconsistency", in: Gabbay, D./Guenthner, F. (Eds.) *Handbook of Philosophical Logic*, 2nd Ed., Vol. 12, 2004.

There are some differences in presenting and systematizing the field of LFIs in these two papers; the latter including also non-truth-functional semantics, tableaus and some ideas on quantificational LFIs.

• See also Bueno, Ottavio/da Costa, Newton/Krause, Devio. "Paraconsistent Logic and Paraconsistency", in: Jacquette, Dale (Ed.) *Philosophy of Logic*. Amsterdam, 2004. Despite the title the paper almost exclusively deals with work related to da Costa-Systems.

9 | Other Systems

The minimal condition to call a logical system "paraconsistent" is that it avoids Explosion or *ex contradictione qoudlibet*. There are many ways to do this. Dialetheism and even weak paraconsistency tie the logical system investigated to more or the less specific programmes in philosophy. There may be other philosophical programs that look out for a suitable paraconsistent system.
One may, further on, completely drop the link to some philosophical program or thesis and investigate a manifold of logical systems for its own sake, as an exercise in the pure investigation of logical structures that may widen the horizon restricted by a narrow focus on standard logics.
In this chapter a couple of systems are presented that either do not fit into one of the programs or approaches presented so far, or are given as mere logical systems, which simply are paraconsistent.

RM3

RM3 is a system that can be characterized truth-functionally (like **LP**), but that in contrast to **LP** keeps *Modus Ponens* for " $\supset$ ". As a consequence of this **RM3** cannot – as does **LP** – keep all **PC** tautologies, since otherwise Explosion would be valid.
RM3 has some features of a Relevant Logic. It is Relevant in having neither *ex contradictione qoudlibet* nor *verum ex qoudlibet sequitur* neither as theorems nor as rules.
Designated truth values in **RM3** are 1 and (0,1).
RM3 can be characterized by the following truth tables:

A	B	A ∧ B	A ∨ B	¬A	A ⊃ B	A ≡ B
1	1	1	1	0	1	1
1	0	0	1	0	0	0
1	0,1	0,1	1	0	0	0
0	1	0	1	1	1	0
0	0	0	0	1	1	1
0	0,1	0	0,1	1	1	0
0,1	1	0,1	1	0,1	1	0
0,1	0	0	0,1	0,1	0	0
0,1	0,1	0,1	0,1	0,1	0,1	0,1

RM3 truth tables differ from **LP** truth tables in the evaluation of " $\supset$ ". In case of a 1 antecedent and a (0,1) consequent the conditional is just false in **RM3** whereas it is true and false in **LP.** The **LP**-evaluation looks more natural, since in the 1:1-reading the conditional is true, and in the 1:0-reading it is false. The same holds for a conditional with a (0,1) antecedent and a 0 consequent, which is only false in **RM3**.
The biconditional, because of this, at first is more natural than in **LP**, since it behaves binary in case of the standard values. In case of a (0,1) right hand and left hand side, however, it only gets the value (0,1).
RM3 has not only *Modus Ponens*, but also Contraposition and so *Modus Tollens*. **RM3** has the Modus Ponens-Theorem, so it falls short of the Strong Anti-Triviality Condition [cf. Chap. 3].
The conditional cannot be defined in the usual way. We have neither

$$(A \supset B) \equiv \neg (A \wedge \neg B)$$

nor

$$(A \supset B) \equiv \neg A \vee B$$

BN4

So far we have not concerned logics which allow for truth value gaps. The existence of gaps is a question that can be kept apart from considerations of paraconsistency. There may be applications of paraconsistency, however, in which the existence of gaps may be useful [if one deals with vagueness or failure of reference in this way (e.g. Blau 1978), see also Chap. 14 on Deontic Logic].
BN4 extends **RM3** by taking also truth value gaps into account (so its theorems are a subset of the **RM3** theorems). [Notice that therefore everything we said about **RM3** theorems and evaluations also applies to **BN4**.]
The fact that some sentence A has no truth value means that the evaluation function (which assigns subsets of the set {0,1} of truth values to each sentence) assigns $\varnothing$ to A.
In **BN4** – in distinction to **LP** – the Deduction Theorem does *not* hold.
BN4 can be given by the following truth tables:

A	B	A ∧ B	A ∨ B	¬A	A ⊃ B	A ≡ B
1	1	1	1	0	1	1
1	0	0	1	0	0	0
1	0,1	0,1	1	0	0	0
1	∅	∅	1	0	∅	∅
0	1	0	1	1	1	0
0	0	0	0	1	1	1
0	0,1	0	0,1	1	1	0
0	∅	0	∅	1	1	∅
0,1	1	0,1	1	0,1	1	0
0,1	0	0	0,1	0,1	0	0
0,1	0,1	0,1	0,1	0,1	0,1	0,1
0,1	∅	0	1	0,1	∅	∅
∅	1	∅	1	∅	1	∅
∅	0	0	∅	∅	∅	∅
∅	0,1	0	1	∅	∅	∅
∅	∅	∅	∅	∅	1	1

Four

BN4 was considered by Belnap to be the appropriate logic of logic programming and artificial intelligence.

Damasio and Pereira (1998) modify **BN4** in changing the truth table for the conditional connective making it bivalent, and defining

$$\models_{FOUR} A \Leftrightarrow v(A)=\{1\} \text{ or } v(A)=\{0,1\}$$

with 1 and (0,1) being the designated truth values.

They call the resulting logic **FOUR**.

The associative, distributive, commutative, identity, double negation and DeMorgan laws all hold in **FOUR**. So does Contraction. *Modus Ponens* holds. The Deduction Theorem applies.

The duals for the conditional do not hold. Neither does *Tertium Non Datur* nor the *Law of Non-Contradiction*. *Modus Tollens* and Disjunctive Syllogism fail.

FOUR truth tables show the corresponding variation to **BN4** truth tables:

A	B	A ∧ B	A ∨ B	¬A	A ⊃ B	A ≡ B
1	1	1	1	0	1	1
1	0	0	1	0	0	0
1	0,1	0,1	1	0	1	0
1	∅	∅	1	0	0	0
0	1	0	1	1	1	0
0	0	0	0	1	1	1
0	0,1	0	0,1	1	1	0
0	∅	0	∅	1	1	1
0,1	1	0,1	1	0,1	1	0
0,1	0	0	0,1	0,1	0	0
0,1	0,1	0,1	0,1	0,1	1	1
0,1	∅	0	1	0,1	0	0
∅	1	∅	1	∅	1	1
∅	0	0	∅	∅	1	1
∅	0,1	0	1	∅	1	1
∅	∅	∅	∅	∅	1	1

Dialogical Paraconsistent Logics

Dialogical Logics are logics in the tradition of Kuno Lorenz and Paul Lorenzen (Lorenzen/Lorenz 1978).

In dialogical logics the rules of the logical particles (connectives as well as quantifiers or modal operators) are introduced as moves of *attack* and *defence* between two players. The proponent proposes a theorem which is then attacked by an opponent.

Frame rules regulate how often an attack can be repeated (e.g. on both sides of a conjunction or on a universal quantifier) and which attack can be chosen to defend against.

One may see dialogical logics as a pedagogical device to introduce the operation of logical rules. (As in everyday argumentation this might be the way we challenge somebody's claims.)

Interestingly the choice of frame rules determines whether one gets standard or – in case the proponent may only defend against the last attack made – intuitionistic logic!

Rahman and Carnielli have introduced a paraconsistent dialogical logic by further modifying the frame rules.

The paraconsistent constraint says that a proponent can attack only those negated sentences of the opponent (by claiming the not negated sentence as

true) that the opponent has attacked in the same dialogue himself (i.e. with respect to which the opponent has claimed the not negated sentence himself).
This further constraints leads to the invalidity of Explosion and several versions of Disjunctive Syllogism. No longer valid – in comparison to intuitionistic logic which is the base for the more restrictive frame rules – are also dualities for the conditional connective. DeMorgan's Laws – even the intuitionistically acceptable direction – however also fail.

Different Names

Some paraconsistent logics that were around before we have dealt with in their LFI-systematisation: **Pac** and **J3** are subsystems or extensions of **LFI1**.

More Systems

If you don't care about the criteria given in chapter 3, you can have the queerest system you like, violating more than one of the criteria, but being paraconsistent by invalidating Explosion.
• (Popov 1988) introduces some other paraconsistent sequential calculi than **SKP**. The semantics seem highly contra-intuitive and leads to the lack of such extensional rules as Conjunction Elimination. Similar calculi you find in (Scotch/Jennings 1989), where also *Modus Ponens* fails!
• Nelson (1949, 1959) developed a version of intuitionism in which appear sentences which are true and false at the same time. To have this Nelson introduces a further – even more "constructive" – negation. In some versions of his systems neither Absorption nor Contraposition hold. The systems are proof theoretically adequate relative to a intuitionistic Kripke semantics.
• (Arruda/da Costa 1984) and (Routley/Loparic 1980) discuss versions of Relevant logics with quite strange five valued truth tables.

Questions

(Q1) **BN4** truth tables including assignments of ∅ look highly arbitrary: Why is a conditional of indeterminate sentences true? Why is a disjunction between an antinomic sentence and an indeterminate sentence simply true? Can you find any *rationale* for this?

(Q2) What can be said about **FOUR** in the light of our criteria for paraconsistent logics?

Exercises

(Ex1) Show by **RM3** truth tables that neither

$$(A \supset B) \equiv \neg (A \wedge \neg B)$$

nor

$$(A \supset B) \equiv \neg A \vee B$$

are valid in **RM3**.

(Ex2) Show by **BN4** truth tables that Contraposition, Double Negation and DeMorgan's Laws hold.

(Ex3) Show by **BN4** truth tables that Contraction does not hold.

(Ex4) Show that Negation Introduction fails in **FOUR**:

$$\nVdash_{FOUR}(A \supset B) \supset ((A \supset \neg B) \supset \neg A)$$

Further Reading

- On the systems **RM3** and **BN4** see: Brady, Ross. "Completeness proofs for the systems **RM3** and **BN4**", *Logique et Analyse*, 25, pp. 9-32.
- On paraconsistent dialogical logic see: Rahman, Shahid/Carnielli, Walter. "The Dialogical Approach to Paraconsistency". Fachrichtung Philosophie der Universität des Saarlandes, Report No. 8. Saarbrücken, 1998, 33pp.; Rahman has worked on several extensions of dialogical logic, including inconsistent ontology and multi-modal systems; you can find there also an introduction – in English – to dialogical logics in general.

10 | Semantics

Corresponding to semantic closure being one of the main motivations of strong paraconsistency semantics is one of the important fields in which paraconsistent logics have to be tested.

The cornerstone is a theory of truth for a language L given within that language itself. A theory of truth that obeys convention (T). A theory of truth that not only gives the truth conditions for the non-semantic vocabulary of L, but also of the semantic vocabulary itself.

The construction of a theory of meaning/truth of a language can follow the general procedure we know from Tarski's theory of truth (Tarski 1936) and Davidson's extension/re-interpretation of that procedure as a theory of meaning (Davidson 1967).

The whole construction that follows mirrors the usual construction of a Tarski style theory of truth for some (formal) language. It employs the usual apparatus and tries to prove the typical lemmas and the essential theorem that every sentence fulfils Convention (T). The crucial difference is "merely" that the whole construction is carried out in some language without caring about the object-language meta-language distinction. The idea of semantic closure demanded doing the semantics of some language in that very language. The somewhat tiresome details that now follow show simply that this is possible.

Language

The basis of the construction can be the language of **SKP** or **LP** (extended with some Relevant conditional).

We take "$\rightarrow$" here as a conditional for which Contraposition holds. [We could avoid using Contraposition by working with more axioms (for every case where we make essential use of contraposition); but for ease of explanation we employ Contraposition.]

Besides the semantic vocabulary we need arithmetical means of *naming* expressions.

"SAT" denotes the relation of satisfaction between sequences of objects and well-formed formula (wff).

"SUC" denotes the successor function. SUC(1)=2. The successor of any non-number is that object itself.

"NUMB" denotes the set of natural numbers.

"FORM" denotes the set of well-formed formula.

"TERM" denotes the set of singular terms of the language.

"FUNC" denotes the set of functors of the language. "FUNC^n" denotes the set of n-ary functors. FUNC does *not* denote the set of *functions*.
"PRED" denotes the set of *predicators* of the language; resp. "PRED^n".
"CONS" denotes a function which takes indices of constants (these indices being a subset of the natural numbers) to the set of constants, and which takes non-numbers to a specific but arbitrarily chosen dummy constant.
"VAR" does the same that CONS does for variables.
"ROW", abbreviated as "( )+( )'" denotes the function that adds the second argument (a sequence) to the first argument (a sequence) building the longer combined sequence.
"APP" denotes a binary function such that APP(x,y) gives the value of the function or sequence denoted by x at the denotation of y (respectively the value of applying the function denoted by x to the argument denoted by y); and if there is no such object gives a specific but arbitrarily chosen dummy object.
"SUB" denotes the triadic function such that "SUB(x,y,z)" denotes the function that agrees with the function denoted by x except that its value at the argument denoted by y is the value of the argument denoted by z.
"DEN" denotes a binary function, such that the value of "DEN(x,y)" is the denotation of the expression y, given that the free variables in y have been given values by the sequence x. For example: If y does contain three free variables x_1, x_2, x_3 their places in y are filled with the first three objects of a sequence s. [Notice: "DEN" does *not* denote the general function of denotation.]
Variables can take as values not only objects of the domain, but also numbers, sequences of objects, and sentences. Since we want to talk about the relation between linguistic entities and their denotation we have to be able to quantify over both and put them into relation.
Each object *o* is identified with its unary sequence <*o*>. This is done to yield a general notion of satisfaction of predicates in relation to sequences that covers also the case of unary predicates.
If s is a sequence and x a number s(x) is the xth object in the sequence s. "s(x/y)" says that in the sequence s y is put at the place of x.

Naming

In general the name of an expression is build by underlining.
For every singular expression of the language we can define its name thus (N being the set of natural numbers):

$\underline{v}_n$ is VAR($\underline{n}$) for $n \in \mathbb{N}$

$\underline{c}_k$ is CONS($\underline{k}$) for $k \in K \subseteq \mathbb{N}$

the variable function VAR applied to the name of a number (a numeral) yields the nth variable's name. The function CONS applied to a numeral yields the kth constant's name.
Given this taken together with the names of the logical vocabulary and the predicates we can build for any sequence *s* of expressions the name $\underline{s}$ of this sequence by using the function ROW: if $s_1s_2...s_n$ is a sequence of expressions $\underline{s_1}+\underline{s_2}+...+\underline{s_n}$ is the name of that expression.
Thus we can talk in L about every expression of that language, quantify over them and can apply predicates – especially semantic predicates – to them.

Axioms for Semantics

To make the structural theory of meaning possible we need *axioms for semantics.* These axioms are not to be confused with *meaning postulates* for the non-logical vocabulary of a specific language. The axioms for semantics are not all semantic axioms, but deal in general with the needed *apparatus* of semantics.
These axioms concern:

- mathematical functions
- syntactic operations
- axioms for the denotation relation DEN
- axioms for the satisfaction relation SAT

First the axioms for mathematical functions:

(Axiom 1) a. $(\forall x)SUC(x) \neq 0$

b. $(\forall x,y)(SUC(x)=SUC(y) \rightarrow x=y)$

c. $NUMB(0)$

d. $(\forall x)(NUMB(x) \rightarrow NUMB(SUC(x)))$

Axiom 1 deals with the successor function in the usual way. Note that (1b) is true also for non-numbers.

(Axiom 2) $(\forall x)(a = APP(s(x/a),x))$

The value at x of a sequence that substitutes a for x is a.

(Axiom 3) $(\forall x,y)(x \neq y \rightarrow APP(s,y)=APP(s(x/a),y))$

If x and y are different the value of a sequence has not changed at y if the value at x has been changed.
Then the axioms for syntactic operations:

(Axiom 4) $(\forall x,y,z)(x+(y+z))=((x+y)+z)$

ROW is associative.

(Axiom 5) a. $(\forall x)\mathrm{TERM}(\mathrm{VAR}(x))$

b. $(\forall x)\mathrm{TERM}(\mathrm{CONS}(x))$

c. $(\forall x_1 \ldots x_n, y)(\mathrm{TERM}(x_i) \wedge \mathrm{FUNC}^n(y) \rightarrow \mathrm{TERM}(y+ x_1+\ldots+x_n)$

Variables and constants are terms, and a n-ary functor builds a new singular term out of the singular term arguments.

(Axiom 6) a. $(\forall x_1 \ldots x_n, y)(\mathrm{TERM}(x_i) \wedge \mathrm{PRED}^n(y) \rightarrow$

$\mathrm{FORM}(y+ x_1+\ldots+x_n)$

b. $(\forall x,y)(\mathrm{FORM}(x) \wedge \mathrm{FORM}(y) \rightarrow$

$\mathrm{FORM}(\ \underline{(} + x + \underline{\triangle} + y + \underline{)}\ ) \wedge$

$\mathrm{FORM}(\ \underline{(} + x + \underline{\rightarrow} + y + \underline{)}\ ) \wedge$

$\mathrm{FORM}(\ \underline{\neg} + x))$

(6a) defines basic formula, (6b) complex formula by the basic connectives ("$\underline{\triangle}$" is the *name* of conjunction, and so on). (6c) correspondingly for quantification.

c. $(\forall x,y)(\mathrm{FORM}(x) \wedge \mathrm{NUMB}(y) \rightarrow$

$\mathrm{FORM}(\ \underline{(} + \underline{\forall} + \mathrm{VAR}(y) + \underline{)}\ + \underline{(} + x + \underline{)}\ )$

Axioms for Denotation:

(Axiom 7) $(\forall x)(\mathrm{NUMB}(x) \rightarrow \mathrm{DEN}(s,\mathrm{VAR}(x))=s(x))$

(Axiom 8) $\mathrm{DEN}(s,\mathrm{CONS}(\underline{k}))=c_k$ for $k \in K$

(Axiom 9) $(\forall x_1 \ldots x_n, y)(\mathrm{TERM}(x_i) \wedge \mathrm{FUNC}^n(y) \rightarrow$

$\mathrm{DEN}(y+ x_1+\ldots+x_n)=y(\mathrm{DEN}(s, x_1)\ldots\mathrm{DEN}(s, x_n))$

These axioms define the denotation of terms recursively. The axiom corresponding to (Axiom 9) for formulas (i.e. with PRED^n) is no topic for DEN, but for SAT.

Axioms for Satisfaction:

(Axiom 10) $(\forall x_1 \ldots x_n, y)(\mathrm{TERM}(x_i) \wedge \mathrm{PRED}^n(y) \rightarrow$

$(\mathrm{SAT}(s,\mathrm{FORM}(y+ x_1+\ldots+x_n) \leftrightarrow$

$y(\mathrm{DEN}(s, x_1)\ldots\mathrm{DEN}(s, x_n))))$

A sequence s satisfies a formula iff the predicate applies to the terms (these maybe completed by s). This is the satisfaction condition for basic formulas. The further axioms deal with complex formula:

(Axiom 11) $(\forall x,y)(FORM(x) \wedge FORM(y) \rightarrow$
$(SAT(s, FORM(\underline{(} + x + \underline{\wedge} + y + \underline{)}\ ) \leftrightarrow$
$SAT(s,x) \wedge SAT(s,y)))$

(Axiom 12) $(\forall x,y)(FORM(x) \rightarrow (SAT(s, FORM(\underline{\neg} + x) \leftrightarrow$
$\neg SAT(s,x)))$

(Axiom 13) $(\forall x,y)(FORM(x) \wedge FORM(y) \rightarrow$
$(SAT(s,FORM(\underline{(} + x + \underline{\rightarrow} + y + \underline{)}) \leftrightarrow$
$SAT(s,x) \rightarrow SAT(s,y)))$

(Axiom 14) $(\forall x,y)(FORM(x) \wedge NUMB(y) \rightarrow$
$(SAT(s, \underline{(} + \underline{\forall} + VAR(y) + \underline{)} + \underline{(} + x + \underline{)}\ ) \leftrightarrow$
$(\forall z)SAT(s(y/z),x)))$

Defining Truth

Truth can be defined in Tarski's way:

(DTRUE) $True(x) \leftrightarrow (\forall s)SAT(s,x)$

A formula (nothing else could be a proper argument of SAT) is true if and only if it is satisfied by all sequences.
Mirroring the usual proof one can derive the following essential theorem:

(THEOREM) For any closed formula x: $\vdash(x \leftrightarrow True(x))$

stating the disquotational character of truth (the (T)-scheme).
This theorem is established by establishing a couple of Lemmas.
By the naming convention and Axiom 5 we get:

(Lemma 1) It t is a term of L, then $\vdash TERM(\underline{t})$

Correspondingly we can establish by Axiom 6:

(Lemma 2) If x is a formula of L, then $\vdash FORM(\underline{x})$

Say that for any term or formula x the *relativisation* of x to s (written "x_s") is obtained by replacing any free variable v_k in x by the kth object in s.
With Axioms 7 to Axiom 9 we can prove for denotation DEN:

(Lemma 3) For any term t of $L \vdash DEN(s,\underline{t})=t_s$

We approach truth more closely with the *essential* lemma:

(Lemma 4) For any formula x of $L \vdash SAT(s,x) \leftrightarrow x_s$

The decisive step is taken – as is in Tarski's construction – by establishing that lemma. Like denotation establishes some link between language and reality, so satisfaction establishes a link between a formula and reality. Some sequence of objects satisfies a formula means that the formula is true of these objects, which in turn can be taken as capturing an essential aspect of the correspondence theory of truth. *Satisfaction* is the concept that does the truth delivering work in a Tarski style truth theory.
So let us look at the proof of (Lemma 4).
Proof (Outline):
The proof proceeds by induction on the complexity of the formulas of L. For basic formulas we get by (Axiom 10):

$$SAT(s,P(t1...tn)) \leftrightarrow P(DEN(s,t1)...DEN(s,tn))$$

By (Lemma 3): $SAT(s,P(t1...tn)) \leftrightarrow P(t1s,...,tns)$
By (Lemma 3) again: $P(t1s,...,tns) \leftrightarrow (P(t1,...,tn))s$
That gives the basic step of the induction (the Induction Hypothesis). Now for complex formula (the Induction Step):
In case of conjunctions: $SAT(s,x \wedge y) \leftrightarrow (xs \wedge ys)$
and: $(xs \wedge ys) \leftrightarrow (x \wedge y)s$
Accordingly for negation and entailment. For quantifiers we get by (Axiom 14) and (Lemmas 2) and (Lemma 3), renaming variables if necessary:

$$SAT(s, (+\exists+VAR(k)+)+x) \leftrightarrow (\exists y)SAT(s(k/y),x)$$

x being the open formula, y being some object to replace vk; by the Induction Hypothesis (i.e. the lemma being true for less complex formula):

$$SAT(s, (+\exists+VAR(k)+)+x) \leftrightarrow (\exists y)xs(k/y)$$

Filling in x other variables other than vk, if any, provided by the objects in s, and using the variable y for vk we get a open formula x' for which we have: $(\exists y)SAT(s(k/y),x) \leftrightarrow (\exists y)x'$
and by construction of x': $(\exists y)x' \leftrightarrow ((\exists y)\ x)s$.
This shows the Inductive Step also for the quantificational case. And thus for all complex formulas of the language. ■

The scheme proved in (Lemma 4) is the satisfaction scheme:

$$\vdash SAT(s,x) \leftrightarrow x_s$$

A formula that does not contain free variables (i.e. a closed formula) is either satisfied by *all* sequences or by none. Being satisfied means in this case that

$$\vdash x_s$$

And since it is a closed formula, this comes to

$\vdash x$

since x does not contain any free variables.
So by the *definition* of truth (DTRUE):

$$\vdash \mathrm{True}(x) \leftrightarrow (\forall s)\mathrm{SAT}(s,x)$$

the right hand side led by assumption (the closed formula being satisfied by all/one sequence) to the formula itself being the case, thus

$$\vdash \mathrm{True}(x) \leftrightarrow x$$

the essential (THEOREM). There we are!

Doing away with Contraposition

As already mentioned our paraconsistent conditional will turn out to be one for which Contraposition does not hold. The corresponding logic (like **SKP**) will be justified in the light of our declared aims of strong paraconsistency only if we can do naive semantics with it, i.e. without Contraposition.
This can in fact be done. We have to supplement the axioms of SAT with axioms for another relation ANTI-SAT, which does the work the negation of SAT does given the presence of Contraposition.
The intuitive sense of ANTI-SAT is that ANTI-SAT(s,x) is true given some sequence s and a formula x iff that sequence makes the formula *false*.
Instead of (Axiom 12) we take

(Axiom 12') $(\forall x,y)(\mathrm{FORM}(x) \rightarrow (\mathrm{SAT}(s, \mathrm{FORM}(\underline{\neg} + x) \leftrightarrow \text{ANTI-SAT}(s,x)))$

Further on we need axioms of making (complex) formula false. These axioms (15) – (17) are obvious for the connectives and quantifiers, given their standard treatment in the axioms (10) – (14).
For entailment we give:

(Axiom 18) $(\forall x,y)(\mathrm{FORM}(x) \wedge \mathrm{FORM}(y) \rightarrow (\text{ANTI-SAT}(s,\mathrm{FORM}(\underline{(} + x + \underline{\rightarrow} + y + \underline{)}) \leftrightarrow \Diamond (\mathrm{SAT}(s,x) \wedge \text{ANTI-SAT}(s,y)))$

In the light of **SKP** semantics an entailment is false if it is possible (there is a accessibility to worlds starting from the actual world @ such) that the antecedent of the conditional is true while the consequent is false. The consequent being false means that ANTI-SAT obtains.
The proof of the essential (THEOREM) then has to be modified accordingly by substituting for each appeal to Contraposition an

application of *Modus Ponens* to some instance of the axioms for ANTI-SAT.

A Theory of Truth

The construction outlined delivers a theory of truth (and correspondingly of meaning) of a language L in that very language.
The theory satisfies that for every sentence of the language we get an instance of convention (T). "every sentence" means *every* sentence, including those dealing with semantic properties themselves. It provides a *systematic presentation of semantic closure.*
Given the expressive power employed and semantic closure, of course the antinomies (or some versions of further antinomies) can be derived in this theory. This semantics is *inconsistent.*
Given the non-triviality of the underlying logic (e.g. **SKP**), this semantics, nevertheless, is *paraconsistent.*
Whether the extended theory for a fuller segment of a natural language is non-explosive depends on how many more axioms with how much logical power we add, for example, which axioms of arithmetic.

Antinomies in this Theory of Truth

The language structure given so far has not the means to formally prove the Liar or other antinomies by diagonalization or other arithmetic means. But since constants can *name sentences* we can form some Liar:

$$(\lambda) \qquad c = \underline{\neg True(c)}$$

Trying to satisfy c will lead us to $SAT(s,c) \leftrightarrow \neg SAT(s,c)$
Replacing in our mathematical axioms the following axiom:

$$\text{(Axiom 1c)} \quad \Box NUMB(0)$$

and adding the axiom that any object is the xth object of some sequence (which should be so given a domain and sequences over it):

$$\text{(Axiom 19)} \quad (\forall x,y)(NUMB(x) \rightarrow (\exists s)(s(x)=y))$$

we can derive a contradiction for the SAT relation.
We define another version of SAT as SAT_1:

$$(1) \qquad SAT_1(x,y) \leftrightarrow (\exists s)(s(\underline{i})=x \wedge SAT(s,y))$$

for some *i* and taking free variables to be universally quantified. That surely is possible and expresses that some formula is satisfied_i by some object x if it is satisfied by some sequence the ith object of which is x.

$$(2) \qquad SAT_1(x,\underline{y_k}) \rightarrow (\exists s)(s(\underline{i})=x \wedge SAT(s, \underline{y_k}))$$

y_k being some formula with some free variable v_i free for x.

(3) $SAT_1(x,\underline{y_k}) \rightarrow (\exists s)(s(\underline{i})=x \wedge y_k(v_i/s(\underline{i})))$

by the definition of satisfaction.

(4) $SAT_1(x,\underline{y_k}) \rightarrow y_k(v_i/x)$

by conjunction elimination and substitution of identicals.

(5) $\Box NUMB(i)$

(6) $y_k(v_i/x) \rightarrow (\exists s)(s(\underline{i})=x \wedge y_k(v_i/s(\underline{i})))$

by our new axioms (1c) and (19), reversing the steps to line (4).

(7) $y_k(v_i/x) \rightarrow SAT_1(x,\underline{y_k})$

(8) $y_k(v_i/x) \leftrightarrow SAT_1(x,\underline{y_k})$

joining (4) and (7).
Into supposedly harmless line (8) we substitute $\neg SAT_1(v_i, v_i)$ for y_k and instantiate x with the *name* of that sentence, so that we get:

(9) $\neg SAT_1(\underline{\neg SAT_1(v_i, v_i)}, \underline{\neg SAT_1(v_i, v_i)}) \leftrightarrow$

$SAT_1(\underline{\neg SAT_1(v_i, v_i)}, \underline{\neg SAT_1(v_i, v_i)})$

an antinomy!

Antinomies of Denotation

Denotation is one core concept of semantics. Self-referential antinomies like the Liar can be modelled in terms of denotation. Let $DEN(\underline{x})$ be a monadic denotation function. For any closed term x, $DEN(\underline{x}) = x$. (The denotation of *the name of* (the) x is x itself.)
The *diagonalization* of a term *a* substitutes *a*'s name ($\underline{a}$) for all free variables in *a*. Let the diagonal *function d* map names of terms to the *names* of their diagonalization. $d(\underline{a(x)}) = \underline{a(a)}$. So this diagonal function does not give us an self-application, but a name of an self-application.
Take an arbitrary term *b* with one free variable *x*. Consider *b*(*dx*)), let us call this *l* (*l* being a name). The diagonali*zation* of *l* is $b(d(\underline{l}))$ (the argument "$d(\underline{l})$" was generated by the diagonal function). Call this *s*. Nothing forbids applying a new name. *s* names the diagonal of *l*, i.e. by the prior definition of the diagonal function $d(\underline{l}) = \underline{s}$. Substituting now identicals within *b* we get $b(d(\underline{l})) = b(\underline{s})$), but by the first definition of s, this means $s = b(\underline{s})$).
Thus:

(Theorem D1) For any term *b* with a free variable there is a closed term *s* such that $s = b(\underline{s})$).

The theorem states *not* a fixed point, since on the left hand side we have the name $\underline{s}$ instead of *s* itself. But the fix point is now within reach:

Consider *b*(DEN(x)). By (Theorem D1) there is a closed term *s* such that for this: *s* = *b*(DEN(*s̲*)). Since *s* is a closed term, *s* = DEN(*s̲*). Thus:

(Theorem D2) For any term *b* with a free variable there is a closed term *s* such that *s*=*b*(*s*)).

This means that there is a term that says/denotes the same as *some* function applied to this term. This gives as fixpoints for *all* functions: Points where the application of the function gives no further object.
The mere existence of fixpoints is not problematic. *Being-identical-with( )* may be employed as often as you like to itself without resulting in a further object. The problem with the two theorems is that the expression *b* can be *any* functional expression of the language!
Within a sufficiently rich language, however, these fixpoints lead into trouble. A fixpoint for the successor function SUC would be a number such that SUC(x)=x, i.e. a number that is its own successor, making arithmetic inconsistent.
Hilbert and Bernays, who discovered the problems with denotation, concluded, therefore, that denotation cannot be represented *within* a consistent arithmetic itself (comparable to Tarski's Theorem concerning the representability of a truth predicate).
The resulting hierarchy is not acceptable for a dialetheist. At least a natural language as semantically closed should be able to represent denotation. So there has to be *some* arithmetic in which some number is identical to its successor. Thus we arrive at paraconsistent mathematics [see Chap. 12]!
Nevertheless we need then some account of non-referring descriptions, because there is an expression available which is a fixpoint with respect to the parity function *f* (mapping even numbers to 1 and odd numbers to 0). This fixpoint s = *f*s . *f* maps 1 (being odd) to 0 and 0 (being even) to 1. If *f* is applicable to s then *f*s = 1 or *f*s = 0. Going through the cases gives us 1=0! Since triviality may ensue from this one may wish that s better not denote at all [see Chap. 20].

Questions

(Q1) What is the difference between denotation and satisfaction?
What different interpretations of antinomies of denotation and satisfaction can be given in terms of the relation of language and reality?

(Q2) What is the difference between diagonalization and the diagonal function, and why is this distinction vital for the argument concerning the fixed points?

Exercises

(Ex1) Give the axioms for ANTI-SAT for conjunction, negation and the universal quantifier.

(Ex2) Spell out in detail the reasoning concerning the fixpoint

$$s = fs$$

Does it go through in an extended **LP**? How does it go in an adaptive version of **LP**?

Further Reading

- The presentation of the truth theory is based on Priest, Graham. *In Contradiction.* A Study of the Transconsistent. Dordrecht, 1987, pp. 157-77.
- On the denotation paradox by Hilbert and Bernays see: Priest, Graham. "On a Paradox of Hilbert and Bernays", *Journal of Philosophical Logic*, 1997, pp. 45-56.

11 | Set Theory

Apart from semantic closure set theory is one of the main motivations for the strong paraconsistent approach. As well as we take convention (T) to be basic for truth so do we take the naive comprehension scheme to be basic to our concept of set:

(COMP) $(\forall F)(\exists y)(\forall x)(F(x) \equiv x \in y)$

There should be a set corresponding to an open formula ascribing some property to the objects.
This comprehension axiom is sometimes called "naive set theory". It was by no means present in all approaches that introduced set theory in the 19th century [Cantor's original set theory was different, concerned with combinatorial multitudes.; but it was present in the logicist approach of Frege and Russell]. "Naive Set Theory" lead to Russell's antinomy. So in today's standard set theory (**ZFC**, Zermelo-Fraenkel Set Theory with Axiom of Choice) there is no unrestricted comprehension axiom or schema [the (COMP) *schema* does not quantify over F].
Paraconsistent set theory regains (COMP).

Russell's Antinomy

Russell's antinomy (usually called "Russell's Paradox") results from defining a set of all sets that are not elements of themselves:

$R \overset{\text{def}}{\equiv} \{x | x \notin x\}$

The formula/property occurring in (COMP) can be any open formula. So it is not forbidden to take "( ) ∉ ( )". We get then:

(1) $(\exists y)(\forall x)(x \notin x \equiv x \in y)$

The y containing all the x that are not members of themselves is the set R, so we get:

(2) $(\forall x)(x \notin x \equiv x \in R)$

Now, what holds for any x (i.e. any set) has to hold for R as well:

(3) $R \notin R \equiv R \in R$

An antinomy!
One can also start reasoning from the definition of R: If R is a member of itself, then R is (by R's definition) not a member of itself. If R is not a member of itself, it is (by R's definition) a member of itself. Contradiction!

Russell's antinomy can be avoided by modifying (COMP) as **ZFC** does by restricting *separation* to an underlying set:

$$\text{(SEP)} \quad (\forall F)(\exists z)(\forall x,y)(x \in y \wedge F(x) \equiv x \in z)$$

(SEP) or the corresponding schema says that we can built a subset of any set given some condition F. (The right to left direction is crucial.)
Now consider a kind of Russell set again. $R' = \{x \mid x \in a \wedge x \notin x\}$ for some arbitrary set a. We take substitution steps like before, and get:

$$(4) \qquad x \in a \wedge x \notin x \equiv x \in R'$$

Is R' an element of a? Either $R' \in R'$ or $R' \notin R'$. Assume $R' \in a$ and the first option, $R' \in R'$. Then we get (by (4) right to left direction):

$$(5) \qquad R' \in a \wedge R' \notin R' \equiv R' \in R'$$

Contradiction! Assume the second option, $R' \notin R'$. We get (by (4) left to right direction) another contradiction:

$$(6) \qquad R' \in a \wedge R' \notin R' \equiv R' \in R'$$

So both options lead to contradiction, and we have to give up the assumption $R' \in a$. The set a does not contain R', so a is not universal. Since a was arbitrary we conclude that *there is no universal set*!

No Universal Set in ZFC

The argument given proves that there is no universal set in **ZFC**. This is mirrored in the way sets are built up in one of the models of **ZFC**, the so called "cumulative hierarchy" of pure sets (i.e. sets with no basic elements): one starts with the empty set $\varnothing$; the powerset of $\varnothing$, $\wp(\varnothing)$, containing all subsets of $\varnothing$ is $\{\varnothing\}$, since $\varnothing$ is a subset of every set (none of its elements in missing!); $\wp(\{\varnothing\})$ is $\{\varnothing,\{\varnothing\}\}$, since besides the empty set all singletons of elements of a set are members of the powerset; going on like that we introduce more and more sets, having k sets at stage n means 2^k sets at stage n+1 (at stage 6 we already have a number with twenty thousand digits!). We arrive at higher and higher cardinalities in a V shape figure. The universe of the cumulative hierarchy is therefore called V. V itself cannot occur in the hierarchy.
Explained otherwise: There can be no universal set V, since $\wp(V)$ would have more elements than V (by *Cantor's Theorem*), but that is impossible if V was the universal set. Contradiction!
That there is no universal set leads to several problems. The standard account of concepts in **FOL** semantics goes like this: What does "( ) is a tree" refer to? It refers to the set of all trees. A concept/property is understood if we understand what its extension is.

Now, what is a set? It cannot be the extension of "( ) is a set", since this extension would be a universal set in the cumulative hierarchy, but there is none. So in standard set theory there is no set/extension corresponding to our usage of "( ) is a set". For restricted usages (set of some kind, cardinality, order etc.) there are sets, but they do not speak of set in general. **ZFC** is *ontologically* restricted.
The problem is the same as with the semantic hierarchy in the Tarski tradition [see Chap. 2]. Standard set theory is using a fundamental notion that cannot be explained *by this theory*! Or uses a fundamental notion that is *incoherent* given that very theory!
Once again this runs against our intuitive understanding of "set", and seems to be a massive performative self-contradiction on side of standard set theory.
The absence of a universal set is not just a problem of understanding what a set is. Some set theoretical explanation of other concepts make use of a universal quantification about sets.
If one defines:

$\Gamma \models A$ $\stackrel{\text{def}}{\equiv}$ A follows from a set of premises Γ if and only if every interpretation that makes all $B \in \Gamma$ makes A true.

one now talks about *any* interpretation. And the domain of an interpretation is arbitrary. It may be a set of arbitrary high rank. So the supposed definition talks about *all* sets of an arbitrary high rank (i.e. of the completed hierarchy), but in **ZFC** we can never get at *all* sets! So it seems that our understanding of consequence cannot be modelled by **ZFC**. **ZFC** can only define an incomplete model thereof.
Further on: If there is no universal set, there is no universal *complement* of a set X (i.e. the set of those x that are not in X, but not just given some basic set of separation Y [i.e. $\{y \mid y \in Y \wedge y \notin X\}$], but the set of *all* x wherever that are not in X [i.e. $\{x \mid x \notin X\}$]). Some theories (category theory) want to talk about such sets, however.
In a version of standard set theory (von Neumann's version taken up by Bernays and Gödel) a distinction between classes and sets is used: Classes are sets that are not elements. The syntax distinguishes between classes and sets and gives a corresponding axiomatization.
The supposed universal set turns out to be a class. The Russell set is a class, and so cannot be a member of itself.
On the one hand this may be considered *ad hoc*, since the introduction of classes seems to play no further role than avoiding antinomies. And on the other hand there seems to be no reason why classes could not be elements of (some) other classes. The general inhibition of elementhood seems to be an exaggeration.

If one then allows for classes to be elements of (some) classes we arrive at a second hierarchy (a hierarchy of classes), and now our old troubles return: There cannot be a universal class.

Extensionality

In naive set theory the basic axiom besides that of Comprehension is that of Extensionality:

(EXT) $(\forall x,y)(Set(x) \wedge Set(y) \wedge (\forall z)(z \in x \equiv z \in y) \supset x = y)$

Sets are identical if they have the same elements; if the domain does not contain any non-sets (i.e. in pure set theory) the first two conjuncts can be dropped. and the conditional be replaced by a biconditional.
The predicate "Set( )" is problematic in **ZFC**, since its extension should be something like the universal set, absent in standard set theory.
If (COMP) is used in its naive form it can be used to prove the existence of sets (like pair or power sets) that have to be introduced by axioms in standard set theory. Its basic supplementation is (EXT) alone!
(EXT) can be used as an axiom, but often in paraconsistent set theory is given in form of extensionality *rules*.

Routley's Paraconsistent Set Theory

Richard Routley uses the logic **DL** [see Chap. 5] with the following quantificational extension (Routley 1979a, p.290):
Additional axiom schemes:

(A14) $(\forall x)P(x) \rightarrow P(á)$

(A15) $(\forall x)(A \rightarrow P(x)) \rightarrow (A \rightarrow (\forall x)P(x))$ *

(A16) $(\forall x)(A \vee P(x)) \rightarrow (A \vee (\forall x)P(x))$ *

(A17) $(\forall x)(P(x) \rightarrow A) \rightarrow ((\exists x)P(x) \rightarrow A)$ * [* x not free in A]

Additional Rules:

(R3) $\vdash A \Rightarrow \vdash (\forall x)A$

Comprehension is expressed with a Relevant conditional:

(COMP') $(\exists y)(\forall x)(x \in y \leftrightarrow P(x))$

(COMP') has no restrictions on "P( )" (like "y does not occur in P( )") so that one can have a set y such that $x \in y \leftrightarrow \neg x \in y$ (taking "$\neg( ) \in y$" as the predicate "P( )"). This is a bizarre set of all things that belong to it iff they do not belong to it!
Such usages of (COMP') immediately raise the question of inconsistent ontology (i.e. *whether* and *where* are objects like the set described?).

(COMP') is no longer well-founded: a set like $\{y \mid x \in y \leftrightarrow \neg x \in y\}$ may contain y itself. (COMP') allows for $\{x \mid x \in x\}$. So the Foundation Axiom of **ZFC** is not part of paraconsistent set theory based on unrestricted comprehension. Foundation was a late comer in **ZFC** any way, has no mathematical applications outside set theory, and is dropped in otherwise standard non-founded set theory (cf. Aczel 1988).
Rephrasing (EXT) using a Relevant biconditional allows to derive even the Axiom of Choice from it, but also Irrelevant theorems, so (EXT) is replaced by a rule:

(EXTR) (i) $x = y \Rightarrow x \in z \rightarrow y \in z$

(ii) $x = y \overset{\text{def}}{=} (\forall z)(z \in x \leftrightarrow z \in y)$

This rules allow for the substitution of identicals and defines how identity of sets is to be taken. For substitution we have:

(SUB) $A \leftrightarrow B \Rightarrow C(A) \rightarrow C(B)$

i.e. if A and B Relevantly imply each other than B can be substituted in any context C of A for A so that the resulting sentence is still Relevantly implied. (Different antinomies do not imply each other.)
(COMP') allows to define sets otherwise introduced by axioms:
Existence of the empty set $\varnothing$:

$(\exists y)(\forall x)(x \in y \leftrightarrow \neg x = x)$

This set is empty, since even in **DL** we have: $(\forall x)x = x$
Existence of the *absolute* complement of some set x:

$(\exists y)(\forall z)(z \in y \leftrightarrow \neg z \in x)$

x is some arbitrary set here, so that we can have the complement of any set we wish. In ZFC there are only relative complements of x (in some superset) because of the restricted version of (COMP).
The antinomies can, of course, be derived in this set theory, but the underlying paraconsistent logic avoids triviality.
That versions of the Axiom of Choice can be derived within his set theory shows, according to Routley, the *realistic* character of paraconsistent set theory (i.e. the domain is simply there, with all functions defined on it, whether we have constructed them from previously constructed material or not).
What about the metalogic of Routley's set theory?
Routley (1979a, pp.931-33) extends his logic **DKQ** by some axioms for arithmetic to his paraconsistent arithmetic **DKA**. He can prove that **DKA** is not trivial, i.e. absolute consistent. A system like **DKA** being inconsistent does not meet the condition of *Gödel's Second Theorem*, so can be used

itself to prove its own consistency. This proof, however, uses a truth functional conditional like that of **LP**. So this proof – because of the Curry Conditions – cannot be extended to paraconsistent set theory.
Routley and Brady (1989) nevertheless proved the non-triviality of a paraconsistent set theory using a logic with a negation semantics in terms of the Routley * and the ternary accessibility relation. Brady improved on that situation by stating his set theory in his logic $\mathbf{DJ^dQ}$.
One can add (COMP) and an axiom version of (EXT) to **LP** and gain a set theory which has non-trivial models, but **LP** without an additional conditional is a logic too weak for standard mathematics.

Brady's Paraconsistent Class Theory

Brady's version of paraconsistent set theory also employs (COMP') and (EXTR). The underlying logic is $\mathbf{DJ^dQ}$.
Given the semantics of content containment Brady has to use (EXTR), since the *content* of $x=y$ seems not to contain $x\in z \leftrightarrow y\in z$.
In facts Brady's theory is a *class theory* (not a set theory). Brady distinguishes classes for which the two axioms hold and for which sentences dealing with them have a Relevant logic from sets, whose memberships sentences obey standard logic! The standard behaviour is needed to have enough countable sets in the classes. On the sets we thus have a completely standard logic and ontology.
The interesting part now is the class theory. Brady has proved his system of class theory to be non-trivial.
In fact Brady tries to avoid the antinomies in the first place, not just their spreading of inconsistency! Brady's version of paraconsistent set theory does *not* contain all of the antinomies and "only" keeps them from spreading triviality elsewhere. Some of the antinomies do not occur. In case of the Russell set one can prove $R\in R \leftrightarrow R\notin R$. To get to the explicit contradiction $R\in R \wedge R\notin R$ once needs either the Law of the Excluded Middle or Negation Introduction. Both are absent in $\mathbf{DJ^dQ}$. Thus given the validity of $R\in R \leftrightarrow R\notin R$ only one can chose to make them both true or both false. Both cases are harmless with respect to the behaviour of the Russell set, but this shows some semantic underdetermination of Brady's theory.
Something similar holds for Curry's Paradox, since Contraction does not hold in $\mathbf{DJ^dQ}$.
Since Brady distinguishes sets from classes he restricts the validity of *Cantor's Theorem* (that the powerset of a set has more elements than the set itself) to sets, avoiding the antinomy that the powerset of the universal

set has to be within the universal set and at the same time larger than the universal set. (The sets are collected into a class.)

Adaptive Set Theory

The problem of recapturing wnough standard set theory and mathematics and avoiding ontologically problematic sentences like

$$a\in b \wedge a\notin b$$

may be (better) solved in a set theory with an adaptive base logic. With a logic like adaptive LP or **UL4** [cf. Chap. 7 and 20] the consistent areas of set theory stay as they are.
With respect to the antinomies and paradoxes created by free usage of unrestricted comprehension the results can be softened. For example, for the Routley set we get

$$(\exists y)(\forall x)(x\in y \equiv x\notin y)$$

or, instantiated,

$$a\in r \equiv a\notin r$$

but detachment will not go through, since either side of the biconditional will be an antinomic sentence, for which ($\supset$E)/($\equiv$E) are not applicable. The standard proof to get a conjunction from a biconditional [cf. Chap. 2] is not available in adaptive logics of this kind. Object r is still queer, but we cannot say that there is an object which is and is not an element of it. We only have that for all objects the membership sentences and their negations are equivalent.

Systematisation of Antinomies

Within paraconsistent set theory the general form of many antinomies can be given [cf. (Priest 1995, pp.142-48); based on (Russell 1905)]:

(i) $\Omega = \{y \mid \varphi(y)\}$ exists and $\psi(\Omega)$

(ii) if $x \subseteq \Omega$ such that $\psi(x)$:

(iia) $\delta(x)\notin x$

(iib) $\delta(x)\in\Omega$

If we have some set Ω of the y satisfying some condition φ and that set satisfies some condition ψ, we get an antinomy if there is some subset of Ω having also the property ψ, and there is some diagonalisation function such that the diagonal of x is not in x itself, but has to be in Ω.
The antinomy occurs by taking Ω itself for x, getting:

$$\delta(\Omega)\in\Omega \wedge \delta(\Omega)\notin\Omega$$

In case of Russell's antinomy Ω is the universal set, φ is the condition of being a member of the universal set. ψ is not important in that antinomy and can be self-identity. The diagonalisation δ concerns not-membership. δ(Ω) is the Russell set {y∈Ω| y∉y}. δ(Ω)∈Ω, since it is a set, and δ(Ω)∉Ω, otherwise δ(Ω)∈δ(Ω). Contradiction in any case.
Taking this "inclosure schema" yields the following overview:

Antinomy' Name	**Set Ω**	**Condition φ**	**Property Ψ**	**Diagonal δ(x)**	**Antinomy**
Russell's Antinomy	Universal Set V	y is a set	z = z	¬x∈x	R∈R and R∉R
Burali-Forti Antinomy	Set of the Ordinals	y is an ordinal	z = z	next greater ordinal	greatest ordinal is no ordinal
Miromanoff's Antinomy	cumulative hierarchy V (of well-founded sets)	y is well-founded	z = z	being contained in V	R∈R since all subsets of R are, and R∉R!
König's Antinomy	definable ordinals	definable	being indefinable	smallest ordinal y∉Ω	y∈Ω, since defined, and y∉Ω

Assessment

Paraconsistent set theory is not only of interest in itself or as formalization of naive set theory. It also may serve as the foundation of paraconsistent arithmetic. It has to be checked what remains of standard mathematics once its foundations in set theory have been restricted to paraconsistent set theories!
Do we need paraconsistency for set theory?
If the justification for a paraconsistent set theory depends on avoiding the antinomies, others approaches that avoid the antinomies might be alternatives [see Chap.18].
If the justification depends on the argument that the notion of set is not clear unless we have a universal set, set theories that combine standard logic with having a universal set might be alternatives. [e.g. Quine's New Foundations (**NF**) set theory, (Quine 1937), or (Church 1974)]

A more decisive point may be keeping unrestricted (naive) Comprehension. That is something that neither **ZFC** nor systems like **NF** can do.
Neither does the distinction between classes and sets capture our naive understanding of sets. A theory not making this difference should be preferred.

Questions

(Q1) Does a comprehension schema that allows for non well-foundedness meet our naive intuitions about sets? Do we usually take sets to be well-founded?

(Q2) One of the major problems of Russell's and Frege's logicist programme (of reducing mathematics to logic) was that some axioms of set theory look very substantial and not purely logical. The main concern of Russell is the Axiom of Infinity (*postulating* a set with infinitely many elements). What is the upshot of paraconsistent set theory for Logicism?

Exercises

(Ex1) Show by defining them that Pairing and Powerset are not needed as axioms in Routley's set theory, but are instances of (COMP').

(Ex2) Take Berry's Antinomy of the smallest number z that cannot be named by less than 99 words. Show how this antinomy fits the inclosure schema.

Further Reading

• On the problem of the missing universal set in the set hierarchy see: Priest's *In Contradiction*, pp.35-47.
• On **ZFC** see a standard text book like: Stoll, Robert. *Set Theory and Logic*. New York, 2nd Ed., 1963. On the different versions of standard set theory and models for **ZFC** see: Lavine, S. *Understanding the Infinite*. Cambridge/MA, 2nd Ed., 1988.

• On paraconsistent set theory see besides the usual references [cf. Chap.1] see the work of Richard Routley (1979a, pp. 914-25) and Ross Brady (2000).
• Compare with Chap. 2 on the problem of semantic closure. See the discussion of Lesniewski's solution of Russell's antinomy in Chap. 18.

12 | Inconsistent Mathematics

Mathematics has traditionally been the hallmark of a science that proceeds by proof, and so is free of falsehoods and more so of inconsistency.
Changing the basic logic used in mathematics to a paraconsistent logic makes mathematics in a weak sense paraconsistent: If there were to turn up some inconsistency in mathematics, it would not explode. But since there are no inconsistencies expected to arise there, a mathematician will not be inclined to forego the deductive power of standard First Order Logic.
Changing set theory to a paraconsistent set theory makes mathematics paraconsistent in a stronger sense, since now the basic axioms are taken as the inconsistent axioms of naive set theory. There are now real inconsistencies – may be even inconsistent objects – in mathematics and the logic, therefore, has to be a paraconsistent one.
And the inconsistency may not only reside with some elusive set theoretic entities, but there may be inconsistent numbers as well!

Inconsistent Mathematical Objects

To have an inconsistent number theory means at least that within the theorems of number theory there is some sentence A with A being a theorem and ¬A being a theorem at the same time.
Supposedly this corresponds to some object/number *o* being an inconsistent object. So inconsistent mathematics is connected to inconsistent ontology. Its underlying logic has to be paraconsistent.
The problems with having F(a) and ¬F(a) for some object *a* seem not so pressing if *a* is some mathematical object than *a* being a physical object [see Chap. 17]: Mathematical objects are either non-existent – *mere* theory, taken instrumentally – or they are in some elusive Platonic realm where strange things may well happen.
If on the other hand one is a reductionist realist about mathematics (mathematics being about structures of reality or mathematical entities rather being concrete entities dealt with by mereology) then inconsistent mathematics is as problematic as your cat being (wholly) black and not being (wholly) black at the same time.
Philosophers when concerned with mathematics focus on number theory, since the ontological questions of mathematics ("What and where are mathematical objects?", "Are there infinite sets?"...) and the epistemological questions of mathematics ("How do we know of

numbers?", "Is mathematics merely conventional?"...) do arise already with number theory.
Taking set and model theory as part of logic anyway, logicians are also mainly concerned with number, since a lot of meta-logical theorems make us of the device of arithemetization.
The same goes for the general theory of automata and computability.
We follow this focus here and so this chapter concerns itself mostly with arithmetic. [Set theory as part of logic is deal with in Chap. 11.] This may not be enough for a mathematician trying to assess the power of inconsistent mathematics. She looks for inconsistent theories at least of the power of the calculus. There are actually such theories, e.g. presented by Chris Mortensen [see Further Reading].

Non-Standard Arithmetic

One of the most fundamental mathematical theories is arithmetic (as given for instance by the Peano axioms). One has to distinguish a first order representation of arithmetic from a second order arithmetic. We are concerned mainly with first order representations.
In distinction to an axiomatic arithmetic theory like Peano Arithmetic there is the arithmetic *N* (being the set of true first order arithmetic sentences in the standard interpretation).
Many of the limitative theorems of meta-logic proceed by having a formal system that includes arithmetic and thus (by Gödelization or arithmetization) is able to represent its own syntax and thus recursive sets like the set containing pairs of proof numbers and numbers of the thus proven sentences.
N is negation complete (either A or ¬A is in *N*), not axiomatisable, not decidable, and, of course, infinitely large.
Given its first order representation there are a lot of well-known theorems about arithmetic (e.g., arithmetic being incomplete).
Given Compactness of **FOL** one can prove that there are non-standard models of arithmetic, which contain additional numbers over and above the natural numbers. These additional numbers behave consistently, however. Consistency provides them in the first place.
Inconsistent arithmetic may concern itself with the opposite deviance: Having arithmetics where there are less numbers than in standard arithmetic.
This is of outmost philosophical interest, since the infinite is a really problematic concept leading to the ever larger cardinalities of "Cantor's paradise", and finitism (in the sense of the assumption that there are only

finitely many objects, even of mathematics) is therefore an option worth exploring and pursuing.

Arithmetic R#

Robert Meyer was the first to give a non-triviality proof of a Relevant (paraconsistent) arithmetic.
The system **R#** is an extension of the first order version of Relevant logic **R** [see Chap. 4] with axioms mirroring those of Peano arithmetic save that the "$\supset$" in them has been replaced by the Relevant "$\rightarrow$". Induction is present as a rule.
Taking the logic **RM3** [see Chap. 9] gives us **RM3#**.
One can extend that system with the ω-rule (to derive a generalization from infinitely many instances), this is **R##** or **RM3##**.
R# is non-trivial in that 0=1 is not provable.
This non-triviality can be established by finitistic methods.
Modus Ponens for "$\supset$" fails in **R#**. If it was valid, Peano arithmetic would be a subsystem of **R#**.
RM3 or **R** may not be one's favourite logics, however, so we look here at inconsistent arithmetic in general, presupposing some basic paraconsistent logic like **LP**.

Inconsistent Arithmetics

Inconsistent Arithmetic that are finite may have any finite size you like. They contain one largest number. Since we do not know which number really is the largest we may assume that one of these arithmetics is true, although we don't know which. Which one it is is not that important, since all these arithmetics have common properties:
Let n be some natural number, then let N_n be a set of arithmetic sentences. These sets have the following properties [cf. (Priest 1994)]:

(i) $N \subset N_n$.

(ii) N_n is inconsistent.

(iii) $A \in N_n$ for a (negated) equation A concerning numbers < n if and only if $A \in N$.

(iv) N_n is decidable.

(v) N_n is representable in N_n (thus we have a N_n truth predicate).

(vi) For the proof predicate B( ) of N_n every instance of

B("A") $\supset$ A is in N_n.

(vii) If A is not a theorem of N_n $\neg$B("A")$\in N_n$.

(viii) For the Gödel sentence G for N_n G$\in N_n$ and $\neg$G$\in N_n$.

An inconsistent arithmetic N_n thus has quite remarkable properties:
• by (i) we have that N_n is complete, since N is.
• by (ii) and (viii) we have, of course, that it is inconsistent.
• by (iv) it has all the nice properties that N does not have, although N_n is complete!
• by (v) we can in the language of arithmetic define a truth predicate for that very same language.
• by (vi) N_n has an ordinary proof predicate.
• by (vii) in conjunction with (iii) we have not only that N_n is not trivial (by excluding some the equations that are excluded by N), but that this non-triviality can be established within N_n itself.

How do we get this?

Proof (Outline):
• A theory with less numbers than N can have less counterexamples to a given arithmetic sentence. Thus it contains at most more sentences (as true). This holds in general (called "Collapsing Lemma"). Therefore (i). So we do not lose any of the power of N by switching to N_n.
• Since N is negation complete *adding* any sentence (as true) means adding a sentence for which the negation is already in N. Thus the resulting theory contains for at least one A, A and $\neg$A. Thus (ii). This means that the logic of these arithmetic theories has to be a paraconsistent logic.
• Representability of truth is a consequence of (iv) and (i). The same holds for the representability of the proof predicate, (vi). Once the proof predicate is representable in the decidable theory N_n we can represent non-provability, and thus have (vii) and finally (viii).
• (iii) is the most interesting property and results from the way the domain of a corresponding model is constructed. ■

A model of a theory N_n is constructed as a filtering of an ordinary arithmetic model. In general one can reduce the cardinality of some domain by substituting for the objects equivalence classes given some equivalence relation (i.e. instead of objects o_1, o_2 ... we have [o_1], [o_2]...). The equivalence classes provide then the substitute objects. Since the objects within the equivalence class are equivalent in the sense of interest in the given context the predicates still apply (now to the substitute object). The trick in case of N_n is to chose the filtering which puts every number $<$ n into its equivalence class, and nothing else; and puts all numbers $\geq$ n into n's equivalence class.

As a result of this for $x < n$ the standard equations are true (of [x]), while in case of $y \geq n$ *everything* that could be said of such a y is true of [n]. So we have immediately $n = n$ (by identity) and $n = n + 1$ (since for $y = n + 1$ in N this is true).
The domain of a theory N_n so is of cardinality n. n now is an inconsistent object of N_n.
If for the moment we picture the successor function by arrows we can picture the structure of a model of N_n thus:

$$
\begin{array}{ccccccc}
0 \rightarrow & 1 \rightarrow & \ldots \rightarrow & n & \rightarrow \\
 & & \uparrow & & \downarrow \\
 & & & \leftarrow &
\end{array}
$$

Such models are called "heap models".
The logic modelling N_n has to be paraconsistent. And it has to have restrictions on standard first oder reasoning as well: (=E) *cannot hold* for n of N_n if triviality is to be avoided, consider:

1. $n - n = n - n$ Theorem (for any number)
2. $n = n + 1$ Assuming n to be the largest number
3. $n - n = n - (n+1)$ (=E) 1, 2
4. $n - n = 0$ Theorem
5. $0 = n - (n+1)$ (=E) 4, 3
6. $0 = (n+1) - n$ Commutativity, 5
7. $((n+1)-n)\times(b-a)/((n+1)-n)=((n+1)-n)\times(b-a)/((n+1)-n)$ Theorem
8. $(0\times(b-a)/((n+1)-n) = ((n+1)-n)\times(b-a)/((n+1)-n)$ (=E) 7, 6
9. $0\times(b-a)/((n+1)-n) = 0$ Theorem
10. $0 = ((n+1)-n)\times(b-a)/((n+1)-n)$ (=E) 8, 9
11. $((n+1)-n)\times(b-a)/((n+1)-n) = b - a$ Theorem
12. $0 = b - a$ (=E) 10, 11

… 18. $a = b$ by some Theorems for "+", "–" ■

A logic with unrestricted (=E) so yields a=b for *any* numbers! [Remember the restriction of (=E) in Chap. 6; see **UL4** in Chap. 20.]

Mortensen chooses **RM3#** as basic system and finitizes it by substituting for a number n the number n *modulo* some m. Thus the domain becomes {0, 1, 2, ... m-1}.
The resulting arithmetic **RM3^m** is complete, non-trivial and decidable. **RM3^m** is *axiomatisable* by adding to **RM3#** the axioms:

$\vdash 0 = m$

and all instances of the following axiom scheme for n $\in$ {0, 1, ... m-1}:

$\vdash (0 = n \leftrightarrow 0 = 1)$.

The approach "*modulo* some m" has at least the same deviant results than the heap models mentioned before: In **RM3^5** we have $4 + 2 = 6$ (since **RM3^5** is complete, i.e. has all theorems of *N*) and $4 \times 6 = 4$ (since "6" denotes 1). And the approach "*modulo* some m" has these deviant sentences for some *known* numbers!

Finitization

Arithmetic is constructed thus as a finite theory. One can generalized the steps of this procedure to apply it to other mathematical theories.
Van Bendegem distinguishes the following steps:

(i) Take any first-order theory T with finitely many predicates. Let M be a model of T.

(ii) Reformulate the semantics of T in a paraconsistenf fashion (i.e. the mapping to truth values and overlapping extensions of P^+ and P^-).

(iii) If the models of M are infinite, define an equivalence relation R over the domain D of M such that D/R is finite.

(iv) The model M/R is a finite paraconsistent model of the given first-order theory T such that validity is at least preserved.

The restriction to theories with finitely many predicates is no real restriction in any field of applied mathematics or formal linguistics, since no physical device (be it human or machine) can store a non-enumerable list of basic predicates.
[Van Bendegem then hints at finite version of the theory of integers and the theory of rational numbers.]

Paraconsistent Löwenheim/Skolem

The *Löwenheim/Skolem-Theorem* is one of the limitative or negative meta-theorems of standard arithmetic and **FOL**. It says that any theory presented in **FOL** has a *denumerable* model. This is strange, since there are first order representations not only of real number theory (the real numbers being presented there as uncountable), but of set theory itself. Thus the denumerable models are deviant models (usually Herbrand models of self-representation), but they cannot be excluded.[29]

Given the general procedure to finitize an existing mathematical first order theory using paraconsistent semantics, there is a paraconsistent strengthened version of the *Löwenheim/Skolem-Theorem*:

> Any mathematical theory presented in first order logic has a *finite* paraconsistent model.

Assessment

A mathematics that does not commit us to the infinite is a nice thing for anyone with reductionist and/or realist leanings.

As far as we know the universe is finite, and if space-time is (quantum) discrete there isn't even an infinity of space-time points.

The largest number may be indefinitely large. So we never get to it (e.g. given our limited resources to produce numerals by writing strokes).

If there is a largest number n there is the corresponding inconsistent arithmetic N_n. We can presuppose N_n being our arithmetic. Since N and N_n agree on all finite and computational mathematics it is hard to see whether we lose anything important at all by switching to N_n.

Since we have paraconsistency anyway for other reasons, we get this finitism *for free*, it seems. So why not take it? In as much as N_n is correct no correct reasoning transcends the finite. Hilbert wouldn't have rejoiced, probably, since N_n of course is inconsistent itself.

The drawback of all this is, of course, the problem of an ontology of inconsistent entities – at least if you are a realist [see Chap. 17].

LFI-Based Inconsistent Arithmetic

Benassi and Gentilini (2003) have developed a paraconsistent provability logic based on a paraconsistent arithmetic that is an extension of a sequent version of the LFI-system **bC** [see Chap. 8].

The system **PCA** consists of axioms:

- defining the primitive recursive functions,
- for "=" (i.e. reflexivity and functionality of "=", as well as substitutivity of identicals within primitive recursive functions),
- defining each numeral as the successor of another, starting with "0".

These axioms are supplemented by a rule of induction. By this **PCA** is recursively axiomatized.

---

29 They can be excluded in some 2nd order semantics for 2nd order set and number theory, see (Shapiro 1991).

Given that standard Primitive Recursive Arithmetic, **PRA**, is non-trivial and negation consistent, so is **PCA**, since any of its proofs is available in **PRA**. For atomic formulas the systems are even identical.
This means that m=n is not provable in **PCA** for different numerals. Thus it is *not* a finite arithmetic like the ones we dealt with before. For one and the same numeral m, however, we can have without trivialization:

$$\varnothing \Vdash (m = m \wedge m \neq m)$$

["$\Vdash$" being the sequent symbol again.]
That

$$\vdash_{PCA} \varnothing \Vdash (m = m \wedge m \neq m)$$

does not trivialize the system means that **PCA** allows for objects/numbers that are (also) *not identical* to themselves. The presence of the contradiction with respect to m=m does not lead to triviality, exhibiting the paraconsistent character of **PCA**.
If P( ) is any arbitrary open formula and á, é any closed terms that represent numbers, then **PCA** does not have substitution of identicals, i.e.

$$\nvdash_{PCA} \varnothing \Vdash (á = é \supset (P(á) \equiv P(é))$$

neither does this hold in sequent form.
PCA as a theory shows the peculiarities of **bC** [cf. Chap. 8], it is interesting for us since Benassi and Gentilini use it to introduce a provability predicate the properties of which can be compared to a standard provability predicate [see Chap. 13]. A provability predicate for **PCA** can be expressed within the system itself, because it contains enough of the primitive recursive functions and so – by arithmetization of its syntax – can represent the provability relation within itself.

Further Perspectives

If there are inconsistent versions of more elaborated mathematical fields like the calculus one may draw some general philosophical conclusions:
• If there are corresponding inconsistent versions of these mathematical theories with comparable strength to the original theories then consistency is not the fundamental mathematical concept, but functionality (of the respective basic concepts) may well be. As Mortensen sums up:

> [T]he fact that the same functional structure can underlie inconsistent, incomplete, or classical theories suggests that the functional aspects of mathematics are more important than squabbles at the sentential level over [Explosion], inconsistency, incompleteness, *etc.*

• If the justification of mathematics depends on its applicability and the inconsistent versions are of comparable applicability then they are justified not just as mathematical theories, but even in the wider perspective of grasping fundamental structures of reality; there no longer will be available the argument from mathematical describability to the consistency of the world.

Questions

(Q1) N_n is decidable – although the procedure maybe quite involved and beyond our limited physical resources. Why? Why is it also finitely axiomatisable?

(Q2) Given that provability is representable in N_n *and* given that N_n is decidable, *and* given a representation of truth, why is the Gödel sentence for N_n

$$(\gamma) \neg B(\gamma)$$

provable, as well as its negation?

Further Reading

• The basic – and only – monograph on inconsistent mathematics is: Mortensen, Chris. *Inconsistent Mathematics*. Dordrecht/Boston/ London, 1995.
• For R# see: Meyer, Robert. "Relevant Arithmetic", *Bulletin of the Section of Logic of the Polish Academy of Science*, 1976, pp. 133-37.
• Graham Priest wrote a couple of papers dealing with inconsistent number theory: (Priest 1994, 1994a, 1996a, 1997).
• On the use of arithmetic in meta-logic and the corresponding results see (Boolos/Jeffrey 1989).
• On the infinite in general, large cardinalities and their role and history in set theory see (Lavine 1998) and (Moore 1990).
• A statement of paraconsistent finitism is: van Bendegem, Jean Paul. "Strict, Yet Rich Finitism", in: Wolkowski, Z. (Ed.) *First International Symposium on Gödel's Theorems*. Singapore, 1993, pp. 61-79.

13 | Meta-Logic

Many famous meta-logical results (e.g. Gödel's Theorems, the Halting Problem, Cantor's Theorem ...) – especially the "negative" ones – make in their proofs use the assumption of consistency or proceed as indirect arguments, arguing from the impossibility of (true) contradictions.
These meta-logical results are often employed to found some philosophical thesis (like Cantor's Theorem being a cornerstone of realism, since it shows that there are more objects than there are names of objects; like Gödel's First Incompleteness Theorem showing that there is a gap between truth and provability; and so on).
In a paraconsistent context in which the logic of meta-logic is a paraconsistent logic itself – as it should be for a dialetheist – it may be that some of these theorems *cannot be proven* at all. It may be that some can still be proven (or some equivalent of them).
Given a dialetheist background philosophy one may re-interpret the philosophical readings given to some of these formal results.

Gödel's 1st Incompleteness Theorem

Gödel's First Incompleteness Theorem is taken standardly as a proof that truth and provability diverge.
Gödel's First Incompleteness Theorem:

> Let T be a theory with a recursive provability relation such that T is able to represent all recursive functions. Then there is some statement/sentence A such that
> (i) in case that T is consistent A is not provable in T, and
> (ii) we can argue by an intuitively sound argument that A is true.

The provability has to be recursive so that we can decide whether a proof has been given; and all theorems go back a basis of recursion. The representability of all recursive functions entails that T is able to speak about its own syntax (by arithmetization) and especially about the recursive proof predicate/relation.
Sentence A says:

> (A) is not provable.

It can be derived by diagonalization like the Liar antinomy.
Sentence A cannot be provable if T is consistent, since otherwise not only a sentence would be provable that *says* of itself that it is not provable one would have an outright contradiction between the statement that A is

provable (that then can be proven, since the provability relation is recursive and representable) and A itself!
So A is not provable – assuming consistency. But this is what A says, so – by Convention (T)! – A is true. That is clause (ii) in the theorem.
The reasoning beyond clause (ii) seems perfectly reasonable to us and uses naive semantics. By *Church's Thesis* (that what is intuitively computable is computable by recursive functions or Turing Machines) there should be some formal system then in which this reasoning is a real *proof.* A system S of semantic closure can be such a system. In this system S sentence A will be provably true. Since S being able to represent its semantics will also be able to represent its syntax, it could contain another sentence that says that A is provable, thus making S inconsistent. But the conflict in S is a new one – it is Gödel's First Incompleteness Theorem put on its head:
Gödel's First Incompleteness Theorem (Second Reading):

1. Naive Semantics is intuitively computable.
2. So there is come recursive computable system S that computes it.
3. In S the reasoning behind clause (ii) is representable.
4. Therefore A is provable in S.
5. There are systems in which truth and provability do not come apart.
6. Given completeness of S the provability of A is provable in S.
7. Representing A's provability gives a sentence B, B $\leftrightarrow \neg$ A.
8. In S the Gödel sentence A is antinomic.

(1) is justified by our intuitive acceptance of basic arithmetic and Convention (T). We also require that we see that something *is* a proof (i.e. conforms to the rules of the formal system) if it is presented to us. (2) need not claim that we have such a system, but that there has to be one. The decisive result against the standard reading is (5). Truth and provability do not have to come apart. What comes apart is rather *completeness* and *consistency.*
The lesson a dialetheist draws from *Gödel's First Incompleteness Theorem* (and *Church's Thesis*, and Naive Semantics) is:

> Given a formal representation of Naive Semantics that is complete, this system will not be consistent.

But a formal representation of Naive Semantics will not be consistent in any case, because of the semantic antinomies! The completeness of a system of Naive Semantics just turns the Gödel sentence into a relative to the Liar.

If truth and provability do not come apart, then Hilbert's program of a complete axiomatization of mathematics can be revived![30]

Gödel's 2nd Incompleteness Theorem

Gödel's Second Incompleteness Theorem is an upshot of the first: If a system T' (with the same properties like T) is able to prove its own consistency, then it is not consistent.
This is so because in T' we also have sentence A. A is not provable by the reasoning presented in the context (i) of the *First Incompleteness Theorem*. A is not provable, since otherwise T' will be inconsistent. If T' now can *prove* its own consistency, it can *prove* (that) A is not provable, but a sentence B representing this is simply equivalent to A!
Gödel's Second Incompleteness Theorem can be weakened – given paraconsistency – to the statement that some non-trivial, but relative inconsistent systems can prove their own consistency (i.e. their non-triviality) [see Chap. 11 & 12].
Depending on the paraconsistent logic one takes as a base of arithmetic one arrives of provability predicates of different strength. Some may be so weak that the completeness or incompleteness results cannot be proven in the first place.

A LFI-Based Provability Predicate

The system **PAC** [cf. Chap. 12] of Benassi and Gentilini can contain its own provability predicate, Pr( ), such that (with #B being the Gödel-number of B) we have:

$$\vdash_{PCA}(\Vdash B) \quad \Rightarrow \quad \vdash_{PCA}(\Vdash Pr(\#B)).$$

Strangely enough – in distinction to standard arithmetic – it is *not* provable in **PCA** for any quantifier free (arithmetic) formula B:

$$B \Vdash Pr(\#B).$$

This is due to the behaviour of negation in **bC**.
Since **PAC**-proofs are available in standard recursive arithmetic **PRA**, if **PAC** could prove its own non-triviality, **PRA** could prove its own non-triviality, but in a standard context the non-triviality of **PRA** comes down to its consistency, and by *Gödel's Second Incompleteness Theorem* **PRA** cannot prove its own consistency, thus **PAC** cannot prove its own non-triviality.

---

30 See van Bendegem (1993); Russell felt uneasy about the Axiom of Infinity as an existence claim, seemingly not purely logical; in Routley's inconsistent set theory the Axiom of Infinity can be derived from Comprehension (Routley 1979a, p.924) – just as logicism would have it.

Since **PAC** is non-trivial, there is a sentence A (stating this non-triviality) such that neither A nor ¬A is provable in **PAC**.
The standard *Diagonal Lemma* (that for any open formula there is a sentence which asserts the application of that formula to its own name) is not available in **PAC**. This is due again to the non-standard behaviour of negation in **bC** and the fact that substitution of identicals does not hold in general in **PAC**.
A proof of the negation incompleteness that we have just seen to hold for **PAC** along the standard lines of *Gödel's First Incompleteness Theorem* is thus not possible for **PAC**.
The provability predicate of **PAC** so seems rather week, mirroring the fact that **bC** is a weak logic.

Tarski's Theorem

Tarski's Theorem says that a consistent theory as strong as standard arithmetic cannot contain its own truth predicate, which is to satisfy Convention (T).
Gödel's First Incompleteness Theorem is understood as saying that truth and provability do not coincide. *Tarski's Theorem* can be understood as saying that the concept of truth is harder than the concept of provability, and it even gives some measure to it: The concept of truth is not arithmetic.
Now, an inconsistent theory containing (inconsistent) arithmetic can contain its own truth predicate without being trivial.
In a paraconsistent context one can thus have what one by *Tarski's Theorem* cannot have in standard logic and arithmetic: a theory dealing *both* with number and truth.

Löb's Theorem

Löb's Theorem is a more general form of *Gödel's Second Incompleteness Theorem*. *Löb's Theorem* says that in a system which can represent its own provability predicate B( ), it holds that if B("A") ⊃ A is *provable*, then A is provable.
Thus *Löb's Theorem* positively claims the partial correctness of the provability predicate. Negatively it is expression of the fact that not

(*) ⊢(B("A") ⊃ A)

in general. (*) cannot hold as theorem, since for a Gödel sentence G we have

⊢(G ⊃ ¬B("G"))

thus

$\vdash(B("G") \supset \neg G)$

and with (*) applied to G we got a contradiction.
But (*) *should* hold: What is said to be provable should be the case! In a paraconsistent system one can have (*).

Cantor's Theorem

Cantor's Theorem states that the power set of a set has a greater cardinality than the set itself.
We have already seen [in Chap.11] that Brady restricts its validity in his paraconsistent class theory. The standard proof of *Cantor's Theorem* does not go through in **SKP**.
The standard proof shows that there is no 1:1 correspondence between the elements of some set x and the elements of its powerset $\wp(x)$. If there was such a 1:1 correspondence each element $z \in x$ would have to have one and only one corresponding subset $y \subseteq x$. Call this correspondence *f*. One defines that subset y' containing all $z \in x$ which are not in the subset of x corresponding to them according to *f*. $y' = \{z \in x \mid z \notin f(z)\}$. If there was *f*, there would be x' such that $y' = f(x')$. But this leads to contradiction $x' \notin y' \rightarrow x' \in y'$, and vice versa.
Now, in **SKP** nothing follows from this, especially not that there is no such correspondence *f*.
That the standard argument does not go through in **SKP** does not show that the powerset of a set is never of greater cardinality than the set itself.
There may be other procedures to show the greater cardinality of some set compared to another (e.g. a grid which by graphic diagonalisation shows that some set cannot be enumerable).
What this example shows, however, is that it is – by far – not clear that all standard theorems have corresponding theorems and proofs in a paraconsistent setting.
Giving up *Cantor's Theorem* has immense effects not only in set theory, but also in philosophical meta-logic. Grim argues by *Cantor's Theorem* that the universe is incomplete, not containing a set of truths, facts, propositions ...
Whether being expelled from "Cantor's paradise" of ever higher infinite cardinalities is a real loss to mathematics and set theory may be doubted [see (Moore 1990), (Lavine 1998), and Chap. 12].

Church's Theorem

Church's Theorem says that **FOL** is undecidable.
This applies then as well to first order representations of mathematical theories like arithmetic.
Now, we have inconsistent arithmetics that are not only axiomatisable, but *are* decidable [see Chap. 12], even if the computational complexity of a corresponding decision procedure on a deterministic Turing machine is exponential.
Thus an extension of *Church's Theorem* to these theories *is not* at hand!

Going Berserk

Proponents of paraconsistent set theory accept the *existence of objects* like the Russell set, i.e. at least some accept that there is a set that is an element of itself and at the same time is not. [The quantificational semantics allows for an object to be within the extension and anti-extension of a predicate P, but only as a realist you are committed to the corresponding objects.]
We will discuss the problem of inconsistent objects and their modes of being in chapter 17, but if you accept inconsistent objects there seems to be no halting to turning limitative theorems of meta-logic around.
Assume there is an inconsistent Turing Machine that halts on its own code number and does not halt at the same time, then the Halting Problem cannot be shown (this way) to be non decidable. And once you assume the Halting Problem to be recursive, then all problems of the same Turing degrees turn out to be recursive. All problems (like decidability of First Order Logic) that are at least as hard as the Halting Problem may turn out to be at least as solvable!

Questions

(Q1) If you are an anti-realist in the sense that truth is conceptually *tied to justifiability*, and these justifications are intuitively computable, what does this mean for the (negation-)completeness of a supposed system S of Naive Semantics?

Exercise

(Ex1) Represent the standard argument for *Cantor's Theorem* in **SKP** (extended by some set theoretic notation). Why can we not conclude that the correspondence *f* does not exist?

Further Reading

• On *Gödel's Incompleteness Theorems* and *Löb's Theorem* see (Smullyan 1992). The re-interpretation of the *First Incompleteness Theorem* is from (Priest 1987, pp.49-63).
• On *Church's Thesis* see: Schultz, Klaus-Dieter. *Die These von Church.* Frankfurt a.M. et al., 1997.
• On *Cantor's Theorem* see (Stoll 1963). On Grim's use of it see (Grim 1991), criticized in (Sylvan 1992).
• On the standard proofs of the basic meta-logical results see (Boolos/Jeffrey 1989).

14 | Deontic Logic and Meta-Ethics

Deontic Logic as been a field in which quite apart from the questions of antinomies "paradoxes" have played a decisive roles, since the field has been invented. These paradoxes (like *Ross' Paradox* or the *Good Samaritan*) are said to show that some intuitively valid logical principles cannot be true in deontic logic, even if the same principles (like deductive closure within a modality) are valid in alethic modal logic. Paraconsistency is not concerned with solutions to these paradoxes.
There are, however, lots of problems with *ex contradictione qoudlibet* in deontic logic, since systems of norms and regulations, even more so if they are historically grown, have a tendency to contain conflicting requirements. To restrict the ensuing problems at least a weak paraconsistent logic is needed.
There may be, further on, real antinomies of deontic logic and meta-ethics (understood comprehensively as including also some basic decision and game theory).

Inconsistent Obligations

It often may happen that one is confronted with inconsistent obligations.
Consider for example the rule that term papers have to be handed in at the institute's office one week before the session in question combined with the rule that one must not disturb the secretary at the institute's office if she is preparing an institute meeting. What if the date of handing in your paper falls on a day when an institute meeting is prepared? Entering the office is now *obligatory* (i.e. it is obligatory that it is the case that N.N. enters the office, O(p)), and at the same time it is *forbidden* (i.e. it is obligatory that it is not the case that N.N. enters the office, $O(\neg p)$).
Now, in standard Deontic Logic we have a conjunction principle

(1) $\vdash O(p \wedge q) \equiv O(p) \wedge O(q)$

If two states are each obligatory, then it is obligatory to have them both realised. Given principle (1) and our little story about papers we get:

(2) $O(p \wedge \neg p)$

Since standard Deontic Logics are extensions of standard logic, they include *ex contradictione qoudlibet*

(3) $\vdash (p \wedge \neg p) \supset q$

As normal modal logics standard Deontic Logics contain their equivalent to the rule of necessitation

(4) $\vdash A \Rightarrow \vdash O(A)$

and the distribution equivalent to the (K)-Axiom

(5) $\vdash O(p \supset q) \supset (O(p) \supset O(q))$

Given the normal character of Deontic Logic we get

(6) $\vdash O((p \wedge \neg p) \supset q)$

(7) $\vdash O(p \wedge \neg p) \supset O(q)$

and thus with (2) and *Modus Ponens*

(8) $\vdash O(q)$

for any sentence "q" whatsoever!
Thus having an inconsistent normative system – as it happens all the day – makes it obligatory to do whatever you like (burning the term paper, blowing up the university ...).
This is unbearable. And that – fortunately – is not how we reason is these situations. In the example given there may be easy solutions, but in normative systems that have a long history the conflicts and the ways to resolve them are not so obvious (the existence of higher courts to solve such conflicts is witness to this).
Given that we have not resolved the conflicts yet the underlying logic has to be a paraconsistent one.
The question is, where paraconsistency has to intervene. Should the underlying logic of the non-deontic language (i.e. **PC**) be changed thus that we no longer have Explosion or similar rules? Or should the behaviour of sentences *within* the scope of deontic operators be changed, maybe by giving up the additivity of "O( )"?

Standard Deontic Logic

We ask ask ourselves if we want to drop any of the principles of standard Deontic Logic. These are:

(DF)	$F(A) \stackrel{\text{def}}{=} O(\neg A)$	
(DP)	$P(A) \stackrel{\text{def}}{=} \neg O(\neg A)$	
(A1)	$\neg(O(p) \wedge O(\neg p))$	[Consistency of Obligation]
(A2)	$O(p) \wedge O(q) \equiv O(p \wedge q)$	[Additivity of Obligation]
(A3)	$O(\top)$	[Inconsistency is forbidden]

Rules: Uniform Substitution and *Modus Ponens*.

Consistency assumption are built into standard Deontic Logic. By (A3) and (DF) we have that inconsistency is forbidden, and it is axiomatically demanded that we have no inconsistent obligations by (A1). Presumably both (A1) and (A3) have to be modified.[31]
In standard Deontic Logic we have a derived (K)-rule and its contrapositive:

$$\vdash(A \supset B) \Rightarrow \vdash(O(A) \supset O(B))$$

$$\vdash F(B), \vdash(A \supset B) \Rightarrow \vdash F(A)$$

Standard Application of Paraconsistency to Obligations

The former strategy of changing the underlying logic may be considered the standard application of a PL to questions of obligation.
If the underlying logic of the normative language is changed to, say, **SKP**, then Explosion is no longer valid, and the argument given above does no longer go through. The principles we find in standard Deontic Logic do not have to be changed then.
Syntactically this approach works by adding formation rules, axioms and rules for deontic operators to your preferred paraconsistent logic. Semantically the typical truth condition given in standard Deontic Logic for "O( )" can be taken over, even more so if the paraconsistent system has a modal semantic already.
Note that this approach can deal with the occurrence of O(A) and $\neg$O(A) as both true at the propositional level, since Explosion does not ensue by $O(A) \wedge \neg O(A)$.

Standard Semantics of Obligations

The paraconsistent treatment of deontic conflicts takes over the standard semantics of standard Deontic Logic. [This is the easier when the underlying paraconsistent logic has already a modal semantics.]
One needs a (further) *deontic accessibility relation* between worlds thus that S(w,w') holds if w' is relative to w a *normatively optimal* world.

> O(A) is true at w if and only if in all worlds w' such that S(w,w') A is true in w' (... false iff in some world w' with S(w,w') A is false).

If *permission* is not defined in the usual way [$P(A) \overset{def}{\equiv} \neg O(\neg A)$] one can give the basic truth condition as:

> P(A) is true at w if and only if in some world w' such that S(w,w') A is true in w'. (... false iff in all worlds w' with S(w,w') A is false).

---

31 "O(A)" with unneeded brackets dropped becomes "OA".

Optimal worlds are intuitively those worlds where everything that should be the case is the case, and everything that is the case is not bad.
Note that in case of inconsistent obligation we have at least one *inconsistent deontic optimal world* w' with A and ¬A true at w' for some sentence A.
The deontic accessibility relation cannot be reflexive, since otherwise we had:

$$OA \supset A$$

which – unfortunately – is not the case.
Iterations of deontic operators are also controversial. Thus it is questionable whether S should be transitive, since this leads to:

$$OA \supset OOA$$

As for natural necessity the **S4** axiom of modal logic [□A⊃□□A] is doubtful, so certainly is OA⊃OOA if the obligations refer to some (accidental) legal system.
The two basic conditions on S are that
- S is serial: (∀w)(∃w')S(w,w'). Seriality means that no world is a deontic dead end. It makes

$$OA \supset PA$$

true. [Remember again the parallel to alethic accessibility conditions, where seriality makes □A⊃◇A true.]

- S is almost reflexive: (∀w,w')(S(w,w') ⊃ S(w',w')). Almost Reflexivity means that no new obligations are violated by doing what is obligatory. It makes true:

$$O(OA \supset A)$$

Something that should hold (in case we allow for iterated deontic operators.

Deontic LP

As an example of extending paraconsistency to deal with normative conflict we can extend **LP** with deontic operators having their standard semantics.
We do not give a axiomatic system here, but extend the propositional LP-trees with rules for deontic operators.
These operators refer to optimal worlds. so that we have to represent within the trees the accessing of an optimal world. We do this by adding *worlds annotated lines* in a tree. A world annotated line looks like this:

in w_1: T(A ⊃ B)

It says – obviously – that in world w_1 it is true that A ⊃ B.
We add world lines to a tree in evaluating deontic sentences. An obligation is true if the content of the obligation is the case in all deontic optimal worlds. We assume that in this case there is at least one deontic optimal world.
For simplicity's sake we assume that there are *no* iterated deontic operators in the language of deontic **LP** (in short: **LPD**).
Within world lines (that is within the scope of a "w_i: " the usual tree rules are applied). [For LP-Trees see Chap. 4]. A branch is closed because of incompatible evaluations on the branch or within a world on the branch. A tree is closed iff all its branches are thus closed.
We define:

• A world w is *reachable* from a node iff that world is on the same branch as that node.

• We *add a world* on a branch iff we add a node with a world line were the world number *i* chosen was not used before in the tree.

• We *add into a world* on a branch iff we add a node with a world line already present on the branch and the sentence mentioned is put into the scope of the world expression "w_i: ".

We lay down the meta-rule: If a rule with the order to add some sentence into all reachable worlds has to be applied, but there are no reachable worlds on the branch, then we add a world to that branch before. [So at least one deontic optimal world is accessible; a requirment needed, since the world of the root of the tree (the actual world) need not be the deontic optimal world.]
We can then give the following rules for deontic operators:

T(OA) add into all reachable worlds T(A)	**F(OA)** add a reachable world with F(A)	**Δ(OA)** add into all reachable worlds Δ(A)	**∇(OA)** add a reachable world with ∇(A)
T(PA) add a reachable world with T(A)	**F(PA)** add into all reachable worlds F(A)	**Δ(PA)** add a reachable world with Δ(A)	**∇(PA)** add into all reachable worlds ∇(A)

Lets us look at some example trees! We show by the following examples that the axioms of standard deontic logic come out *valid* in **LPD**. This means that one can have the standard understanding of the deontic operators and have a non-explosive logic at the same time!

$\vdash_{LPD} O(p) \wedge O(q) \supset O(p \wedge q)$

Proof

```
Δ(O(p) ∧ O(q))
∇(O(p ∧ q))
      |                      (Δ∧)
    ΔO(p)
    ΔO(q)
   /      \                  (∇∧)
∇O(p)       ∇O(q)
  |           |              (∇O)
in w2: ∇p   in w3: ∇q
  |           |              (ΔO)
in w2: Δp   in w3: Δq
```

Both branches of this tree are closed because of incompatible evaluations in the respective worlds w_2 and w_3, and thus the tree is closed, so that the sentences to be refuted turns out to be valid. Like with quantifier rules it is recommended to apply those rules that introduce (worlds) first.

$\vdash_{LPD} O(\top)$

Proof

```
∇(O(⊤))
∇(O(p ∨ ¬p)            [definition of "⊤"]
   |                   (∇O)
in w1: ∇(p ∨ ¬p)
   |                   (∇∨)
in w1: ∇p
in w1: ∇(¬p)
   |                   (∇¬)
in w1: Δp
```

The tree is closed because of incompatible evaluations Δp, ∇p in w_1.

Strangeley enough also the consistency axiom of standard deontic logic is valid in **LPD**.

$\vdash_{LPD} \neg(O(p) \wedge O(\neg p))$

Proof

$\nabla(\neg(O(p) \wedge O(\neg p)))$

| $(\nabla\neg)$

$\Delta(O(p) \wedge O(\neg p))$

| $(\Delta\wedge)$

$\Delta(O(p)$

$\Delta(O(\neg p)$

| (ΔO)

in w_1: Δp

| (ΔO)

in w_1: $\Delta(\neg p)$

| $(\Delta\neg)$

in w_1: ∇p

The tree is closed because of incompatible Δp, ∇p in w_1. The validity of this gives us with each deontic inconsistency (the conjunction of two inconsistent obligations) immediately another deontic inconsistency (*vis.* the conjunction of this deontic inconsistency with the stated theorem)!

Inconsistent Obligations in a Consistent World

Casey McGinnis takes the latter option mentioned of keeping the underlying standard logic: The basic idea is to have a logic that can deal with normative conflicts, but makes no further changes in logic, especially not at the non-modal level of ordinary sentences. So the world is considered to be consistent, therefore **PC** can be applied in its full strength. Obligations may be inconsistent, so the logic *within* the scope of deontic operators has to be a paraconsistent logic.
This approach assumes:

- the world is consistent
- obligations may be inconsistent
- additivity of obligations and other intuitive principles should hold
- there may be gaps with respect to obligation (i.e. states such that O(A) is neither true or false, or at least that neither of O(A) and O(¬A) is true).

The idea of keeping the logic within the deontic operators apart from the underlying logic is modelled by keeping **PC** at the non-modal level and having **BN4** [see Chap. 9] at the deontic level. The system is called **SPDL** (for "Semi-Paraconsistent Deontic Logic").

SDPL like **SKP** singles out a "home world" w_0 as the starting point of accessibility. w_0 is required to be consistent and complete, i.e. atomic sentences receive either {0} or {1} as truth value. { } or {1,0} occur *only* at worlds different from w_0. Semantic consequence is truth preservation at w_0. "P" is *not* defined in terms of "O".
The semantic rules have to ensure that inconsistency does not travel back from an accessible world *via* the rules of "O" into the home world: If a w_0-accessible world is inconsistent for A, then – according to the standard semantic rule for "O" given above – OA is true at w_0 *and* false at w_0, *and* O(¬A) is true at w_0. So there would be sentences with non-standard values at w_0.
This problem can be solved by invoking a double standard in revising the falsity conditions of the standard semantics of "O" and "P". The revised rules are:

(SO) $0 \in v(\mathrm{OA},w)$ iff ($w = w_0$ and $1 \notin v(\mathrm{OA},w)$) *or*

($w \neq w_0$ and $(\exists w')S(w,w')$ and $0 \in v(A,w')$)

(SP) $0 \in v(\mathrm{PA},w)$ iff ($w = w_0$ and $1 \notin v(\mathrm{PA},w)$) *or*

($w \neq w_0$ and $(\forall w')(S(w,w') \supset 0 \in v(A,w'))$)

The parts for $1 \in v(\mathrm{OA},w)$ and $1 \in v(\mathrm{PA},w)$ remain the same. Thus **SPDL** makes a norm only false if it is not already true; one could say that SPDL-semantics favours *positive* evidence from the normatively optimal worlds.
Now one can prove that at w_0 *all* sentences are *bivalent*. [Look at the **BN4** truth tables for binary values and (S0) and (SP) above.]
The Deduction Theorem holds for **SPDL**.
Proven equivalents *cannot* be substituted for each other in **SPDL**, since in **PC** all contradictions are provably equivalent, but for obligations $O(p \wedge \neg p)$ need not say the same as $O(q \wedge \neg q)$, and the presence of deontic conjunction elimination in addition to substitution of proven equivalents would lead to deontic explosion (that is explosion within the scope of deontic operators).
SPDL is not a normal modal logic, i.e. neither do "oughtification" for *any* tautology nor the (K)-rule hold:

$\vdash_{\mathbf{SPDL}} \top$

because of the base logic **PC**, and

$\nvdash_{\mathbf{SPDL}} O\top$

SPDL has as theorems:

(T1) $P(p \wedge q) \supset Pp \wedge Pq$

(T2) $Op \supset Pp$

(T3) $O(p \supset q) \supset (Op \supset Oq)$

(T4) $O(p \supset Pp)$

(T5) $OOp \supset Op$

(T6) $O(p \wedge q) \equiv Op \wedge Oq$

(T7) $P(p \vee q) \equiv Pp \vee Pq$

SPDL invalidates:

(*1) $Op \supset OOp$

(*2) $Pp \supset OPp$

(*3) $Op \supset O(q \supset p)$

(*4) $O(p \vee \neg p)$

(*5) $F(p \wedge \neg p)$

(*6) $\neg O(p \wedge \neg p)$

(*7) $Pp \vee P\neg p$

SPDL thus does not validate all theorems of standard Deontic Logic (especially not Axiom (3) that the inconsistent is forbidden). Invalidating (*7) seems questionable, since we certainly should be either allowed to do some act or abstain from it, otherwise we are in a limbo.

Note: Explosion holds in **SPDL** (since it has **PC** as underlying logic).

Normative conflicts of the sort $OA \wedge O(\neg A)$ can be solved by **SPDL** and lead neither to deontic explosion nor to general explosion. If, however, we had $OA \wedge \neg OA$ this would be a case of an ordinary contradiction (at the home world) and would by the validity of Explosion allow to infer any B whatsoever!

The occurrence of this problem is softened by not having $PA \equiv \neg O \neg A$, such that the observation of a permission to $\neg A$ does not in conjunction with the norm to have A realized lead to everything. Thus the question is, whether we could ordinarily come into situations where we can ascertain that OA and can ascertain that $\neg OA$. It seems to me that we can: Imagine a situation where there are two sources of laws/rules, one demanding A the other being quiet on A. Thus according to the one: OA. And by the other being quite: $\neg OA$.

The absence of $PA \equiv \neg O \neg A$ also deviates from our ordinary notion of permission, as does the absence of $PA \vee P(\neg A)$.

These may be reasons to have a paraconsistent logic also as the underlying logic in deontic reasoning.

Questions

(Q1) The case of inconsistent obligations, is that a case of weak paraconsistency or of strong paraconsistency, and what does the answer to this question depend upon?

(Q2) What does Almost Reflexivity correspond to in alethic modal logic (respectively the logic of provability)?

Exercises

(Ex1) That some thing is forbidden means that its negation is obligatory. Consider the deontic necessitation rule

$$\vdash A \Rightarrow \vdash O(A)$$

Why does it say that is *forbidden* to realise *something inconsistent* (given the background of standard logic)?

(Ex2) If in **SPDL** one did not revise the falsity condition of "O", but required $0 \in v(OA,w) \Leftrightarrow 1 \notin v(OA,w)$ – why does this make

$$O(OA \supset A)$$

invalid? [Draw an accessibility diagram.]

(Ex3) Show for some of the **SPDL** theorems/non-theorems why they are valid/invalid.

(Ex4) Show that $OA \supset PA$ is valid in **LPD**.

Further Reading

• An introduction to Deontic Logic in general is: Åqvist, Lennart. *Introduction to Deontic Logic and the Theory of Normative Systems*. Neapels, 1987. The deontic "paradoxes" are also dealt with there, as well as Diadic Deontic Logic, which takes conditional obligation to be formalized by "O(A/B)" instead of "$B \supset OA$".

• Casey McGinnis' ideas are taken from his forthcoming PhD thesis *Paraconsistency and Deontic Logic*, (2004). McGinnis also gives a tableau style proof system for **BN4** and its deontic application.

15 | Epistemology and Philosophy of Science

Dealing with and treating inconsistencies in theories as a topic of the philosophy of science is the fundamental justification of the weak paraconsistent approach.

The use of a paraconsistent logic in that context is not only avoiding Explosion; the real confirmation of the thesis that scientists proceed with their theory development in the face of inconsistencies is a reconstruction of how this containment of inconsistencies and usage of inconsistent theories really is effected or can be effected.

Supplementing the view on the actual workings of theory revision and updating the historical reconstruction of theory development and change as it really took place may foster the paraconsistent picture.

Epistemic logic – as a branch of modal logic, like deontic logic – also has its own paradoxes. Deductive closure of belief has been considered paradoxical in epistemic logic. The theory of confirmation and probability theory contain the *Raven Paradox* or the *Lottery Paradox*. These are not antinomies, so it is not clear whether paraconsistent logics have a job here, but there might be more severe cases!

Inconsistent Theories

Paraconsistent modelling can be employed diagnostically in case of historic examples of theories which are/were inconsistent, although they are/were not thought to be trivial or are/were not even known to be inconsistent.

Examples given are:

• the classic calculus of infinitesimals in which the infinitely small amounts are taken as *being nil* sometimes and as *being something* after all (one may divide through) at other times [cf. (Moore 1990, chap. 4)].

• quantum mechanics if you take the double slit experiments thus that some particle cannot pass both slits, but does so nevertheless; but this commits you to an inconsistent ontology at the quantum level if you take this literally; weak paraconsistency might say that we only *talk* like that, but that this way of talking has to be superseded.[32]

---

[32] A quantum logic giving up distributive laws (Putnam 1968) turned out to be not able to circumvent the problem (Gibbins 1981).

• Bohr's theory of the atom, Bohr combing hypotheses *both* of classical electrodynamics with incompatible quantum hypotheses.
• Carnot's Theorem in thermodynamics. The theorem was derived by Clausius in two ways using an inconsistent premise set, but he accepted the second proof, since it did not use the inconsistency.
• Planck's Law. Planck approached black body radiation is terms of *both* classical and quantum hypotheses.
• Newtonian Gravitation Theory, since for any nominated force on a test mass we can find a way of dividing the source masses of Newtonian cosmology so that we get the wanted resultant force.

The *historical thesis* behind these examples is that as long as there is no superseding new theory or grounds to resolve the inconsistencies in a particular way, scientists will go on working with an inconsistent mixture of theory (elements), but avoid trivialisation. Thus the logic used here can only be paraconsistent!
A *systematic thesis* behind these examples is that reasoning from the inconsistent mixture can serve as a heuristics towards the looked for consistent unified theory. [Lavoisier is cited as an example for this.]

Realism or Instrumentalism?

Instrumentalism is the view that the posits of science need not be taken at face value. Whether there are fifteen quarks or thirty-five is not of decisive importance, but whether the corresponding theoretical framework allows for successful predictions and technical applications in the field in question.
From an instrumentalist perspective one may go as far as not caring whether the theoretical part of a science contains contradictions, as long as this is the best working theory; paraconsistent logic, in this case, preventing disastrous logical behaviour.
From a *realist* perspective the contradictions posited by some theory which is held to be the best theory have to taken as true. In the case of empirical sciences this amounts to accepting inconsistent objects in reality! That seems just too much [cf. Chap. 17 on inconsistent ontology].
So one may be, although a realist in general, an instrumentalist about contradictions (thus advocating weak paraconsistency here). Without the realist attitude, however, there seems to be less motivation to solve the inconsistencies.

Inconsistent Observation

The *basis* of empirical sciences is observation. Can there be inconsistent observations? [Notice: "Observe" is factive (i.e. entails the existence of the observed scene), whereas "it seems" is not factive.]
There are inconsistent observations in the weak sense that one observation A may lead to accept thesis B, while another observation C leads to a rejection of thesis B. Observations (A and C) are then inconsistent with each other. This is an unproblematic everyday case.
There are optical illusions, think of a picture by Escher. One seems to see an inconsistent objects. Of course, since these are illusions, there *is* no such object, but the *seeming* nevertheless is real. That seeming is, however, not stable (as you recognise if you try to fix both the contradictory perspectives on such a drawing in question).
As one can observe A, one may observe $\neg A$ (by noting the absence of A). As one can observe A and B, one may observe $A \wedge B$. Now if observation is thus compositional, one may observe $A \wedge \neg A$, as Priest (2002) claims. But $A \wedge \neg A$ being *observable* (a modal claim) can only mean that there are situations/worlds where $A \wedge \neg A$ really is *observed.*

Sources of Inconsistency

One can try to give a systematisation how inconsistency *can arise* within a scientific theory [cf. (Miller 2002)]:

(a) reasoning from incorrect, or unknowingly restrictive, experimental data.

This leads to inconsistency when the incorrect data are confronted with correct data, or when the over-generalisation founded in the too restrictive data is put to the general test. As examples are given Galileo with several of his experiments and the famous Michelson/Morley experiment!

(b) reasoning from incorrectly interpreted premises.

As example the supposed inconsistency of the wave/particle duality is given, taking "wave" and "particle" as *ordinarily* understood.

(c) reasoning on the basis of concepts that are later jettisoned.

This by way of equation or by implicitly reasoning with principles (valid for the jettisoned concepts) the negations of which are in force in the updated theory. An example may be Lorentz' ether theory.

Theory Revision

Another application of weak paraconsistency can be theory revision. Theory revision or updating is standardly modelled by operations like theory expansion (throwing in more sentences), or contraction (throwing

out some sentences). The standard methodology of the AGM-approach aims at preserving or regaining *consistency* [see (Gärdenfors 1988)].
A paraconsistent logic could claim to be *the* logic of theory revision in that it can accommodate inconsistent belief sets and their evolution into a new theory.
The central concept of revision and the occasion to give up some belief by contraction can then no longer be consistency, but some other quality of belief systems. *Coherence* may be a candidate. Consistency no longer would be the first requirement on coherence, but other criteria of coherence like explanatory power, simplicity or data adequacy would not be modified. Even an inconsistent belief system might aim at coherence in that respect – as far as possible.[33]
Formally the standard methodology of the AGM-approach is developed by axioms for expansion, contraction and revision (as comprised of the two former operations).
If inconsistent beliefs are allowed the underlying logic has to be changed to a paraconsistent one, since trivial belief systems still do not make sense.
Those axioms that lay down consistency [axiom (K5) for revision in (Gärdenfors 1988), basically] have to be given up.
Revision has to be defined in a new way along the lines of the so-called "Levi Identity":

Revision is expanding with A a contraction with $\neg$A.

Revision in this sense is paraconsistently meaningful and may increase coherence [another AGM-axiom, (K7), has to be given up, however].

Coherence and Universality

Epistemology itself may be considered to be at least implicitly inconsistent, since it is universal (employing semantic concepts).
Epistemology is universal in that it talks *in general* and *universally* about the conditions of being true or being justified, including the justifiability or truth of epistemological theories. It has to be universal given its philosophical aims and the implausibility of a hierarchy.
Universality is especially obvious in case of coherence theories. Coherence theories claim that given an alternative of theories we shall chose the theory that is more *coherent* than the other – whatever that may mean in detail.
The coherence comparison is necessary, since more than one theory can cope with the data given, so that there are no "external" points of

---

[33] On coherence and its criteria see: (Bender 1989), (BonJour 1985), (Rescher 1979), (Thagard 1978).

comparison if that meant confronting theories with the world. Rather theories have also to be compared with each other in the light of the coherence criteria (like explanatory power, completeness...).

Now, if they are comparable – and arguments against inconsummerability show that they are – there has to be a *super-frame* in which we do the comparison, or an *area of overlap of methodology*.

This area of overlap or the super-frame consists of universal concepts of (theory) appraisal like *justified, explanatory, contained in* etc., concepts that also include the structural concepts of language.

That we need this super-frame has to be justified within a theory of coherence (starting from a rejection of both naive realism and relativism), and it is another way – besides insisting on semantic closure [Chap. 2] – to justify and outline the proper place of philosophy (as the general reflection on our (linguistic) ways of accessing reality).

The standpoint of the super-frame or the standpoint of comparing complete webs of beliefs are universal in character and thus – at least for their containing semantics – are beset with antinomies.

Coherence needs paraconsistency, even if consistency is a *criterion* of coherence for some lower level theories.

Epistemic Logic

Standard Epistemic Logic is a version of modal logic. As such it has been controversial in its closure assumptions like

(1) $\vdash A \Rightarrow \vdash KA$

(2) $\vdash (A \supset B) \Rightarrow \vdash (KA \supset KB)$

(3) $\vdash KA \Rightarrow \vdash KKA$

where "K" is the knowledge operator. (1) claims complete knowledge of logic, (2) closure of our knowledge under valid implications, and (3) the self-accessibility of our knowledge. All these claims have been criticised.

If one tries to make epistemic logic applicable to inconsistent belief systems one has to drop the axiom schemes requiring consistency of belief:

(4) $\neg B(A \wedge \neg A)$

(5) $B(\neg A) \supset \neg B(A)$

where "B" for the moment is the belief operator. Somebody may believe either an explicit contradiction – vs. (4) – or she may have an inconsistent set of beliefs, such that (5) is not true.

Giving up (1) – (5) for reasons of psychological adequacy, however, does not leave much of a logic worth its name!

Paradoxes of Confirmation

Although this is not directly related to paraconsistency, Relevant Logics are able avoid some of the paradoxes of confirmation theory.
One standard is the *Raven Paradox*. The hypothesis

(1) All Ravens are black.

(1') $(\forall x)(\text{Raven}(x) \supset \text{Black}(x))$

can be confirmed, supposedly by positive instances. If a sentence is confirmed, then so should be all the sentences that are logical equivalent to it; and these are in **FOL**, for example,

(2) $(\forall x)(\text{Raven}(x) \wedge \neg\, \text{Black}(x) \supset \text{Raven}(x) \wedge \neg\, \text{Raven}(x))$

(3) $(\forall x)(\neg\, \text{Black}(x) \supset \neg\, \text{Raven}(x))$

Now, (2) it seems can never be confirmed, since its consequence contains a contradiction; (3) has the – supposedly paradoxical – consequence that every instance of a non-black thing (e.g. a piece of chalk) supports a thesis about ravens.
In many paraconsistent logics (e.g. in **SKP**) neither (2) nor (3) is logical equivalent to (1), so even maintaining the thesis of confirmation equivalence of logical equivalents the *Raven Paradox* does not ensue.

Assessment

Within the philosophy of science we can see weak paraconsistency at work. There is plenty of evidence that we need some weak paraconsistent modelling in some examples from the history of science and in theory change.
There is no need for dialetheism in the philosophy of science, since scientists, although working for some time with inconsistent theories, still assume that reality is consistent and thus the ultimate theory will be consistent.
In case of epistemology the general argument tying universality in philosophy to dialetheism applies. A universalist – "transcendental" – philosophy of knowledge can only be dialetheist.

Questions

(Q1) Why does the Raven Paradox not arise in **SKP**? That is: Why can (2) or (3) not be derived from (1)?

(Q2) $A \wedge \neg A$ being *observable* (a modal claim) can only mean that there are situations/worlds where $A \wedge \neg A$ really is *observed*. It is not just a seeming! How could that be? – Try it for yourself!

(Q3) Within philosophy of science there has been a shift from a model of theories as logically closed sets of sentences towards the so called *structuralist* theory (Sneed 1979, Stegmüller 1986), which sees theories as defined by models in the manner of set theory. The structualist picture distinguishes between the core of a theory and its full models and intended applications. Is this picture less opposed to the idea of inconsistent theories than the standard view (the so called "statement view") of theories?

Exercises

(Ex1) In case you are familiar with the AGM-approach to belief revision, try to find a paraconsistently possible case of belief revision in which axiom (K7) for revision is invalidated.

Further Reading

• A reader dedicated solely to paraconsistent modelling and interpretation of inconsistency in science is: Meheus, Joke (Ed.) *Inconsistency in Science*. Dordrecht, 2002.
The examples in this chapter are mostly taken from that book. The essays in it deal both with static as well as dynamic inconsistency (using adaptive logics). In that book you also find (Priest 2002) and (Miller 2002).
• On paraconsistent belief revision cf. Fuhrmann, Andre. "Theory Contraction Through Base Contraction", *Journal of Philosophical Logic*, 20 (1991), and especially: Tanaka, K. "What Does Paraconsistency Do? The Case of Belief Revision", *The Logica Yearbook 1997*, ed. by T. Childers, Prague, 1998, pp. 188–197.
• On standard Epistemic Logic see (Lenzen 1980). A critic of its closure conditions you find in (Hintikka 1970 and 1973). On its paraconsistent restriction see (Routley 1979a, pp. 884-94).

16 | Hypercontradictions

The worst thing that could happen to a premise set in standard logic is that it becomes or turns out to be inconsistent. A contradiction (a sentence A, such that A and ¬A are given or even provable) is the worst case for standard logic. The set of consequences is thereby trivialized. Everything can be deduced, since *ex contradictione qoudlibet sequitur* holds.
Such a simple contradiction is no problem for paraconsistent logics. To deal with such contradictions is the purpose of paraconsistent logics.
The question is whether there are sentences that are as disastrous to a paraconsistent logical system as contradictions are for a system of standard logic. One may first define such *hypercontradictions* and then see whether there are actually any. If there are provable hyper-contradictions a paraconsistent logic is as trivial as standard logic!
Another problem may be the implausibility of the self-application of some of the dialetheist's basic statements. This may not be as bad as hypercontradictions, but disastrous for a (philosophical) presentation of the dialetheist's position. [We first look at the second problem, then at hypercontradictions.]

Truth without Assertability?

Strong paraconsistency (dialetheism) claims that some contradictions are true. Theories which entail contradictions might be correct. So some contradictions have to be true, since they are provable. Take, for example, the Liar in naive semantics

(λ) is false.

by familiar reasoning (valid in at least some paraconsistent logics) we arrive at the conclusions that (λ) is both true and false, its truth being derivable by *reductio* from the assumption of its being false.
Now, something that is true should be assertible by any speaker towards an audience. Furthermore, being provable (λ) fulfils even the strictest condition that a semantics of assertability could insist on. The semantic battle between truth and assertibility does not apply to (λ).
However, there might be another battle to be fought. I will explore some *pragmatic* constraints on assertability that might be strong enough to make (λ), although provable, not assertible.
What about the truth of "A is true" in case A is a dialetheia?
In a many-valued logic it is possible that statements/sentences concerning the value of other statements/sentences are bivalent: "A is true" is true

only if A is true; in case A is undecided "A is true" is simply false [cf. (Blau 1978, pp. 82-84) and the truth operators in Chap. 4].
What if A is dialetheia? Graham Priest claims that in this case "A is true" is a dialetheia itself [see (Priest 1979, pp. 238-40)]!
The difficulty arises because of convention (T), which – neglecting paraconsistently the difference between object and meta language – we can state as:

(T) A is true $\leftrightarrow$ A

By Contraposition we arrive at:

(T') $\neg$A $\leftrightarrow$ $\neg$(A is true)

If A is a dialetheia we have v(A,0) so by the definition of negation in **LP** we have v($\neg$A,1). And with *Modus Ponens* applied to (T') we get:

v($\neg$(A is true),1)

and once again by the definition of negation:

v(A is true,0)

Furthermore it is true that A is true, since it is a dialetheia, therefore:

v(A is true,0) *and* v(A is true,1) ↯

"A is true" now is a dialetheia itself. We would have the truth table:

A	A is true
1	1
0	0
0,1	0,1

and similar for "A is false".
This, however, would have paradoxical consequences. The main thesis of (strong) paraconsistency is that some contradictions are true. Now, this should have the form "($\exists$A)A is true" with respect to at least some contradiction/dialetheia "A". Since "A is true" is a dialetheia itself, the thesis of dialetheism will be a dialetheia.
The main thesis of (strong) paraconsistency *would be antinomic*![34]
A minimal condition on a philosophical thesis, however, should be that it claims to be true *only*. Otherwise the triviality which should be avoided in case of theories containing contradictions would reappear.

---

34 (Priest 1979) accepts this result – even feels happier about it (?). To me this consequence seems absurd.

An antinomy *asserts* nothing (in a pragmatic sense of "assertion" to be specified). There might be statements which are true and false at the same time, but there can be no reason to assert them in a theoretical debate (i.e. reasons besides training one's vocal chords or being on stage etc.), since nothing is excluded by claiming them to be true. No possible state of the world (no piece of information) is rejected because of their assertion.

The *act of asserting* something can only fail with respect to a dialetheia, since the *felicity conditions of assertion* contain, at least:

(i) that we claim something to be the case by citing reasons or giving a justification and

(ii) see this information as worthy of being uttered, because the acceptance of this information would make a difference in the following discourse or action.

But in case of a dialetheia this only can misfire. The aim of assertion is truth, and *nothing but the truth*: only the "true only" excludes its opposite and, thereby, commits itself. In asserting something we commit ourselves against some opponent. Usually we do not consider this, since usually we do not argue in antinomic contexts. In non-antinomic context it is sufficient to show the falsity of the claim of the opponent to infer to the truth of our claim. In the case of a dialetheia we are not able to argue for it in this ordinary fashion, since in its case the success or the failure of our argumentation is irrelevant to justify the claim made. The dialetheia is validated in any case. Any justification given by us plays only in the hands of the opponent. Any argument that I will present to make the case of a dialetheia "A" will be an argument for "$\neg$A" (i.e. the claim of my opponent).

Therefore, we cannot assert contradictions/dialetheias with the *knowledge* of them being contradictory, since then asserting them is irrelevant or not preferable to the assertion of their negation.

Contradictions – at least if we know them to be such things – violate the conversation maxim of *relevance*. We will be unable to commit ourselves.

It will not help here to take the informational content of a sentence to be not those worlds or sentences it excludes but the information "it carries", i.e. the sentences it implies, since a dialetheia *by its very definition* and by the usual reasoning as applied, for example to the Liar, implies its own negation, and, therefore, implies everything its negation implies. A dialetheia and its negation have the same content. A dialetheia implies its own negation, and so, by transitivity, all that the negation implies, and *vice versa*: the share their set of consequences.

Considering such pragmatic constraints asserting something is *more* than having a true belief accompanied by some justification.
Because of these constraints asserting something fails in case of dialetheias or known contradictions. Notwithstanding that we have proved them we are not able to assert them. Therefore, dialetheism as a philosophical position cannot be a dialetheia itself on pains of being not assertible, i.e. being no contender in the debate at all.

A Problem with LNC?

The mere validity of the Law of Non-Contradiction (LNC) in some PLs does not commit the adherent of such a system to an antinomic thesis of dialetheism itself: from

$\models(\neg(A \wedge \neg A))$

we get by the definition of validity the statement:

(2) $\text{True}(\neg(A \wedge \neg A))$

From this we get by the definition of negation:

(3) $\text{False}(A \wedge \neg A)$

The argument of the Aristotelian, who claims that there are *no* true contradictions, will continue:

(4) $\neg\text{True}((A \wedge \neg A)$

and

(5) $(\forall A)(\neg\text{True}(A \wedge \neg A))$

since A has been chosen arbitrarily. So by the duality of quantifiers:

(6) $\neg(\exists A)\text{True}(A \wedge \neg A)$

which could be considered to be the thesis of the Aristotelian. A dialetheist, however, is not committed to this conclusion, even if she accepts LNC. The step from (3) to (4) is not paraconsistently valid, since one cannot conclude paraconsistently from the *falsity* of a statement that it is not true (as well). That is the very issue of dialetheias.
The negation of the thesis of the dialetheist [i.e., (6)], therefore, cannot be derived from the acceptance of the Law of Non-Contradiction.

Accepting *falsum*?

The following argument (where D stands for the doctrine of dialetheism), which may be taken as refuting dialetheism by showing that it implies *falsum*, which in turn no-one can really assert of believe, is also problematic:

1.<1>	D	Assumption
2.<2>	$D \supset T(A \wedge \neg A)$	Dialetheists claim for some A
3.<1,2>	$T(A \wedge \neg A)$	($\supset$E) 1,2
4.<1,2>	$A \wedge \neg A$	Convention (T) 3
5.<>	$\neg C \equiv C \supset \bot$	Df. "$\neg$", or duality
6.<>	$\bot \equiv A \wedge \neg A$	Df. "$\bot$", or duality
7.<1,2>	$\bot$	($\supset$E) 4,6
8.<2>	$D \supset \bot$	($\supset$I) <u>1</u>, 7
9.<2>	$\neg D$	($\equiv$E) 5,8 C/D ■

The problem with this argument is not just using ($\supset$E) with an inconsistent antecedent – which may be problematic for its own right – but this use of "$\bot$". If *falsum* is really a bottom particle, then (6) is simply not true for a dialetheist, since $A \wedge \neg A$ is evaluated (0,1) in case of a dialetheia, and one need not accept $(0,1) \equiv 0$ as being evaluated either (0,1) or 1 like in **LP**. *falsum* either has to be introduced as primitive into such a system, or it has to be defined using some strong negation "~" as $A \wedge {\sim}A$. Both moves need not be taken or be accepted by a dialetheist.

An Assertibility Principle

The two foregoing arguments against dialetheism are not convincing. The real problem is having to assert the truth of a dialetheia without wanting to assert the dialetheia itself.

How can we satisfy the constraints on assertibility and keep the thesis of dialetheism from becoming a dialetheia itself?

The dialethist should say: Antinomies are true, but they are *not* assertible.

Concerning an operator or predicate of assertion "ASSERT" it would *not* be valid:

(*) ASSERT(True(A)) $\rightarrow$ ASSERT(A)

Even if we can assert the truth of a dialetheia A (since, for example, we have a proof of A), this should not imply that we can assert A itself. The reason for this – given above – is that antinomies have no cognitive content.

For meta-logical reasons I might (or should) be motivated to be a dialetheist and to assert that some contradictions are true, but I have no inclination to assert any antinomy simpliciter. I believe that the Liar is true, but I am not the Liar myself, I hope. What would I assert by it?

Proof-Theoretic Adjustments

The denial of the just mentioned principle or even stating its negation (that contradictions just cannot be asserted) could point to a *pragmatic* solution of the problem posed by Priest's "self-referential postscript".

On the other hand we have the problem that our proof-theory and our semantics may result in the thesis of dialetheism being a dialetheia itself. If we *adopt* the principle that dialetheias should not be asserted that would make it not assertible. Since we want and have to assert it we have to adjust our proof theory.

The argumentation so far saves us from asserting dialetheias which are, nevertheless, true. To *assert* dialetheism we have to ensure that dialetheism is no dialetheia *at all*. We have to block the derivation of it being antinomic.

How could we block the derivation in if we consider Convention (T) as beyond doubt? *Modus Ponens* seems even more beyond doubt. The truth conditions of negation cannot be altered without being deviant with respect to extensional operators (i.e., being deviant on too large a scale). The culprit has to be Contraposition. Without contraposition in Convention (T) we could infer nothing from the falsehood of A (i.e. the truth of ¬A) concerning the truth value of "A is true". And this is how it should be in a paraconsistent semantics, since the truth values "true" and "false" should be independent enough from each other to allow for paraconsistent evaluations.

In **LP** semantics Contraposition is valid as a consequence relation. The corresponding conditional is valid in **LP** anyway, since **LP** is an extension of classical propositional logic. It is difficult to see how to block the validity of Contraposition in **LP**, but because of its invalidation of *Modus Ponens* **LP**'s conditional "⊃" is doomed anyway as a representation of a real conditional. This means that the conditional in Convention (T) cannot be taken to be "⊃". Either **LP** has to be extended by another conditional invalidating Contraposition or **LP** cannot be the logic of dialetheism!

As we have seen in chapter 6 **SKP** does not have Contraposition as a rule of inference. The modal semantics of entailment can falsify it. Contraposition can be added to give us $\mathbf{SKP}^+$, but that system then cannot be the logic of dialetheism.[35]

[35] As we have seen, as a consequence of dropping Contraposition indirect argumentation (e.g. Negation Introduction) is severely limited in **SKP**.

Afterthoughts about the Liar

Suppose you accept the proposal. It seems to work well with respect to a lot of antinomies. I might even assert that the Liar is true, since that is what we prove in naive semantics.
But what about the corresponding claim that the Liar is false? If I claim that the Liar is a dialetheia I claim that it is true and false. By conjunction elimination I should arrive at

(1) The Liar is false.

Now, this sentence speaks about the Liar, and it says just what the Liar says, i.e.

(2) $(1) \leftrightarrow (\lambda)$

We seem to face a dilemma: either we assert a dialetheia itself, what we should not do, or if we block the procedure just outlined we face a problem of expressibility: Some semantic fact about the Liar (its being false) would become ineffable. And ineffability of semantic facts is unacceptable since it bereaves dialetheism of its main argument against hierarchy conceptions of semantics which are ineffable themselves.
Two ad hoc solutions could be: either to weaken the ban on asserting dialetheias (allowing some exceptions to a default rule) or to invent some other description of the Liar.
If the Liar is the dialetheia paraconsistent logicians are most concerned with I could assert

(3) "The dialetheia that paraconsistent logicians are most concerned with" is false.

If we treat "is false" as a predicate we are still allowed to substitute different *names* of an expression for each other (i.e. substitute (λ) for "the dialetheia that paraconsistent logicians are most concerned with"), but if we now assert of (3) that it is true or that it is false, i.e.

(4) "The dialetheia that paraconsistent logicians are most concerned with is false" is true.

we have *inside* the scope of the truth predicate a name of (3) and into this we cannot substitute (λ) for "the dialetheia that paraconsistent logicians are most concerned with" (this being substitution into quotation marks).
This blocks:

(*) $(4) \leftrightarrow (\lambda)$

So we can assert that it is true that the Liar is false and, therefore, that the Liar is false, i.e. we could assert our semantic fact concerning the falsity of

the Liar. So some assertions about dialetheias are dialetheias themselves, like (1) is. Some are not, like (4).
And that is all we need for consistently asserting the thesis of dialetheism. If only we can express the thesis of dialetheism in some way – and in some way with respect to any single dialetheia like the Liar – Priest's problem of self-application is solved.
Since we already have seen that the thesis of the Aristotelian cannot be proven, we are saved.
Surely more needs to be said about this.

Hypercontradictions Defined

Classical logic system become trivial because of paradoxes like the Liar and rules of inference like *ex contradictione qoudlibet*. Dealing with the Liar a paraconsistent system (by revision of some logical principles) blocks spreading triviality.
A *hypercontradiction* is a paradox that can arise within this new paraconsistent system and threatens it with triviality (e.g. by proving "1 = 0", so that *all* statements will be both true and false, taking the numbers to represent truth values in interpretations v).
The philosophical merits of dialetheism (especially being able to have a semantically closed language) are endangered by hypercontradictions, since they would make this theory trivial.
[Note: To have an exact concept of x does imply neither that there is an x nor that one would like to have an x around.]

The Everett Case

Everett was one of the first to come up with hypercontradictions. They are a semantic version of the Strengthened Liar:

(λ') (λ') is not true

The Strengthened Liar (λ') is still mapped to $\{0,1\}$, arguing by cases for some interpretation function v: Suppose $0 \in v(\lambda')$, then (λ') is true, so $1 \in v(\lambda')$, so $v(\lambda') = \{0,1\}$, and if $1 \in v(\lambda')$ then accordingly.
Given the four evaluations we can have in a **LP** style semantics (i.e. Truth, Falsity, Simple Truth, Simple Falsity) another Liar is:

(λ'') (λ'') is simply false.

This sentence takes into account that some sentences are both true and false, and claims of itself to be false *only* ("simply false").
Syntactically it just leads to the contradiction (λ'') $\wedge \neg$ (λ'') within a suitable paraconsistent system, but from a semantic point of view it leads into disaster:

Suppose (λ") is true, then the set of truth values (λ") is mapped to are either {1} or {0,1}. But, on the other hand, if (λ") is true, by convention (T) (λ") obtains, so that the set of truth values (λ") is mapped to is {0}. So, if (λ") is true {0} = {1} or {0} = {0,1}, which gives by extensionality of sets that 1 = 0, i.e. triviality!
So we end with 1 = 0, which is the end of all distinctions between true and false sentences in the semantics given so far.

Evaluation Relations

To avoid this case we switch to an evaluation relation [as we have already done in previous chapters]:

$$\neg(v(A,1) \Rightarrow \neg v(A,0)) \wedge \neg(v(A,0) \Rightarrow \neg v(A,1))$$

Truth and validity are defined then:

(D1) A is true in $M_i \overset{\text{def}}{=} v_i(A,1)$

(D2) A is valid $\overset{\text{def}}{=} (\forall v)v(A,1)$

Considering now (λ") we have

(λ") $(v((\lambda''),0) \wedge \neg v((\lambda''),1))$

Take (λ") to be true, i.e. $v((\lambda''),1)$, then $v((\lambda''),0)$. Take (λ") to be false, i.e. $v((\lambda''),0)$, then $\neg v((\lambda''),0)$ or $\neg\neg v((\lambda''),1)$. By a property of negation we have that $\neg v((\lambda''),0)$ implies $v((\lambda''),1)$, since we have no truth value gaps here. So $v((\lambda''),1)$ implies $v((\lambda''),0)$, and vice versa. This comes, at most, to:

$v((\lambda''),1)$ *and* $v((\lambda''),0)$

(λ") being a dialetheia as it should be.

Bromand's Hypercontradiction

Joachim Bromand developed two versions of a hypercontradiction that is supposed to work *even* for a semantics using an evaluation relation!
One of them can be presented in the form of this deduction:

1. $(\forall A,v)(\exists x)(x=\{y \mid v(A,y)\})$ (Naïve) Comprehension
2. $d(A)=\{y \mid v(A,y)\}$ function picking out the set of truth values given some formula A
3. $(\lambda''') \Leftrightarrow (d(\lambda''')=\{0\})$ Definition of some Liar sentence,
4. $(\forall A)(d(A)=\{0\} \vee d(A)=\{1\} \vee d(A)=\{0,1\})$ Semantic principle
5. $d(\lambda''')=\{0\} \vee d(\lambda''')=\{1\} \vee d(\lambda''')=\{0,1\}$ (∀E) 4

6. $(\forall A)v(A,1) \Leftrightarrow A$	Convention (T)
7. $v((\lambda'''),1) \Leftrightarrow (\lambda''')$	$(\forall E)$ 6
8. $d(\lambda''')=\{0\}$	Assumption
9. (λ''')	Substitution of Equivalents 3, 8
10. $v((\lambda'''),1)$	Detachment 7, 8
11. $d(\lambda''')=\{y \mid v((\lambda'''),y)\}$	d-function for (λ''')
12. $1 \in d(\lambda''')$	Definition of d 11, 10
13. $1 \in \{0\}$	(=E) 8, 12
14. $1=0$	Extensionality of sets 13
15. $d(\lambda''')=\{1\}$	Assumption
16. $1 \in d(\lambda''')$	Definition of d 15
17. $v((\lambda'''),1)$	Definition of d 16
18. (λ''')	Detachment 7, 17
19. $d(\lambda''')=\{0\}$	Substitution of Equivalents 3, 18
20. $1 \in \{0\}$	(=E) 16, 19
21. $1=0$	Extensionality of sets 20
22. $d(\lambda''')=\{1,0\}$	Assumption
… 28. $1 = 0$	see (16)-(21)
29. $1=0$	Dilemma 5, 8, 15, 21

Line (29) states the needed result, which can be then employed thus:

…	
30. $v(C,1) \vee v(C,0)$	Semantic principle ("no gaps")
31. $v(C,1)$	Assumption
32. $v(C,0)$	(=E) 29, 31
33. $v(C,0)$	Assumption
34. $v(C,1)$	(=E) 29, 33
35. $v(C,1) \wedge v(C,0)$	$(\wedge I)$ 32, 34
36. $(\forall C)(v(C,1) \wedge v(C,0))$	$(\forall I)$ 35 ■

– That is triviality!

The hypercontradiction starts by defining by (naïve) comprehension for each sentence the set of its truth-values (i.e. the set of all values assigned to the sentence by the evaluation relation). Allowing no truth value gaps we have that for any sentence this set has to be either $\{0\}$, $\{1\}$ or $\{0,1\}$. Then some Liar is defined who asserts that its set of truth value is the singleton$\{0\}$ (saying thus that it is only false). Going through the cases and applying Convention (T) on the way yields for each case the worrisome identity 1=0, which thus can be derived by Dilemma. Once we have this identity and given our representation of truth by 1 and falsity by 0 we end with triviality by substituting the identicals within evaluation sentences.

Getting Back on My Rocker

Does the presence of a hypercontradiction bring us back to the classical solution of the paradoxes?

That is not so. For the simple reason that there is no solution to the paradoxes in classical logic. The hierarchy conception says we are always talking from some level in the hierarchy, and *at the same time* makes a general statement to the effect that constructing the semantics of a language (level) we just go one level up. – This I called the MYSTERY [see Chap. 2]. So it is instructive that Brendel (1992) after "rejecting" paraconsistency starts talking about Wittgenstein's ladder or that which cannot be expressed at all, Bromand (2001) sums up his investigation that it "can be" that his thesis of inexpressibility (of the hierarchy, respectively of truth) cannot be expressed. That is no "can be", it just *cannot* be expressed, if true. Dialetheism avoids MYSTERY at the price of accepting some true contradictions.

Inconsistent Numbers to the Rescue

Inconsistent arithmetic can have finite models. In a finite model there is a largest number. One might suppose that the largest number is a *vastly* large number beyond these limits. Therefore we do not know what this number is, but – realistically speaking – it is there. Let us call it "m". So for this number we have m = m+1, since there is no larger number. In fact there are no numbers m+1, m+2..., we only express the fact that there are no such numbers by m = m+1 = m+2 ... [See Chap. 12 and (Priest 1994)].

The number m (respectively the numeral "m") has to be an exception to the rule of substitution of identicals, otherwise one could reason to a=b for all numbers (by principles valid even in inconsistent mathematics).

In Chap. 5 on **SKP** we said:

In case of Substitution of Identicals we introduce the set Ξ of inconsistent objects (i.e. objects such that: $F(a) \wedge \neg F(a)$ for some F).

Let δ be the denotation function of quantificational semantics. Then:

$$(R13)\ \delta(á) \notin \Xi\ \&\ \Gamma \Vdash á=é\ \&\ \Pi \Vdash P(é) \Rightarrow \Pi \cup \Gamma \Vdash P(á)$$

If á does not denote an inconsistent object then substitution applies. We could also modify the rule (R13), using the least inconsistent number m and a denotation function *d( )*:

$$(R13')\quad d(á) \neq m\ \&\ \prod \Vdash á=é\ \&\ \Gamma \Vdash P(é) \rightarrow \prod \cup \Gamma \Vdash P(á)$$

Now for a bold claim. A sufficiently rich semantically closed language has to contain inconsistent arithmetic, so it contains m.
Which number we take to represent the truth value "true" is conventional, so let us take m instead of 1!
If we do not take "*v(*C,1)" as atomic – although it certainly looks that way from a syntactic point of view –, we may just give up transparency. If we take "*v(*C,1)" to be atomic, we have to give up functionality as well.
Then lines 30-35 of applying Bromand's hypercontradiction will not go through! Even if 0 = m, we cannot derive disaster. Triviality does not ensue.
– Can one keep a straight face proposing this? Is this an ***ad hoc*** solution or an *ad hoc* **solution**? Another solution – not committed to the inconsistent number m – would be the logic of (weak) identity that some extension of **LP** offers [see Chap. 4].
This solution is not *ad hoc* in restriction (=E), since we have seen already some occasions where this has been dropped for other reasons in some paraconsistent logic. Restricting (=E) further on need not be connected to paraconsistency at all.
Starting from the work of Peter Geach there has been established a field called "Relative Identity (Logic)". The basic idea is that it makes no sense to speak of absolute identity (at least not in all contexts and concerning all questions of identity). Identity is (at least sometimes) relative to being the same x of a kind *F*. Van Inwagen (1995) develops some of these ideas in a little logical system of relative identity. Symmetry and Transitivity of relative identity hold, but substitution of identicals *fails*, since otherwise the absolute concept of identity could be regained. (Absolute identities are *substantial* assumptions then.)
Pardey (1994) argues that in ordinary language contexts R(a,a) cannot be seen as substituting into R(a,b) in case that a=b. The idea that R(a,a) is a special case of R(a,b) he calls the "reflexivity thesis" in distinction to which he claims that in ordinary R(a,b) statements it is *presupposed* that a ≠ b. A presupposition cannot just be made a part of the sentence without producing strange sentences like "He reminded all of his audience, except himself, that ..." Given this it is not valid in general that transparency

holds, "a = b" is rather used to cancel the presupposition of non-identity made with "R(a,b)"

Krause and Beziau (1997) discuss several versions of stating Leibniz' Law and claim that quantum objects fail to meet it, since they are identical within their group although being different objects. They discuss some logics that violate identity in the form that the so called identity law for the conditional

$$A \vdash A$$

is not valid in them.

The deviant behaviour of the quantum objects is, however, not mainly a problem of functionality (since quantum objects of some group indeed inherit their properties fulfilling functionality), but with identity in general; they demand something *stronger* than Leibniz' Law.

One we see that there is something wrong with substitution of identicals [(=E)] we can reject the criticism that the avoidance of Bromand's hypercontradiction is *ad hoc*. In fact we do not need to consult inconsistent arithmetics to recruit an unconventional representant of the truth value "true". Once we lay down that (=E) does not hold for inconsistent objects we can block the whole derivation of "0=1" in Bromand's case. The deduction makes use at several lines [(13),(20),(27)] of (=E) with respect to $d(\lambda''')$, but $d(\lambda''')$ is an inconsistent object: We can derive

$$d(\lambda''')=\{1\} \wedge \neg\, d(\lambda''')=\{1\}$$

since we can derive $d(\lambda''')=\{0\}$ [see lines (15)-(19)].

Assessment

The implausibility of asserting contradictions and of the philosophical positions held by oneself to be true and false at the same time can be avoided given a further restriction of the preferred paraconsistent logical system (here: dropping Contraposition).

Dialetheism is/remains a clearly statable theoretical position.

The danger of the known hypercontradictions can be banned. This again requires a restriction of paraconsistent logic, in this case with respect to the logic of identity. This solution is not optimal, since it works either with the idea of inconsistent objects, which is problematic itself [see Chap. 17], or with a notion of identity (in **LPQ**$^{=}$) that is very weak. Dialetheist's should go on looking for a better solution to this problem. There has to be one, since there is no going back to MYSTERY.

Tomorrow somebody may come around with a new supposed hypercontradiction. So this problem remains virulent. The same is true, however, for standard set theory or many other interesting theories.

Questions

(Q1) Priest sometimes defends dialetheism by denying that a rule of reasoning just employed by his critics is valid in "the paraconsistent logic". How could Priest react to the argument that a dialetheia and its negation share their information content, since by transitivity the dialetheia implying its negation implies what the negation implies? What can be said against this defence in turn?

(Q2) Someone may say that to avoid giving up Contraposition in general the conditional in Convention (T) should be *sui generis*. What is the problem with that proposal?

Exercises

(Ex1) Show by tableaus that Contraposition as a consequence relationship holds in **LP**. [see Chap. 4]

(Ex2) Go through the argument assuming (λ") false.

Further Reading

• For the problem of self-application see: (Priest 1979, Postscript). This part of the presentation here uses (Bremer 1999). On assertibility conditions see (Sainsbury 1988, Chap. 6).
• On the Everett hypercontradictions see: Everett, Anthony. "A Note on Priest´s 'Hypercontradictions'", *Logique et Analyse*, 1993, pp. 39-43; "Absorbing Dialetheia?", *Mind*, 103, 1994, pp. 413-19; "A Dilemma for Priest`s Dialethism", *Australasian Journal of Philosophy*, 74, 1996, pp. 657-67.
• On Bromand's hypercontradictions see: Bromand, Joachim. *Philosophie der semantischen Paradoxien*. Paderborn (Mentis), 2001; "Why Paraconsistent Logic Can Only Tell Half the Truth", *Mind*, 111, 2002, pp.741-50.
• The part on hypercontradictions uses (Bremer 200x).
• On the involved inconsistent mathematics see Chap. 12.

17 | Inconsistent Ontology

An ontology of inconsistent objects is – in my eyes – the greatest challenge of/to paraconsistent mathematics and set theory.
Given the strong paraconsistent program of true contradictions and a even mildly realistic theory of truth (containing in some – maybe even restricted – fashion the idea of correspondence), a true contradiction is *supposedly* made true by either an inconsistent fact (taking facts – at least for the moment – to be truth makers of statements) or by inconsistent objects. Like true contradictions they are just *there*.
The challenge may not be that great for Naive Semantics given some mildly anti-realistic theory of truth (containing in some – maybe even restricted – fashion the idea that truth depends on justification), and observing that the inconsistent *objects* in that area are *sentences* only.
The real problem are objects like the Russell set or the least inconsistent number. Isn't that too much to bear, even for a dialetheist?
The most famous theory in the field is Meinong's ontology of possible, of inconsistent and of impossible objects, and their modes of being.

Inconsistent Ontology and Realism

As a realist – even if you do not adhere to naive realism or extreme versions of metaphysical realism – you adhere to some principle that there correspond structured entities (facts or objects with properties) to true statements. The entities are – at least as much as our linguistic resources to describe them are partly sufficient – as the true statements say they are.
This means that a truth like $F(a) \wedge \neg F(a)$ means at first sight that the object *a* has property F and does not have property F. On second sight we worked with the idea of an extension of "F( )" and an anti-extension of "F( )", the extension being the set of entities fulfilling the criteria of F-ness, and thus being F; and the anti-extension being the set of entities fulfilling criteria of not being F, thus being not-F.
For an anti-realist this may solve the problem of inconsistent objects, since being an inconsistent objects means nothing more for an anti-realist than that the objects fulfils inconsistent criteria. There is no claim on the anti-realist's side that there corresponds something to this in reality. The anti-realist can even explain how this may happen in case of ordinary objects: If predicates are employed to more or the less vague criteria or family resemblances to some prototype it may happen that one route of

resemblance leads from the prototype of F to *a*, and another route leads *via* some intermediaries from *a* to a prototype of non-F.
In the manner of weak paraconsistency one may argue that we have to be able to model theories that depict – at least implicitly – the world as containing inconsistent objects without ourselves to be committed to this picture. We need the formal tools (like **LPQ**) for this, but these tools themselves have no negative ontological impact. That is just like we need a logic to draw inferences in works of fiction (or about art) where some works are essentially inconsistent with respect to some object (e.g., some stories about time travelling or drawings by M. C. Escher).
A realist cannot take this easy way out. For (most) realists properties are *structures* of objects – or parts or tropes... – and either you have them or not.
In case of *sentences* – i.e. for a dialetheist view on naive semantics – the way out may be that a sentence is really an object that can have inconsistent properties without us having ontological scruples: A sentence being a dialetheia means that itself and its negation are provable. These are clear cut properties.
What about the content of the dialetheia? If the Liar is really true there has to be some fact corresponding to this truth!
The content of the semantic antinomies, once again, concerns facts *about language*. Given our mild form of realism that incorporates some idea that truth is also – besides aiming at correspondence – tied to justification we can accept inconsistent objects here, since this "merely" points to the inconsistent nature of our linguistic access to reality. That is a deep philosophical point – as dialetheism is – but it locates the inconsistent objects somewhere in the objects having the job of mediating between our mind and the rest of reality, these objects often being constituted by linguistic conventions.
The problem of inconsistent objects is much harder with respect to ordinary objects. If properties are structures of objects, and this means in the last analysis structures of distribution of matter and energy, then an inconsistent objects cannot exist, it seems, since either at some location there is matter or not.
For a dialetheist the problem is naive set theory, given one is a realist about sets. A set, it seems, either is a member of another set or it is not, otherwise the including set could not be well-defined.

Meinong's Ontology

The most promising place to turn to for an ontology of inconsistent objects is Alexius Meinong's *Gegenstandstheorie*. The logic of Meinong's ontology has to be, it seems, some kind of paraconsistent logic; and strong paraconsistent semantics may need something like Meinong's ontology. Thus the focus in this chapter is on Meinong's ontology and its formalisation by analytic philosophers.

Meinong's theory has been ridiculed by analytic philosophers from Russell to Ryle. The idea of there being an object for any name or description (including the golden mountain or the round square) seems too strange.

There has been a growing interest in Meinong's theory, however, with the advent of Free Logics (logics that allow for individual expressions that do not refer) and the intricacies of the semantic and logical analysis of context of belief. The logic of fictional objects also can be hardly referential. Semantics of modal logics talk about different modes of being (being actual, i.e. part of the actual world, vs. being merely possible) – so there may be a relationship to Meinong's ideas.

In Meinong's theory are – in sense of "are" to be explained – *all* objects. There are also inconsistent and impossible objects. With inconsistent objects there seem to be inconsistencies, since the round square is round and is square, thus round and not-round.

Meinong himself did not develop a logic to deal with inconsistent objects. He saw standard logic as fit for *existing* objects (these are the objects in space and time). Inconsistent objects are for him, because of their inconsistency, *impossible objects* (i.e. it is impossible that they exist [somewhere in space and time]).

Meinong's *basic idea* is the rejection of any inherent connection between having properties (i.e. predication) and existence (i.e. metaphysics, in Meinong's use of the term). [This idea can be spelled out into several theses – to be explored shortly.]

The point of attack is the *Ontological Assumption* saying

(OA) Predication implies existence.

or the *Referential Assumption* saying

(RA) Every singular term refers to some kind of being.

Noneism

This attack on the Ontological and the Referential Assumption is generalised by Richard Routley (1979a) into *noneism*.

Noneism is the theory of non-being. Meinong's more fundamental idea – behind his attack on (OA) and (RA) – is the claim that objects are *beyond being*. That idea is supposedly hard to grasp.

Meinong does *not* claim that there are realms of being *besides* being in space and time (i.e. existence). There are no domains of *possibilia* (possible objects). And there are no "outer-domains" (like in some Free Logics) where even more strange objects like the round square reside.

Meinong claims that objects *are* without *being*! The philosophical field that deals with objects in this generality is *Gegenstandstheorie [Object Theory]* (whereas metaphysics is concerned with existents only).

"Noneism" is a name to Meinong's claim. *Noneism* claims, for example, that mathematics does not deal with anything having being; so there is no problem of *abstract entities*: numbers etc. are objects and nothing beyond that. The same goes for sets and properties (if taken as *abstract* entities). Noneism is *the* alternative to Platonism, it claims.

Noneism goes beyond a *dual aspect theory* of meaning (that separates sense/meaning from reference), since it sees in such dual aspect theories only a version of (RA) in that these theories take (as in Frege) the sense sometimes as the referent of an expression.

Any kind of shifting (like in Frege) *or* using intensions in intensional contexts (like in Carnap) is said to less adequate to our understanding of intensional contexts than a *straightforward* noneism such that

(1) Peter believes Holmes to live in Bakerstreet.

expresses a relation between Peter and (the object) Holmes.

Objects can be *quantified*; there will be different kind of quantifiers though – some with existential impact, others not.

Noneism can be characterised by a set of postulates:

(P1) Everything is an object.

(P2) Many objects have no way of being.

(P3) Nonexistent objects have properties and are constituted in some way.

(P4) Existence is no characteristic property of an object.

(P5) Every object has an essence independent of its existence.

(P6) Every object has its characterising properties.

These postulates have some immediate consequences:
• by (P1) anything can be the object of belief, desire, fear – any propositional attitude – whether the object is possible or impossible.
• by (P6) – also called the *Characterisation Postulate* – the golden mountain is golden, and the round square is round and is square.
• by (P4) versions of the ontological proof of God's existence should be blocked.
• by (P3) and (P5) the round square and the triangular square are *different* impossible objects.
• by (P5) and the existence of *impossibilia* we can say:

(2) There is something which necessarily does not exist.

The first quantifier having no existential impact here.
Postulate (P3) is called the *Principle of Independence.* As a universal claim it is the contrary to (OA).
The *Characterisation Postulate* is a further claim to the well defined *nature* of nonexistents. It allows to draw modal conclusions (like (2)) from the definition of an object.
As mentioned above, by (P1) anything can be the object of belief, desire, fear – any propositional attitude – whether the object is possible or impossible. The attitude is directed to the object *itself,* not to its representation or to the sense of the object's name.
And given that we have quantifiers at our disposal that carry no ontological commitment we can freely *quantify into* intensional contexts:

(3) Peter thinks of the round square.

(4) (∃x)(Peter thinks of x)

goes through.[36]
The postulates have some immediate consequences as well for our way of using arbitrary individual expressions.
We can recast the *Postulate of Independence* as a statement about sentences [cf. Routley 1979a, p. 14]:

(P3') Sentences about singular objects have meaning independent from the existence or the possibility of these objects.

[36] Note that the failure of substitutivity in intensional contexts still obtains in noneism. If

(5) The round square is Meinong's famous example for an impossible object.

we still need not have that (6) is true if (3) is true, given Peter's ignorance:

(6) Peter thinks of Meinong's famous example for an impossible object.

(P3") Many sentences about nonexistents have a truth value.

Not every sentence about a nonexistent object has a truth value, since nonexistents are in most cases only partially characterised. We do not know how many rolls Holmes ate during his observation of the Baskervilles. [So a noneist logic may allow for truth value gaps.][37]

Ascertaining which properties an existent has may be observable or be based on observation. Which properties a nonexistent has has to be determined differently.

Whatever can be said with truth value (be it "true" or "false") about nonexistents can only be due to their *definitions* (as in the case of the round square) or due to *the story told about them* (as in the case of Holmes).

So what we have here is basically a way to get sentences from other sentences. We do not access objects of any kind.

Given that we already have the definitions or the stories before us, all these sentences about nonexistents have their truth value *a priori*.

Meinongian Logic

The logic corresponding to Meinong's ontology cannot be a standard logic because of the presence of inconsistent objects.

It cannot, as well, be a paraconsistent logic in which *Tertium Non Datur* holds, since Meinong allows not only for inconsistent, but also for incomplete objects (i.e. objects such that there is some property P such that neither P nor $\neg$P are true of them) – unless one introduces a distinction between sentence negation and predicate negation. Then *Tertium Non Datur* may hold for sentence negation (the non-application of the property making the negated sentence true), but not for predicate negation. Given two negations one needs to know what interrelations hold between these negations. Does, for example, $\neg{\sim}P(a) \equiv P(a)$ hold? There has to be some *logic* for predicate negation if it is not just a tool of introducing additional predicates. Further on one may wonder whether natural languages have these two negations.

If one kept a single negation the logic of Meinongian ontology might be some 4-valued logic like **BN4** [cf. Chap. 9] or **FDE** [cf. Chap 5].

Assessment

Dialetheism in semantics needs no special ontology of inconsistent objects if the inconsistencies are located within our linguistic frameworks. That a sentence can be shown to be true and can be shown to be not true points to

[37] Note that (P3') and (P3") are true in many Free Logics as well, cf. (Lambert 1991). The distinguished nature of noneism is due to postulates (P1), (P2), (P5) and (P6).

the fact of inconsistent evaluations or derivations, but to no deep ontological mystery.

Inconsistent theories in the sciences can be understood in the sense of weak paraconsistency, i.e. they may be modelled by **LPQ**-style quantificational semantics with inconsistent objects, but one does not believe that there *really are* these objects.

You really *need* an ontology of inconsistent objects if you are a mathematical realist and your favourite mathematics is inconsistent, or if you are a dialetheist in set theory, sets again taken realistically.

You can have a dialetheist set theory with inconsistent objects if you are a *noneist*. Noneism in denying being to inconsistent objects is, however, to weak as foundation of paraconsistent set theory, since sets – unless you believe in noneism – are usually taken to exist (even if not in space in time). Noneism certainly is no version of realism.

Noneism is either

– a version of a *substitutional* understanding of individual expressions (such that we can use a non-referring expression and *tell a story* in which this expression occurs [for example a story about a unicorn]) in which case intensional contexts are to be understood in some way paratactically [in the tradition of Carnap's intensional isomorphy or Davidson's *saying that*],

– or noneism is not comprehensible at all. The distinction between existents and *possibilia* is a clear one in modal semantics. Noneism claims even less being than possible being, but still uses the forms of "to be". – What an object beyond all being is supposed to be, is beyond me.

The main argument that in any context we need an "item" to be talked about is not convincing. Given a dual aspect theory of meaning (i.e., reference vs. meaning in the narrow sense) some talk may have no referent, but still has *meaning*. Referentially it is about nothing, but we can rephrase the *content* of such talk. Giving this content does not presuppose an "item" that these sentences are "about".

In Free Logic we are free to use any singular term we like. It just may turn out that it does not refer. This accounts for the free use of names and descriptions in ordinary discourse. We do not need the – further – assumption that everytime we use an expression that might refer to an object there "is" some object, although it might be non-existent and completely without being.

Questions

(Q1) Why can we say that the basic First Order principle of noneism is: F(ιxF(x))?

(Q2) Noneism claims that mathematics is a "just so" story about objects that have *no* way of being. What are the fundamental epistemological and ontological problems of this view, especially in light of the usage of mathematics in the sciences?

Further Reading

• On the wisdom of the middleway in matters of realism between (extreme) metaphysical realism and idealism cf. (Bremer 1999a, 2000).

• Meinong's theory is presented in his *Über Gegenstandstheorie* (Leipzig, 1904 [in the volume *Untersuchungen zur Gegenstandstheorie und Psychologie*]) and *Über Annahmen* (Leipzig, 1902).

• A monograph on the Independence Thesis alone is: Lambert, Karel. *Meinong and the Principle of Independence.* Cambridge et al., 1983.

• Richard Routley, one of the founding fathers of paraconsistency and dialetheism, wrote a monumental monograph (1000 type scripted pages) *Exploring Meinong's Jungle and Beyond* (Routley 1979a) expousing not only his interpretation of Meinong's work, but also attacking the referential assumptions of standard semantics in his own right. Routley aims at a wider theory of *noneism* (and paraconsistency)

• An exposition on the supposed logic of Meinong's theory is: Jaquette, Dale. *Meinongian Logic.* Berlin/New York, 1996. Jacquette does not use a paraconsistent logic, since he distinguishes between predicate and sentence negation. The inconsistent objects just have a property and its contrary, where predicate negation is not explosive. Jacquette also uses Meinong's distinction between nuclear properties, which are part of the essence of some object, and extra-nuclear properties, which are not allowed to enter into the definition of an object. But why should this be forbidden? The main reason to forbid this is to avoid the resulting antinomies, it seems.

• See also: Pasniczek, Jacek. "Paraconsistent vs. Meinongian Logic", in: (Carnielli/Coniglio/Ottaviano 2002), pp. 523-34.

• An application of Routley's logic **DL** to fictional discourse is argued for in: Heintz, John. "Reference and Inference in Fiction", *Poetics*, 8 (1979), pp. 85-99.

18 | Alternatives Solutions of the Paradoxes?

Paraconsistency seems to be a desperate measure. If there is any other way out of the antinomies ("paradoxes") one may rather go that way.
In this chapter we look at some suggestions for some antinomies.
Whereas paraconsistency provides a *universal* method to deal with any antinomy whatsoever, or even some proponents proclaim a universal logic providing the framework for all antinomy related reasoning the alternatives are a rag back of solutions many of which deal only with just one antinomy. Nevertheless the case by case comparison may be fruitful given the philosophical worries accompanying paraconsistency.

Russell's Antinomy and Lesniewski

Russell's antinomy (usually called "Russell's Paradox") was one of the main motivations for Lesniewski to develop his *mereology*.
Mereology is the theory of parts and wholes. It substitutes the concept of an aggregate for the concept of a set. Usually mereology is pursued for ontological reasons within a nominalist programme. Lesniewski, however, saw it also as superior to set theory in its avoidance of the antinomies.
We look at some version of Lesniewski's mereology (ideas from 1913-1914) in which he avoids the Russell Paradox by having all classes (i.e. aggregates) being members of themselves. Further on in this version of mereology there is no empty class. So the Russell Set – or the corresponding mereological class – looking for the classes that are not members of themselves just does not exist!
Lesniewski's mereology is built on a few definitions and axioms:

(1) x is element of the class y if there is a z such that

(i) y is the class of objects z

(ii) x is a z.

formally: $(\forall x,y)(x \,\varepsilon\, el(y) \equiv (\exists z)(y \,\varepsilon\, Cl(z) \wedge x \,\varepsilon\, z))$

This is the definition of being *an element*. Lesniewski uses "ε" as elementary predication/being-such relation. [Notice also that by merely being a part of an aggregate the part has not a defining property, therefore this twofold definition.] (1) has to do some of the work Comprehension does in set theory.

Classes are objects:

(2) If y is a class, then y is an object.

formally: $(\forall y)(y \varepsilon C \supset y \varepsilon y)$

So "ε" has ontological impact. If something is an object, it is its own class:

(3) If x is an object, then x is the class of objects x.

formally: $(\forall x)(x \varepsilon x \supset x \varepsilon Cl(x))$

So an object also defines its own kind, so to say. (3) rejects the concrete/abstract division of set theory.
From (2) and (3) we get:

(4) If y is a class, then y is a class of objects y, and y is a y.

By generalizing on the second "y"s:

(5) If y is a class, then there is a z, such that y is the class of objects z and y is a z.

From (5) and (1) taking "x" in (1) to be "y":

(6) If y is a class, then y is an element of the class y.

Thus we have established that all classes are self-members!
Mereology takes classes as existing aggregates/heaps. As an axiom we have that the aggregation of objects is *not nothing*, i.e. the class cannot be empty:

(7) If some object is the class of objects y, then some object is y.

Thus in this version of mereology there is no empty set. As a dual of (6) we get:

(8) No object is a class which is not element of itself.

Notice that, by (7), if y is not element of x, still both are objects, so the negation of a statement of elementhood cannot mean that the class x does not exist. And now from (7) and (8) we derive the non-existence of the Russell Set:

(9) No object is a class of classes which are not elements of themselves.

We argue by (8) that there are no objects corresponding to the definition of the Russell Set, and by (7) that there is no aggregate of nothing.
Lesniewski's later system (1916) – as mereologies today – focuses more on the relation of being *a part*. In that system no object is a part of itself (being a part is defined as asymmetrical), but still all classes are members of themselves, there is no empty class, and being a member of x is equivalent to being a subset of x.

That system still remains in a countable domain.

Lesniewski's Mereology can avoid Russell's Paradox. Some other antinomies do not occur in Lesniewski's mereology because of its limitations of cardinality.
The main problem with mereology is whether it is a revision of standard mathematics, by giving up its foundation (standard set theory) in favour of mereology. Lesniewski's mereology is such a revision. Lewis' mereology is not. It is just a recasting/reduction of standard set theory as a *facon de parler* founded in mereological axioms. Lewis achieves (with the residual problem of singletons) the nominalistic reduction of set theory to heaps. Lewis also provides the higher cardinalities. Since it is a reduction, however, Lewis has still all the problems we had with standard set theory (e.g. absence of a universal set). A revision of standard mathematics is not so easily advertised to mathematicians, who usually don't care about the philosophical problems given with **ZFC** or ontology. The problem of an adherent of a Lesniewski like mereology, therefore, is to regain standard mathematics. [The fundamental idea of Lewis was to avoid just this.]

Set Theories with Universal Sets

One philosophical problem with standard set theory besides restricted Comprehension is the absence of a universal set (as the extension of the concept *set*). Some set theories with universal sets have been proposed.
The widest known set theory with a universal set V – for which we have $V \in V$ – is Quine's **NF** (from his paper "New Foundations of Mathematics", 1937). This system has been explored in its relation to type theory and **ZFC**. Another such set theory is (Church 1974).
Like dialetheist set theories, which work "only" by Extensionality and Naive Comprehension, **NF** also works by having Extensionality and an Comprehension Scheme that is not as restricted as in **ZFC**.
Quine's Comprehension Scheme uses the idea of *stratified formula* (similar to the theory of types):

$$(\exists y)(\forall x)(x \in y \equiv P(x))$$

where "y" is not free in "P( )" and "P( )" is stratified. [A formula is stratified if the set on the right hand side of "$\in$" is of a higher level than that on the left, and its definition does not include that on the left.]
NF has the power to introduce Pairing, (Absolute) Complement, Powerset, Union as instances of Comprehension.
Non-stratified formula can be used in **NF** (this is different to Type Theory), but they cannot be used to define sets. Since non-stratified formulas can be used in **NF** one does not need a universal set or an empty

set for every level (as in Russell's Type Theory) to have well-formed formula.

The antinomies – especially the Russell Set – are avoided, since the corresponding open formulas in the Comprehension Scheme are not stratified.

$V \in V$ means that Cantor's Theorem does not hold (in general) in **NF**. **NF** has other highly controversial features like the existence of infinite descending chains of cardinals, which conflicts with the Axiom of Choice.[38]

Giving Up Convention (T)?

The main reason for dialetheism given in chapter 2 was the need for semantic universality. This universality requires defining semantic concepts within the language under investigation itself. The antinomies then ensue, most famously that of the Liar, involving the concept of truth.

Formalizing the semantic antinomies, especially the Liar, makes use of the Tarskian idea of defining truth and Convention (T). Convention (T) is taken as a universal disquotational or correspondence fixing device:

(T) "p" is true (in L) if and only if p.

One may think now that one can avoid some of the antinomies by giving up Convention (T).

Giving up Convention (T) runs against its intuitive plausibility. So a compromise might be to restrict Convention (T) to some – consistent – contexts. [Remember that **ZFC** solved the Russell Paradox by restricting the naive/unrestricted comprehension axiom.]

We take the biconditional in (T) to be mutual entailment ("$\leftrightarrow$") to have detachment [cf. Chap. 16].

We can distinguish in Convention (T) the two directions

(T$\rightarrow$) $T(\text{"A"}) \rightarrow A$ [or with "T" as operator: $T(A) \rightarrow A$]

(T$\leftarrow$) $A \rightarrow T(\text{"A"})$ [or with "T" as operator: $A \rightarrow T(A)$]

Antinomies ensue only if (T) is employed to statements with semantic vocabulary (like "( ) is true", "( ) donates ( )'", "( ) means ( )'"...). So we can start with:

(T1) If A is a statement not containing semantic vocabulary: $T(\text{"A"}) \leftrightarrow A$.

---

[38] The discussion of the features, merits and disadvantages of **NF** cannot be delivered here; see *Further Reading*.

For statements about extra-lingual reality (T) holds, and this may be the reason for its intuitive force, since these are the statements we mostly care for.
The problems with (T) concerns statements containing semantic vocabulary, but not all of them. We can even state:

(T2) If A is not a statement referring to another statement containing semantic vocabulary: T("A") $\leftrightarrow$ A

In this case A refers to some non-semantic statement B, and A is true, according to (T), if B has the semantic property A says B has.
We have problems if a semantic statement A refers to another semantic statement B. In case of Liar chains A and B can be different statements:

(1) Statement (2) is false.

(2) Statement (1) is true.

But not even all these cases lead to antinomies:

(3) Statement (4) is false.

(4) Statement (3) is false.

lead to no antinomy, since (3) may be true, whereas (4) is false. The Truth-Teller is another case of harmless semantic circularity:

(5) Statement (5) is true.

The Truth-Teller may be taken either as true or as false, it certainly leads to no antinomy. So we can state as a fact:

(F) Only in some cases of semantic statements referring to other semantic statements this leads to antinomies.

Given that only sometimes problems ensue we might see (T) as a rule with minor exceptions, as *a default*. We can state the default:

(T3) If A is a semantic statement referring to a semantic statement B, *by default* we have T("A") $\leftrightarrow$ A.

one may also say "as a rule we have...".
Default rules are nothing extraordinary. Within science and everyday life we often use them. Consider: "All birds can fly", "At the main station you get the connection", "Lessons are on Tuesday"... In all these cases we do not give up the generalization once we hear of a penguin, miss a bus on a day with very bad weather or don't have lesson on a national holiday. We treat these cases as understandable exceptions to the otherwise true rule/generalization. There even are logics for this phenomenon: Default Logic or Non-Monotonic Logic!

The problematic direction of Convention (T) is (T←). One can argue *ad hominem* against the default idea: Even if (T←) is not *true* [i.e. T("A → T("A")") is false], just *as you say* it may be that A → T("A"), such that still antinomies ensue [cf. (Priest 1987, p.21)]. On the other hand the exceptions to (T) are taken to be antinomic contexts, default theory *itself* is not one.

Assessment

Restricting Convention (T) may block some of the semantic antinomies. Nevertheless there are three main problems with this approach:

• The measure seems *ad hoc* in that we have to see the antinomy first to declare then that this was not the right context to apply Convention (T). On the other hand Default Logic is a general framework, i.e. it was not invented to deal with the antinomies. Taking (T) as a default is so only an application of this wider approach. In this concrete case, however, it is still *ad hoc* and not algorithmic.

• The approach was not fully formalized here. The problem with supposed solutions to antinomies is often that once we have formalized them we have a semantic machinery in place that allows to introduce new antinomies for the old (as with the Strengthened Liar in many-valued approaches).

• If there are exceptions to Convention (T) we seem to have statements with absent/restricted semantic properties. How is that possible?

Schemata

The semantic hierarchy failed in talking about the hierarchy itself and the general way to define semantic concepts.

If one looks at the definitions repeated at ever higher levels, these definitions are very similar. They only differ in their indexes of levels. One might think, therefore, that one can give the *schematic form* of such a definition. That schema then would *express* what it is to define a semantic concept. Why shouldn't that be enough?

This leads to a difficult question: What is it to understand a schema? Compare:

$$A \supset (B \supset A)$$

with

$$p \supset (q \supset p)$$

The latter is an instance of the former. How do we take the former?

If understanding the schema means "we know that *all* instances are valid" we are back at universal quantification.

Quantifying over indexes that are only implicit – in case of a meta-semantic schema – does not make quantification about indexes and the resulting contradictions go away.
The problem is old: Hilbert's finitism was founded on the usage of schemata in contrast to generalizations. Using a schema was taken by Hilbert to mean "given *any* instance we accept it". So a schema talks about *arbitrary instances*, not about *the totality* of its instances.
It certainly is no solution to take our ability to understand schemata as inexpressible. That would bring us back to some mystery.
Furthermore one might doubt whether the understanding of any presented instance of a *restricted* definition is enough to understand the *universal* semantic concepts.
Whether there is anything to this distinction between "any" and "all" seems to be an open question to me.
For the moment I take it that the use of schemata is no alternative to non-hierarchical semantic concepts (and so to paraconsistency).

Questions

(Q1) Why can't the discrimination that we have an exception case to Convention (T) as a default rule not be algorithmic?

(Q2) Lesniewski's argument against the Russell Set proceeds by definitions and axioms. (1) looks like set theoretical Comprehension. (2) merely says that classes are objects. (4), (5), (6), (8) are just consequences. So where is the decisive assumption? (3), (7)?

Exercises

(Ex1) Take the Liar and show that (T←) is the more problematic direction of Convention (T).

(Ex2) Starting with the formalizations of (1) – (3) give a formalization of Lesniewski's argument.

Further Reading

• On mereology see: Ridder, Lothar. *Mereologie*. Frankfurt a.M., 2002; Simons, Peter. *Parts*. Oxford, 1987. Some of Lesniewski's original papers are translated; see: "On the Foundations of Mathematics", *Topoi*, 2 (1983), pp. 7-52. Lewis, David. *Parts of Classes*. Oxford, 1991. On the residual problem of singletons see (Bremer 1999b, §II.b).

• On giving up Convention (T) as universal see: Harman, Gilbert. *Change in View*. Cambridge/MA, 1986. On Default Logic see: (Besnard 1989), (Brewka 1991).

• On Hilbert's finitism and the use of schemata see Lavine's *Understanding the Infinite* [see reference in Chap.11].

• Frode Bjordal in "Truth in Perspective" (*International Philosophical Preprint Exchange*, 1996) takes (T←) as the culprit, but needs a modal logic with specially designed accessibility relations for his results.

• On set theories with a universal set see the papers (Quine 1937) and (Church 1974) and: Forster, T. *Set Theory with a Universal Set*. Exploring an Untyped Universe. Oxford, 1992.

19 | Paraconsistency and Programming

This introduction has covered several fields in which paraconsistency is explored and developed. We have seen its merits, but also some problems and unsolved questions in these areas.
Paraconsistent logics are more and more becoming an acceptable tool of work in the formal sciences and in modelling in the cognitive sciences and philosophy. With that development the fields of application are increasing.
Here we look at an area that is often mentioned as one of the main areas of future – commercial? – applications of paraconsistency: Data-management and programming.
The focus here lays on weak paraconsistency, since the contradictions we find in a database are supposedly due to our imperfect ways of gathering data about a non-contradictory part of the world.[39]

Databases

Databases are sets of data that change with time, typically because new data are entered or old data are updated. Further on procedures programmed to execute (regularly) on the database change data in other areas/tables accordance with the new data.
Depending on the organization developers invested in a database the integrity of the data is defined first (according to the standards of normalization used in standard data servers like Microsoft SQL-Server or Oracle or Sybase) and hopefully kept with procedures and dependency constraints that fire in case new data may affect the database integrity. This is far from trivial and can amount to enormously large code for large databases. These integrity constraints and the respective procedures *define* what counts as inconsistent data.
Notwithstanding the cautious design of the database and the amount of integrity checking usually sooner or later the problem of inconsistent data arises.
Nevertheless a typical database (server) will not deduce anything from inconsistent data, for example fill tables now with arbitrary entries.
The entries computed by stored procedures running on an inconsistent database typically make sense although integrity and consistency are corrupted in the database.

---

[39] Since otherwise we would have to go into details of logic and database programming that are beyond the scope and intent of this introduction this chapter only presents the basic points and refers you to the literature.

Factually the logic of such databases is not explosive.

In case you know SQL, consistency keeping comes down to the typical normalization constraints and checking inserts or updates, as in:

```
CREATE TABLE employee (
emp_id int NOT NULL PRIMARY KEY CHECK
   (emp_id BETWEEN 0 AND 1000),
emp_name varchar(30) NOT NULL CONSTRAINT no_nums CHECK
   (emp_name NOT LIKE '%[0-9]%'),
mgr_id int NOT NULL REFERENCES employee(emp_id),
entered_date datetime NULL CHECK
   (entered_date >= CURRENT_TIMESTAMP),
entered_by int CHECK (entered_by IS NOT NULL),
   CONSTRAINT valid_entered_by CHECK (entered_by =
   SUSER_ID(NULL) AND entered_by <> emp_id)
)
```

Revision of Databases

Even if the inconsistency of a database is seen as something that should be overcome immediately be revision of the relevant parts of it one needs some form of paraconsistent reasoning during or modelling the revision process itself.

All – non-trivial – consequences of the inconsistent data should be present to identify the desirable ones.

In fact revision algorithms often possess a higher computational complexity than paraconsistent logic programming does, which can be of polynominal complexity [cf. (Damasio 1996, Chap. 10)].

Resolution

Queries against data sets (in a language like PROLOG) or queries in automated theorem proving are typically answered by *resolution*. Resolution works by *Horn clauses*. Horn clauses are right to left conditionals: their *head* states what can be derived given we have what is said in their *body*. A query asks whether some statement is derivable. Resolution now checks whether this statement is the head of some Horn clause and if it finds one tries to work out whether it can derive the body of that clause (and so on with this new *goal* until the derivation is founded in some fact statement).

Now, *ex contradictione qoudlibet* does not apply in resolution in as much as there is not in general a sequence of steps by which an arbitrary query can be satisfied from an inconsistent theory/database.

Negation as Finite Failure

Negation (in a language like PROLOG) is often taken as the absence of positive evidence. So if one queries for a statement and no derivation (either from basic data or by resolution) is available the answer is "No". If the language's dialect involves a negation sign and one queries for the negated statement the answer will be "Yes". Thus a negation is derivable as finite failure to derive the not negated statement.

Negation as finite failure is obviously non-monotonic: Once you add something the statement queried for may become derivable.

Negation as finite failure does not lead to an application of *ex contradictione qoudlibet*. Negation as finite failure, however, means that typically one has only positive left hand sides of Horn clauses. One can circumvent this by inventing negative predicates like "`non_coloured(X)`" but this is not an *in-built* negation (operator), but depending on our understanding of this predicate. For these predicates – depending on their definition and the database – one can, of course, have `coloured(apple)` and `non_coloured(apple)` thus simulating real (strong) negation.

For a better capturing of real live examples involving strong negation the proof engine (or programming language) should be extended by an in-built strong negation, that can also occur on the left hand side of a Horn clause [cf. (Damásio 1996)]. This negation is monotonic. A programming language PARLOG has been proposed as a paraconsistent version of PROLOG [cf. (Avila/Abe/Prado 1997)].

Whereas negation as finite failure is merely non-explosive (and thus paraconsistent) the addition of a strong negation allows for arriving at *proven* contradictions: `A,not-A`.

Applications

There are several research groups that work on extended logic programming (with different kinds of negation) and dealing with inconsistency.

For example, SNePS is a propositional semantic network system designed to support (or model) agents competent in some natural language. SNePS contains routines (an inference machine) that allow for some automatic revision/contraction and dectection of inconsistencies. If a contradiction occurs SNePS is not explosive but interacts with the user providing options how to remove the inconsistency.

Paraconsistency as Meta-Theory

Since even before the advent of paraconsistent logics the factual behaviour of – at least a great many – databases and proving techniques was paraconsistent one simply needs some version of paraconsistent logic to adequately *describe* what logic is really implemented in them.
Paraconsistent Logic has a job as meta-theory of (database) programming here. The question is whether the paraconsistent *behaviour* of programmed systems is due to them following some kind of non-explosive logic or is due to them just working on restricted – supposedly consistent – sub-areas of the system/the data.
Resolution can work very well in an inconsistent theory, since proving the goal works its way only through subject related parts of the theory, so that some other part of the theory may well be inconsistent without ever coming into contact with the resolution going on.

GVII

Ginsberg has developed a 7-valued paraconsistent logic, called **VII**, that combines paraconsistency with non-monotonicity.
The truth values are: true, true by default, false, false by default, indetermined, indetermined by default, contradictory. The designated truth values are: true, and contradictory.
There is a strong negation meaning that there is positive evidence for the falsity of a statement, and there is a weak (finite failure) negation meaning that according to the stored state of knowledge the statement is false.
The conditional is designated if either the antecedent is not designated or the consequent is designated (just the standard behaviour).
Several standard theorems are not valid: Excluded Middle, Contraposition. DeMorgan Laws do not hold for weak negation. LNC does not hold for strong negation. *Modus Tollens* does not hold. Disjunctive Syllogism holds only for weak negation.
Modus Ponens, the Deduction Theorem, Contraction, Double Negation, Distribution Laws, Associativity and more all hold in **VII**.

QC

Anthony Hunter and Philippe Besnard have introduced the paraconsistent propositional logic **QC**. The logic is called "QC" for "quasi-classical". **QC** does not deal with defaults and is monotonic. (The intended application of

QC is to measure the amount of inconsistent information in a database by counting non-equivalent interpretations.)
QC works by taking the classical rules of natural deduction (dividing them into composition and decomposition rules) and imposing the constraint that (∨I) – as the one rules that introduces new and possibly Irrelevant sentence letters – and other composition rules are to be applied only after the decomposition rules have been applied.
QC by this (since no decomposition rule can be applied to an empty set of premises) has no theorems!
Further on the derivability relation of **QC** is not transitive!

Questions

(Q1) Why does the constraint defining **QC** block the standard derivation of *ex contradictione qoudlibet*?

(Q2) Apart from algebraic considerations, what may be a reason to have in **VII** for each truth value X a *simply X* and a *by default X* version, but not for the value of being contradictory?

(Q3) In case you are familiar with *normalization* as applied in typical (SQL) databases: Why does a violation of first and second degree normalization (of *primary* and *foreign keys*) come down to inconsistent data?

Excercises

(Ex1) In case you are familiar with PROLOG try to implement the typical "penguin Tweety is a bird" example so that in one version non-monotonicity is shown and in another version by use of a defined `non_fly(X)` predicate inconsistency occurs.

Further Reading

• On databases in general focussed to a typical commercial product cf. Soukup, Ron/Delaney, Kalen. *Inside Microsoft SQL Server*. 1999.
• On key concepts like *resolution* and *unification* see (Ben-Ari 1993).

• On PROLOG in general and negation as finite failure see Clocksin, W./Mellish, C. *Programming in Prolog*. Berlin et al., 3rd Ed. 1987.
• On paraconsistency as meta-theory see: (Damásio/Pereira 1998) and (Damásio 1996).
• On **QC** cf. Besnard, Philippe/Hunter, Anthony. "Quasi-classical Logic.", in: *Symbolic and Quantitative Approaches to Reasoning and Uncertainty*, Lecture Notes in Artificial Intelligence, 946, Berlin et al., 1995, pp. 44-51; Hunter's "Paraconsistent Logics", in: (Gabbay/Smets 1998); and: Wong, Paul/Besnard, Philippe. "Paraconsistent Reasoning as an Analytic Tool", *Logic Journal of the IGPL*, 9 (2001), pp. 217-29.
• On **VII** see: Ginsberg, M. "Multivalued Logics. A Uniform Approach to Inference in Artificial Intelligence", *Computer Intelligence*, 4 (1988), pp. 265-316.
• For SNePS look at: http://www.cse.buffalo.edu/sneps/.

20 | Universal Logic

There is no simple summary to all of paraconsistent logic, since there are so many paraconsistent logical systems, divergent approaches and applications. There is, however, an interesting question that may arise at least for a dialetheist: Are we to be logical relativists, choosing a different system for each different purpose, or shouldn't we – in the spirit of semantic closure, so to speak – look out for a system that is able to deal with all these purposes.

Such a system would be a *universal* logic.

For philosophy one might wish for a universal logic. Philosophy was taken here as a field of universal inquiry/reflection. In case universality is only possible with a severely restricted logic, however, all philosophical reasoning in the decisive fields – including this introduction – had to be recast in that logic, where many standard arguments simply do not go through. So on the other hand the universal logic in question should be *adaptive* to distinguish consistent from paraconsistent contexts. Standard logic should simply be correct – not only semi-correct [cf. (Priest 1987, pp.137-53)] – in consistent contexts.

Weak Universal Logic

A universal logic might be universal as a paraconsistent logic, i.e. in all fields in which we need *a paraconsistent* logic this logic can be employed and gives acceptable results. This may be called *the weak universalist program.*

One may take the weak universalist program as being extremely cautious: One takes one's favoured paraconsistent logics – and sticks to it in *all* contexts. Since this paraconsistent logic can deal with contradictory contexts it can deal with any context, so it really is universally applicable.

The problem with this extreme caution is that one loses all otherwise available consequences in consistent contexts. Therefore one rather tried to distinguish the type of context one is reasoning in. In praxis this meant that we employ standard First Order Logic for all non-semantic or non-antinomic contexts and switch to paraconsistency only in our formalization of complete semantics (or, maybe, set theory).

Strong Universal Logic

Or a truly universal logic can be employed everywhere, supposedly containing a way to distinguish consistent from inconsistent contexts, without loss of proper logical power in comparison to **FOL**. This may be called *the strong universalist program.*

In case philosophy contains consistent contexts and uses arguments valid only in consistent contexts it seems to need to follow either a strong universalist or a corresponding adaptive program [cf. Chap.7].

Both the LFI-approach and Adaptive Logics follow the idea to be able *within the system used* to distinguish contexts of a stronger logic (usually **FOL**) and contexts for a paraconsistent logic. The way they do it is completely different, however. In the LFI-approach the distinction what kind of context we have has to be given *beforehand*; only given the corresponding knowledge can we choose the appropriate formalization (i.e. use °A or not); in Adaptive Logics we mark the supposition that some formula has to be consistent, a supposition that may be *revised* in the process of reasoning; no prior knowledge about the consistency behaviour of a context is required.

Universal Logic 1

Richard Routley has in his (1979a) an appendix with the nice title "Ultralogic as Universal". He defines: "A universal logic, in the intended sense, is one which is applicable in every situation whether realised or, possible or not." So this idea is tied to question of modality and inconsistent ontology – and Routley's *noneism* [see Chap. 17].

Standard logic should be recaptured in those areas where it is valid, according to Routley. He keeps *Tertium Non Datur*, but claims that universal logic should allow for truth value gaps.

He proposes the Relevant system **DKQ** the first degree structures (i.e. without nested entailments) of which are those of the Relevant logic **RQ** (i.e. a quantified version of system **R**). [Remember from Chap. 5 that **R** contains all **PC**-theorems, for "⊃". *Modus Ponens* is only given for "→".]

The semantics of **RQ** needs something like the Routley Star and the ternary accessibility relation; **DKQ** has, according to Routley, no finite characteristic truth tables for its sentential part!

Given the last point one may better look elsewhere for universal logic.

Universal Logic 2

Brady's Logic $\mathbf{DJ^dQ}$ [cf. Chap. 5] is announced as a universal logic.
Brady explicitly says that the aim should be to have a universal logic and not chose one's logic for each department of research. Standard reasoning should be recaptured in consistent contexts, again.
In $\mathbf{DJ^dQ}$ neither Disjunctive Syllogism, nor Absorption, nor the *Modus Ponens*-Theorem (for "→") nor *Tertium Non Datur* are valid! So Brady introduces "classical sentences" (p', q' ...) for which Disjunctive Syllogism and *Tertium Non Datur* should hold.
Brady uses his system not just to avoid trivialization from antinomies, but to avoid the antinomies in the first place by the invalidity of *TND*! [The Liar and its negation are *both* taken as false, against the spirit of Convention (T) and what the Liar says, it seems.]
In this – two sorted – formal system the power of standard logic is indeed recaptured, but in the process of *formalization* we have to know already which sentences (or predicates) *are* "classical", i.e. consistent!
Negation Introduction may be a problem since in $\mathbf{DJ^dQ}$ not even:

$$(A \rightarrow \neg A) \rightarrow \neg A.$$

holds.

Universal Logic 3

Jean-Yves Beziau works on a programme he calls "universal logic"; but in his case the title is not meant as referring to some specific logical system, but to a study of the most universal features that logics have. Beziau's "universal logic" is rather a general theory of logics.
The key question is that enterprise is: "What have all logical systems in common?" or even simpler "What is logic?"
Beziau sees the common ground in the *abstract* idea of a *consequence relation* (abstract in the sense of not being specified by certain axioms or rules) and the abstract notion of a *non-trivial maximal set*, the set being maximal with respect to a consequence relation; non-triviality being the more universal notion than consistency (as in maximally consistent sets in standard model theory), as shown by paraconsistent logics.
The study of logics in this generality comprises the study of abstract/non-specific proof theory.
The general study of logics is even more general than the study of algebraic logical structures.

More Universal Logics

One may take one's favourite LFI-system or adaptive logic system as a universal logic. Both approaches have it as part of their official doctrine that it should be possible to recapture standard reasoning (remember da Costa's original idea, [Chap. 8]).

Proponents of the corresponding camps within paraconsistency (like Diderik Batens) are, however, outspoken logical particularists, i.e. they propose that one chooses a logic given a particular task or topic at hand.

We will not pick some particular of these systems here, since – as we have seen in Chap. 7 and Chap. 8 – both approaches have virtues and shortcomings in comparison to versions of **LP**.

So let us try a little mixing of ideas! As a little summary overview, and as a statement to a supposed universal logic, let us develop here a universal logic as a system of natural deduction with adaptive features and extended with operators of modalities and inconsistency with some relative of **LP** as the lower limit logic.

Universal Natural Deduction

The adaptive idea corresponds to the dynamic character of our knowledge concerning the consistency of some context; it also incorporates the *bona fide* epistemic principle that given no other information we should by default reason with the strongest available logic.

Natural deduction stays closer to the actual process of deriving consequences from premises than axiomatic systems, not to speak of trees and other *ex post* decision procedures (where you test a specific formalization of a specific supposed consequence).

Natural deduction – although redundantly – can often characterize the connectives by introduction and elimination rules that give the meaning of the connectives. It may be supplemented by axioms (rules with empty antecedents) and definitions.

For ease of application we develop a mixed system here, proposing rules for basic connectives, but also having some definitions.

We take the format of natural deduction shown in Chap.7: We number the line, then include in "< >" the number of *assumptions* this line depends on, then give the formula, then the operation by which this line was generated, then the set of formulas *presupposed* to be *true* (to apply the restricted rules, [see below]), and if needed the marked individual constants for the quantifier rules.

We built this system by using the following ingredients:

- an adaptive version of standard **PC** (cf. Minimal Inconsistent **LP**),
- quantifier rules in the vain of *Minimal Free Description Theory* (allowing for the use of descriptions, including those that are – as are some individual constants – non-referring),

- identity rules that restrict substitution to consistent objects,
- rules for a stronger conditional, whether we really need this or not,
- basic rules for modalities.

The system thus is dynamic and maybe incomplete; but it is a truly universal logic incorporating the basic ideas we have been going through in this book. We could call the logic "Adaptive Extended LP with Minmal Free Description Theory, restricted Identity, Basic Entailment and S5 Modalities" or "**ALPeMFDrIES5**" for short, or just **UL4**.

The definition of the language and the built up of derivations are as usual, with the modifications mentioned above.

A typical derivation looks similar to the one's already given in chapter 7.

We now give the rules for the connectives/quantifiers used in **UL4**. One may doubt whether they are all needed – as one may doubt whether one really needs modal logic or a modal entailment if there is an adaptive conditional already – but in any case we invest **UL4** with some extra expressive power, in case applications arise.

As mentioned, we do not follow the strict format of natural deduction in giving *only* the meaning of all connectives – as far as possible – in introduction and elimination rules. The benefit of using **LP** as our fall back paraconsistent logic is that all standard tautologies are **LP** valid. So we can simply include all **PC** tautologies in **UL4**!

UL4 Rules

Let us then go through the rules that define **UL4**. First notice that a line that reads:

n.< >   A

contains a *theorem*, since the sentence A does not depend on any assumption (the dependency set noted within "< >" is empty). Theorems can be introduced into derivations at any time.

[Letters "n", "m" etc. are used to refer to unspecified line numbers. Remember: "A" is a schematic letter, the object language having sentences like "p", "F(a)" etc.]

To include **PC**-tautologies, which we know already, we have the PC Rule:

n.< >   A   PC   ∅

where A is any **PC**-theorem. The column with markings is empty.

For any other theorems (i.e. already proven **UL4**-theorems) we have the Theorem Rule:

n.< >   A   TH   Γ

where A is any **UL4**-theorem. Γ contains the presuppositions. There cannot be a list of marked individual constants in theorems.
To introduce *assumptions* into a derivation we have the rule of Assumption Introduction:

(AE)	n.<n>	A	AE	$\varnothing$

Conjunction Introduction has the form:

n.<m>	A	...	Γ	
o.<k>	B	...	Λ	
p.<m,k>	$A \wedge B$		($\wedge$I) n, o	$\Gamma \cup \Lambda$

Conjunction Elimination has the two forms:

n.<m>	$A \wedge B$	...	Γ
o.<m>	A	($\wedge$E) n	Γ

n.<m>	$A \wedge B$	...	Γ
o.<m>	B	($\wedge$E) n	Γ

[Here and in the following rules "<m>" refers to an unspecific (number) of assumptions that the line depends on. Γ can, of course, be empty; if there are marked individual constants they are marked only in the line where the quantificational rule is employed, see below.]
Disjunction Introduction has the two forms:

n.<m>	A	...	Γ
o.<m>	$A \vee B$	($\vee$I) n	Γ

n.<m>	A	...	Γ
o.<m>	$B \vee A$	($\vee$I) n	Γ

Disjunction Elimination has the form:

n.<m>	$A \vee B$	...	Γ
o.<k>	$\neg A$	...	Λ
p.<m,k>	B	($\vee$E) n,o	$\Gamma \cup \Lambda \cup \{°A\}$

This is the restricted form of Disjunctive Syllogism.
Negation Introduction has the form:

n.<n>	A	AE	$\varnothing$
o.<m,n>	$\neg A$	...	Γ
p.<m>	$\neg A$	($\neg$I) n,o	Γ

If some assumption allows to derive its own negation, then this sentence can be stated negated *simpliciter* [i.e. the status as assumption is discharged, as indicated by the underlining in the line using (¬I)]. The usual form of Negation Introduction leads to trivialization in inconsistent contexts.

Negation Elimination has the form:

n.<m>	$\neg\neg A$	...	Γ
o.<m>	A	(¬E) n	Γ

This double negation elimination is anti-intuitionistic.

Conditional Introduction (*Conditionalization*) has the form:

n.<n>	A	AE	$\varnothing$
o.<m,n>	B	...	Γ
p.<m>	$A \supset B$	(⊃I) n,o	Γ

This rule mirrors the Deduction Theorem, which is valid both for **PC** and **LP**. If the conditionalization is the last step of a derivation the restrictions on not having marked individual constants in it have to be kept.

Conditional Elimination (*Modus Ponens*) has the form:

n.<m>	$A \supset B$	...	Γ
o.<k>	A	...	Λ
p.<m,k>	B	(⊃E) n,o	$\Gamma \cup \Lambda \cup \{^\circ A\}$

This is the restricted form of *Modus Ponens* corresponding to the restricted Disjunctive Syllogism. We have, of course:

$$\vdash_{UL4}(A \supset B) \equiv (\neg A \vee B)$$

The truth operators used in chapters 4 and 8 can be introduced as well, in a syntactically extended language. Truth Introduction/Elimination follow the disquotational (T)-schema. Strict Truth/Falsity will be defined notions. The Inconsistency operator is treated by rules as well.

Truth Introduction has the form:

n.<m>	A	...	Γ
o.<m>	TA	(TI) n	Γ

Truth Elimination is the converse:

n.<m>	TA	...	Γ
o.<m>	A	(TE) n	Γ

Falsity Introduction has the form:

n.<m>	$\neg A$	...	Γ
o.<m>	FA	(FI) n	Γ

Falsity Elimination is the converse:

n.<m>	FA	...	Γ
o.<m>	$\neg A$	(FE) n	Γ

Inconsistency Introduction has the form:

n.<m>	$A \wedge \neg A$	...	Γ
o.<m>	$^{\bullet}A$	($^{\bullet}$I) n	Γ

Inconsistency Elimination is the converse:

n.<m>	$^{\bullet}A$	...	Γ
o.<m>	$A \wedge \neg A \wedge \neg{}^{\circ}A$	($^{\bullet}$E) n	Γ

These two rules follow the idea that an "$^{\bullet}$" formula is a hidden conjunction [cf. Chap. 8]. For Simple Truth we introduce its version of Convention (T):

n.<>	$\Delta A \equiv A$	(Δ)	$\varnothing$

This works since detachment [as ($\supset$E) or ($\equiv$E)] and Contraposition are restricted to consistent sentences. Defining ΔA as $TA \wedge \neg FA$ will not do, since $TA \wedge \neg FA$ is true for antinomies! Restricting rules for "T" or "F" would leave the truth or falsity of antinomies inexpressible. The consistency operator "$^{\circ}$" is taken as defined notion then.
Necessity Introduction (*Necessitation*) has the form:

n.< >	A	...	Γ
o.< >	$\Box A$	($\Box$I) n	Γ

A theorem (but not any sentence depending on further assumptions) can be necessitated, like in *normal* modal logics.
Necessity Elimination has the form:

n.<m>	$\Box A$	...	Γ
o.<m>	A	($\Box$E) n	Γ

What is necessary is also the case. This corresponds to the basic axiom of standard modal logic **T**: $\Box A \supset A$.
Since necessity is taken here to be semantic necessity (not natural necessity or some more restricted version of necessity) it has to be governed in the way of a normal modal logic of the strength of modal system **S5**. Therefore we need two further rules for a normal modal logic. The K Rule corresponding to the K-Axiom of modal logic has the form:

n.<m>	$\Box(A \supset B)$	...	Γ
o.<k >	$\Box A \supset \Box B$	(K) n,o	Γ

Note that employing *Modus Ponens* now with $\Box A$ requires $\Box A$ to be consistent (otherwise provable contradictions would lead to triviality).

The <u>S5 Rule</u> corresponding to the **S5**-Axiom has the form:

n.<m>	$\Diamond A$	...	Γ
o.<m>	$\Box\Diamond A$	(S5) n	Γ

For (S5) it is not required that $\Diamond A$ is a theorem.
One may consider having also an entailment connective "$\rightarrow$". Whether one needs one is another question. The reason "$\rightarrow$" was introduced in the first part of this book was either that whereas principles failed for "$\supset$" one liked to have a conditional for which they hold, or that too Irrelevant consequences hold for "$\supset$". The latter reason has no force in the context of discussing universality: The more can be inferred the better may be the chances to capture consequences universally. The former reason is weakened by the adaptive approach: The principles we like to be valid sometimes are valid in these circumstances. So the *rationale* for having a further conditional connective is not clear.
Further on, the semantics considered for "$\rightarrow$" were mostly – with the possible exception of Brady's semantics of *contents* – not very convincing. The ternary accessibility relation may be sometimes/somewhat understood in information terms, but meaning relations are not adequately pictured thus.
Once one has a modal semantics for "$\rightarrow$", these modal frames should also provide the semantics for modal operators like "$\Box$".
Even **SKP** semantics is problematic then, since it [cf. Chap. 6] has to use a non-reflexive accessibility relation. If the modal accessibility relation is non-reflexive $\Box A \supset A$ is not valid, although it is one of the most intuitive principles concerning necessity. If the modal accessibility relation was reflexive, Absorption would not be invalid in **SKP**, however!
One could solves this problem by either distinguishing several modal accessibility relations between worlds (one for each modal basic notion) or by taking the conditional in the problematic cases of Curry like paradoxes to be "$\supset$" instead of "$\rightarrow$", so that *Modus Ponens* is not in general valid and trivialization is blocked [cf. Chap. 3]. Both options are not satisfactory.
Thus one may add some weak principles of entailment (like natural deduction versions of the sequent rules of **SKP**) *or* – and that is the approach I favour – one takes entailment like in standard modal logic to be *semantic entailment* in the sense that: $A \rightarrow B \Leftrightarrow \Box(A \supset B)$.
Taking entailment to be *semantic entailment* in the sense that:

$$A \rightarrow B \Leftrightarrow_{UL4} \Box(A \supset B)$$

gives us *derived* introduction and elimination rules for "$\rightarrow$".

Entailment Introduction is a strict form of Conditionalization:

n.<n>	A	AE	$\varnothing$
o.<o>	B	AE	$\varnothing$
...			
r.<n,o>	C	...	Γ
s.< >	$A \wedge B \rightarrow C$	$(\rightarrow I)$ $\underline{n},\underline{o}$,r	Γ

In strict conditionalization all assumptions have to be conditionalized (thus we get a theorem to be necessitated to yield the entailment).
Entailment Elimination is a version of *Modus Ponens*:

n.<m>	$A \rightarrow C$	...	Γ
o.<k>	A	...	Λ
p.<m,k>	C	$(\rightarrow E)$ n,o	$\Gamma \cup \Lambda \cup \{°A\}$

Since Entailment Elimination is a version of *Modus Ponens* it is not valid in inconsistent contexts, so there is not a universally valid version of *Modus Ponens*, even if semantic entailment is around.
This might be a reason to take "$\rightarrow$" not to be semantic entailment, but a Relevant conditional, characterized by the principles of some Relevant Logic, such that *Modus Ponens* holds universally – even in inconsistent contexts. This would cover the intuition that there are no exceptions at all to *Modus Ponens*.
We introduce some further connectives just by definitions. There are, of course, derivable introduction and elimination rules then.
Within a derivation we use the definitions by referring to their name:

(D$\equiv$) $A \equiv B \overset{\text{def}}{=} (A \supset B) \wedge (B \supset A)$

(D$\leftrightarrow$) $A \leftrightarrow B \overset{\text{def}}{=} (A \rightarrow B) \wedge (B \rightarrow A)$

(D$\Diamond$) $\Diamond A \overset{\text{def}}{=} \neg\Box\neg A$

(D∇) $\nabla A \overset{\text{def}}{=} \Delta\neg A$

(D°) $°A \overset{\text{def}}{=} \Delta A \vee \nabla A$

(D$\top$) $\top \overset{\text{def}}{=} (A \vee \neg A)$

(D$\bot$) $\bot \overset{\text{def}}{=} \nabla(A \vee \neg A)$

We use a quantificational logic in the manner of Minimal Free Description Theory. This version of Free Logic maintains that we may use individual expression – especially descriptions – that do not refer.

Given these non-referring expressions the quantificational rules have to be revised, since one can only generalize from an arbitrary *existing* object or specify to an arbitrary objects if one knows that this object exists.
The objects are divided into the mere *possible objects* and the *existing objects*. The existing objects give the domain of a given possible world.
One may consider the broader domain as comprising just names and descriptions, and the existence claim as saying that some name or description is instantiated, thus avoiding the ontologically controversial *possibilia*, but this is a debate independent from paraconsistency, so let us just follow the usual modelling here.
We have to give the usual requirements on marking individual terms in case of applying Universal Generalization or Existential Specialization within a derivation [cf. for example (Quine 1974), (Essler/Martinez 1991)]. These are:

- terms generalized in Universal Generalization and specialized to in Existential Specialization are *marked* at the *right* of such a line,
- the marking also notes the dependencies on other individual terms in that line (in the form "a(e)" "a" being marked depended on "e"),
- markings may not be circular (i.e. we do not have "a(e)" *and* "e(a)"),
- no term may be marked twice,
- marked terms may neither occur in the premises nor in the conclusion of a supposed valid derivation.

In applications of the quantifier rules one also has to meet the requirement that by generalising one constant to a variable "x", "x" will not be bound by already otherwise existing quantifiers. (∀I) and (∃I) require further on that "x" and the individual term occur at *exactly* the same places in a given sentence.
E!(á) says that the object denoted by á exists, "E!( )" being the existence predicate. [Of course it is a logical constant (i.e. not free for substitution).]
Quantifiers refer to existing objects only. "(∃x)F(x)" really means there is an *existing* objects that is F.
As **FOL** does implicitly – by demanding that the domain is not empty – here we also assume that there *is* something, the Existence Assumption:[40]

n.< >   (∃x)E!(x)   (E!)   ∅

[40] There are versions of Free Logic (so called "Universally Free Logics") that do not assume that anything exists whatever – so making logic free of any assumptions of existence – but they have hardly any interesting applications, of course.

Identity Introduction is valid for any object, existing or not:

n.< >	$a = a$	(=I)	$\varnothing$

Identity Elimination (i.e. substitution of identicals) is more critical. It has to be restricted to avoid trivialization in a paraconsistent logic with as much expressive power as **UL4**.

We have to presuppose that some object is not an inconsistent object to apply (=E) to it. We define a *consistency predicate* "K( )" for objects (as a logical constant, of course) to do this:

(DK) $K(á) \stackrel{\text{def}}{=} \neg(\exists P)(P(á) \wedge \neg P(á))$

UL4 is no 2nd order system, but we may employ (DK) in that way that we note $\neg K(á)$ in some line if for the object named á we could have a line with an instance of the scheme: $P(á) \wedge \neg P(á)$.

Identity Elimination then takes the form:

n.<m>	$P(á)$	...	Γ
o.<k>	$á = é$	...	Λ
p.<m,k>	$P(é)$	(=E) n,o	$\Gamma \cup \Lambda \cup \{K(é)\}$

Since we want to use description and modal operators we have to provide (=E) with a *provisio* in case descriptions are involved.

In modal logic **S5** all modalities can be reduced to modalities of degree 1 (i.e. all modal operators except the most right ones can be dropped [cf. Hughes/Cresswell 1990, pp. 51-54]).

We require as a *provisio* for Identity Elimination:

In case we have $á = é$, then

(i) if á is a description and é an individual constant, é cannot be substituted into a modal context of "$\Diamond$",

(ii) if á is an individual constant and é a description, é cannot be substituted into a modal context of "$\Box$".

Thus we avoid the typical counterexamples to modal (=E):

(1)	The-number-of-planetes = 9
(2)	$\Box(9 > 7)$
(3)	$\Diamond$(The-number-of-planets > 9)
(*)	$\Box$(The-number-of-planets > 7)
(**)	$\Diamond(9 > 9)$

The following quantifier rules require following the rules of marking the constant generalized/specialized in (∀I) and (∃E), and the renaming of variables mentioned before. Relations are used here to show the case of marking dependencies.

∀-Introduction (Universal Generalization) has the form:

n.<m>	R(á,é)	...	Γ	
o.<m>	(∀x)R(x,é)	(∀I),n	Γ ∪ {E!(á)}	á(é)

Thus the application of (∀I) requires an existence assumption concerning á, since we conclude to a generalization about all *existing* objects. á is marked, here as depending on é.

∀-Elimination (Universal Instantiation) has the form:

n.<m>	(∀x)P(x)	...	Γ
o.<m>	P(é)	(∀E),n	Γ ∪ {E!(é)}

Since the generalization is (maybe) true of existing objects only the application of (∀E) presupposes that the constant specialized to names an existing object.

∃-Introduction (Existential Generalization) has the form:

n.<m>	P(á)	...	Γ
o.<m>	(∃x)P(x)	(∃I),n	Γ ∪ {E!(á)}

Thus the application of (∃I) requires an existence assumption concerning á, since we conclude to a generalization about some *existing* objects.

∃-Elimination (Existential Instantiation) has the form:

n.<m>	(∃x)R(x,á)	...	Γ	
o.<m>	R(é,á)	(∃E),n	Γ ∪ {E!(é)}	é(á)

Since the generalization is (maybe) true of existing objects only the application of (∃E) presupposes that the variable is specialized to a name of an existing object. The name of the object is marked in its dependencies in the formula in question.

Minimal Free Description theory allows that there are non-referring names and descriptions. It assume that there is something [see (E!)]. It requires the uniqueness of a description with respect to the existing objects only – so to say: if the thing does not exist, the question of its uniqueness does not arise. Otherwise it looks like the standard Russellian account of descriptions.

We use the usual "ι"-notation, so that "ιxF(x)" means "*the* (unique) F". The (MFD) Rule can be stated as the following two ways of interchangability:

n.<m>	$\iota x P(x) = \acute{a}$	...	Γ
o.<m>	$(\forall y)(\acute{a}=y \equiv P(y) \wedge (\forall z)(P(z) \supset z=y)$	(MFD),n	Γ

n.<m>	$(\forall y)(\acute{a}=y \equiv P(y) \wedge (\forall z)(P(z) \supset z=y)$	...	Γ
o.<m>	$\iota x P(x) = \acute{a}$	(MFD),n	Γ

The first conjunct in the equivalence states satisfaction of the defining property, the second expresses uniqueness.

In the context of quantificational rules we can now make clear the reference to a set of *presuppositions* above.

Adaptive Logics speak of Dab-formula and corresponding sets of consistency assumptions. In **UL4** we note these consistency assumptions as presuppositions to employ some restricted rules. Actually the consistency presupposition is "°A".

In Minimal Free Description Theory usually a conjunct "E!(a)" is needed (e.g. as derivable line or *assumption*) to employ one of the quantifier rules. Since **UL4** is a dynamic logic already we need not work with "E!(a)" as a line in a derivation, but can note this also as a presupposition in the presupposition set Γ noted on the right. [This save us some work within the derivation and makes them more similar to standard ones. Existence presuppositions are dynamic!]

In case of Identity Elimination the presupposition is that we have a consistent object. We note this as the presupposition "K(a)" for an object a in question.

Each of the sentences in the presupposition set has a negation. Once the negation of such a presupposition can be derived, all lines are retracted which depend on that presupposition (like in the original adaptive dynamics). The retraction thus does not only concern the disappointment of consistency assumptions (either for a sentence or an object), but also the disappointment of existence presuppositions.

If the last line A of a derivation has a non-empty presupposition set Γ, this means that the sentence in that line is derivable from the assumptions noted within "< >" given these further presuppositions.

Let Φ be the (possibly empty) set of assumptions and Γ the (possibly empty) set of presuppositions. We have:

$$\neg(\exists B \in \Gamma)\ \Phi \vdash_{\mathbf{UL4}} \neg B \Rightarrow \Phi \vdash_{\mathbf{UL4}} A$$

To save labour and have derivation looking more closely like standard derivations we adopt the convention to drop noting Γ if Γ is empty.

UL4 – Examples!

Let us see some examples of **UL4**-derivations!
The first shows a principle of interchange given an object is the unique F:

1.<1>	$G(\iota xF(x))$	AE	
2.<2>	$a = \iota xF(x)$	AE	
3.<2>	$G(a)$	$(=E)$	$\{K(a)\}$
4.<1>	$a = \iota xF(x) \supset G(a)$	$(\supset I)\underline{2},3$	$\{K(a)\}$
5.<>	$G(\iota xF(x)) \supset (a = \iota xF(x) \supset G(a))$	$(\supset I)\underline{1},4$	$\{K(a)\}$

Descriptions carry no existence assumptions themselves, thus:

1.<1>	$a = \iota xF(x)$	AE	
2.<1>	$(\forall y)(a=y \equiv F(y) \wedge (\forall z)(F(z) \supset z=y)$	MFD,1	
3.<1>	$a=a \equiv F(a) \wedge (\forall z)(F(z) \supset z=a)$	$(\forall E)2$	$\{E!(a)\}$
4.<>	$a=a$	$(=I)$	
5.<1>	$F(a) \wedge (\forall z)(F(z) \supset z=a)$	$(\supset E)3$	$\{E!(a),°(a=a)\}$
6.<1>	$F(a)$	$(\wedge E)5$	$\{E!(a),°(a=a)\}$
7.<1>	$(\exists x)F(x)$	$(\exists E)6$	$\{E!(a),°(a=a)\}$
8.<>	$a = \iota xF(x) \supset (\exists x)F(x)$	$(\supset E)\underline{1},7$	$\{E!(a),°(a=a)\}$

Proving a duality:

1.<1>	p	AE	
2.<>	$p \supset \neg\neg p$	PC	
3.<1>	$\neg\neg p$	$(\supset E)1,2$	$\{°p\}$
4.<2>	$\neg p \vee q$	AE	
5.<1,2>	q	$(\vee E)3,4$	$\{°p,°\neg\neg p\}$
6.<2>	$p \supset q$	$(\supset I)\underline{1},5$	$\{°p,°\neg\neg p\}$
7.<>	$(\neg p \vee q) \supset (p \supset q)$	$(\supset I)\underline{2},6$	$\{°p,°\neg\neg p\}$

Proving something this way doesn't make too much sense, since one could have (7) by **PC**, detachment requires "$°(\neg p \vee q)$" anyway.
So that some sentence is provable given some assumptions relative to some presuppositions does not mean that there is no other derivation which does not make so many presuppositions.

Proving some modal theorem:

1.<>	$\Diamond\neg p \supset \Box\Diamond\neg p$	$(S5)(\supset I)$	
2.<>	$\neg\Box\Diamond\neg p \supset \neg\Diamond\neg p$	$(PC)(\supset E)1$	$\{°(\Diamond\neg p \supset \Box\Diamond\neg p)\}$
3.<>	$\Diamond\Box p \supset \Box p$	$(D\Diamond)2$	$\{°(\Diamond\neg p \supset \Box\Diamond\neg p)\}$
4.<>	$\Box p \supset \Diamond\Box p$	(TH)	

5.<>	$\Box p \supset \Box\Box p$	$(\supset E)(\supset I)3,4\ \{°\Box p, °(\Diamond\neg p \supset \Box\Diamond\neg p)\}$
6.<6>	$\Box p$	AE
7.<6>	p	$(\Box E)6$
8.<6>	$p \lor q$	$(\lor I)7$
9.< >	$\Box p \supset p \lor q$	$(\supset I)\underline{6},8$
10.< >	$\Box(\Box p \supset p \lor q)$	$(\Box I)9$
11.<>	$\Box\Box p \supset \Box(p \lor q)$	(K)10
12.<>	$\Box p \supset \Box(p \lor q)$	$(\supset E)(\supset I)\ 5,11\ \{°\Box p, °(\Diamond\neg p \supset \Box\Diamond\neg p)\}$

"$(\supset E)(\supset I)$" abbreviates an application of *transitivity* (with a temporary assumption to the antecedent of the first conditional). The restrictions on *Modus Ponens* may – like in this example – introduce a long list of presuppositions, sometimes even requiring consistency of *theorems*.

UL4 – Consequence

I will not go into the details of UL4-semantics here; it is a combination of the extensional semantics for the truth-functional junctors of an extended **LP** we have seen in Chap. 4 with the modal ersatzism of a quantificational semantics in the vain of the Minimal Free Description Theory [see *Further Reading*]. The correctness of **UL4** results from combining the relevant parts of the corresponding correctness proofs. Obviously

$$\nvDash_{UL4} \nabla \mathrm{T}$$

and thus with the – supposed – correctness of **UL4** we have its non-triviality. We make use here of a more restricted definition of consequence. Consequence in **UL4** is defined:

$\Gamma \vDash_{UL4} A$ iff
in case that all $B \in \Gamma$ are true at least, then A is true at least.

Nothing needs to be said concerning the case that any $B \in \Gamma$ is false *only*. One has not to hold that then a consequence relationship holds. To do so would be Irrelevant.
To do so may come close to reintroducing Explosion, as well. ΔA and ∇A are incompatible, so both can never be true at the same time, so allowing for Irrelevant consequences would yield, for example,

$$(*)\ \nabla A, \mathrm{T}A \vDash_{UL4} C$$

for any C.

Suppose a Liar like:

(λ) $\nabla\lambda$

Luckily the following derivation is *not* **UL4** valid:

1.	$T\lambda \vee \neg T\lambda$	(PC)
2.	$T\lambda \supset \lambda$	Convention (T)
3.	$\neg T\lambda \supset \nabla\lambda$	Definition "∇"
4.	$\nabla\lambda \wedge T\lambda$	1,2,3, Convention (T), Definition λ

UL4 – Assessment

This universal logic **UL4** has several merits:

- it is paraconsistent, correct and non-trivial,
- it may model inconsistent ontology – if needed,
- it obeys Convention (T) with disquotational "T"-rules,
- it expresses (in)consistency within the language – if needed,
- it is as standard a logic as possible without trivialization, so fulfils the methodological criteria of chapter 3,
- it does not validate *Modus Ponens* in general, so avoids Curry's Paradox,
- it does not validate Contraposition in general, so dialetheism is not a dialetheia itself,
- it restricts substitution of identicals, so can avoid hypercontradictions,
- replacement of provably equivalents [$A \dashv\vdash B$] holds, but not replacement of proven equivalents [$\vdash A \equiv B$].

The main shortcoming of **UL4** – as an adaptive logic – is that its provability relation is not recursively enumerable, because of its dynamic.

Questions

(Q1) Why does the usual form of Negation Introduction lead to trivialization in inconsistent contexts? The rule is:

n.<n>	A	...	$\varnothing$
o.<m,n>	$\neg B \wedge B$	...	Γ
p.<m>	$\neg A$	$(\neg I)$ n,o	Γ

(Q2) Why do we have to assume that A is consistent in Entailment Elimination in **UL4**?

(Q3) Why can't we have the LFI-style definition of "°" in **UL4**?

$$(D^\circ)\ {}^\circ A \overset{\text{def}}{\equiv} \neg{}^\bullet A$$

(Q4) Why can we have replacement of provably equivalents in **UL4**, but not replacement of proven equivalents [$\vdash A \equiv B$]?

(Q5) Even though "a=a" we note in **UL4** the presupposition of its consistency "°a=a" if required by some rule. Why can't we drop this in case even of theorems?

Exercises

(Ex1) State the introduction and elimination rules corresponding to $(D\equiv)$, $(D\Delta)$, $(D\nabla)$ and $(D\leftrightarrow)$ in **UL4**.

(Ex2) Why does the Liar reasoning concerning $\nabla\lambda$ not go through in **UL4**?

(Ex3) Prove the sentence in the right column from the premises in the left. What presuppositions do you need?

$p \supset p, \neg q$	$\neg p$
$\neg p, \neg q$	$\neg(p \vee q)$
$p \supset q$	$(q \supset r) \supset (p \supset r)$
$p \vee q, p \supset r, q \supset r$	r

	$(\forall x)E!(x)$
$(\forall x)F(x)$	$\neg(\exists x)\neg F(x)$
$(\forall x)(F(x) \supset G(x))$	$(\forall x)F(x) \supset G(x)$

Further Reading

• On the Relevant Logics of Routley and Brady see Chap. 5.

• On Beziau's work see his (1995) and his self-description "From Paraconsistent Logic to Universal Logic", a version of which appeared in: *Sorites*, 12 (2001), pp. 12-32. One may see (Wolenski 1995) as an exercise in universalizing logic in that Wolenski argues that logic is not mainly concerned with inheriting truth but designated values even if the designated value of a "dual logic" was falsity.

• On Minimal Free Description Theory see the essays in (Lambert 1991); on the format of natural deduction used here and the ersatzist interpretation of outer and inner domain see (Bremer 2000a); on Priest's own version of a Free Logic variant of **LP** see (Priest 1999).

Epilogue

This introduction has covered several fields in which paraconsistency is explored and developed. We have seen its merits, but also some problems and unsolved questions in these areas. Paraconsistent logics are more and more becoming an acceptable tool of work in the formal sciences and in modelling in the cognitive sciences and philosophy. With that development the fields of application are increasing.
Problems so far unresolved or difficult to approach in meta-ethics or epistemology may gain from a fresh look from the paraconsistent perspective – not to speak of semantics and meta-logic itself.
The major decisions to be made are:

1. The decision whether one goes for a pluralism of logics from the different camps of paraconsistency or one tries to give a unified treatment of consistency related topics with one universally applied logic.
2. The decision which of the approaches within paraconsistency seems to be on the one hand the most promising and on the other hand the one that keeps closest to our (philosophical) intuitions.

See the Evil in Beauty

Standard logic is dear to most raised in it and realising the beauty of its proofs and the naturalness of much of its semantics.
First Order Logic and (some) realism is where many philosopher's heart rests.
Even the limitative theorems of meta-logic are revealing insights about language and logic then.
Wait – are they really? Here the problems start. We are not talking about language in general here, we get messed up in the troubles of the hierarchies of ever higher meta-languages without even being able to state either something (semantic) about logic and language *in general* or merely explaining what *we are doing* at the moment.
Our fascination with beauty now put into question we see more problems around: Is the material conditional the natural conditional after all? Is it really true that we cannot believe something inconsistent without falling into triviality immediately?
And then: Has beauty blinded us to forego one set for each condition? Isn't there not just one universal set of truths dealing with everything?

See the Beauty in Evil

Hearing of true contradictions for the first time may make your mind boggle: How could anyone believe this? Hasn't she falling through the rock bottom of rationality? – and so on.

Believing in true contradictions – further on – has an embarrassing tradition in philosophy, theories one rather does not associate with.

Nevertheless, if you are (some) realist and given you stick to universality in logic and semantics – against the luring of first order beauties – then you take what you get by this: dialetheism.

One of the deeper meta-insights on philosophy is: Every philosophical system has its quandaries and implausibilities, the only question is *where* they are located.

The aim of this introduction was to argue that paraconsistency in general – and dialetheism especially – has the better overall coherence than does a thorough going adherence to standard logic.

As a dialetheist for universal semantics and logic and (mild) realist with reductionist leanings you can avoid instrumentalism, (strong) anti-realism, belief in (manifolds) of queer truth values, truth value gaps, ineffable concepts, abstract objects or whatever strange ontology is in store – just in case you accept that some sentences are true and false at the same time.

So now that you have gone over the edge into the abyss of logical evil, revel in it!

Further References

These references supplement the "Further Reading" list of each chapter, and contain work referred to at some point in the presentation. Items of the "Further Reading" section are mostly not listed again here.

Aczel, Peter (1988). *Non-Well-Founded Sets*. Stanford.

Akama, Seiki (1998). "Nelson's Paraconsistent Logics", manuscript, 12 pp. (read at the Stanislaw Jaskowski Memorial Symposium, Torun, 1998).

Al-Hibri, Azizah (1978). *Deontic Logic*. Washington.

Alves, Elias (1992). "The First Axiomatization of a Paraconsistent Logic", *Bulletin of the Section of Logic*, 21, pp. 19-20.

Anderson, Alan/Belnap, Nuel/Dunn, Michael (1992). *Entailment*. The Logic of Relevance and Necessity. Princeton, Vol. II 1992.

Aqvist, Lennart (1987). *Introduction to Deontic Logic and the Theory of Normative Systems*. Neapels.

Armour-Garb, Bradley/Beall, J.C. (2003). "Minimalism and the Dialetheic Challenge", *Australasian Journal of Philosophy*, 81, pp. 383-401.

Arruda, Ayda (1989). "Aspects of the Historical Development of Paraconsistent Logic", in: (Priest/Routley/Norman 1989), pp. 99-130.

-/da Costa, Newton (1984). "On the Relevant Systems P and P* and Some Related Systems", *Studia Logica*, pp. 33-49.

Avila, B./Abe, J./Prado, J. (1997). "Reasoning in Paraconsistent Frame Systems", in: Siriruchatapong, Z./Barthes, J. (Eds.) *The Second International Workshop on CSCW in Design*. Bangkok, pp. 239-44.

Avron, Arnon (200x). "Combining Classical Logic, Paraconsistency and Relevance", *Journal of Applied Logic*, forthcoming.

Batens, Diderik (1989). "Dynamic Dialectical Logics", in: (Priest/Routley/Normann 1989), pp. 187-217.

Batens, Diderik et. al. (1999). (Eds.) *Frontiers of Paraconsistent Logic*. Baldock.

Barwise, Jon/Seligman, Jerry (1997). *Information Flow*. The Logic of Distributed Systems. Cambridge.

Bazhanov, V. (1998). "Towards the Reconstruction of the Early History of Paraconsistent Logic", *Logique et Analyse*, 161, pp. 17-20.

Beall, J.C./van Fraasen, Bas (2003). *Possibilities and Paradox*. An Introduction to Modal and Many-Valued Logic. Oxford.

Ben-Ari, M. (1993). *Mathematical Logic for Computer Science*, New York et. al.

Benassi, Corrado/Gentilini, Paolo (2003). "Paraconsistent Provability Logic and Rational Epistemic Agents", manuscript, 38 pp. (read at the Third World Congress on Paraconsistency, Toulouse, 2003).

Bendegem, Jean van (1993). "The Strong Hilbert Program", *Revue International Philosophie*, 47, pp. 343-53.

Bender, John (1989). (Ed.) *The Current State of the Coherence Theory*. Critical Essays on the Epistemic Theories of Keith Lehrer and Laurence BonJour with Replies. Dordrecht et al.

Bentham, Jeremy van (1979). "What is Dialectical Logic?", *Erkenntnis*, 14, pp. 333-47.

Berk, Lon (2003). "Why the Liar Does Not Matter", *Journal of Philosophical Logic*, 32, pp. 323-41.

Besnard, Philippe (1989). *An Introduction to Default Logic*. Berlin.

Beziau, Jean-Yves (1995). "Universal Logic", in: Childers, T./Majer, O. (Eds.) *Logica '94*. Prague, 1995, pp. 73-94.

- (2002). "Are Paraconsistent Negations Negations?", in: (Carnielli/Coniglio/D'Ottavanio 2002), pp.465-86.

Blau, Ulrich (1978). *Die dreiwertige Logik der Sprache*. Berlin/New York.

Bloesch, Anthony (1993). "A Tableau Style Proof System for Two Paraconsistent Logics", *Notre Dame Journal of Symbolic Logic*, pp. 295-301.

Bochvar, D. (1939). "On a Three-Valued Calculus and Its Application to the Analysis of Contradictories", *Mathematceskij Sbornik*, 4, pp. 287-308.

BonJour, Laurence (1985). *The Structure of Empirical Knowledge*. Cambrige MA/London.

Boolos, George/Jeffrey, Richard (1989). *Computability and Logic*. Cambridge, 3rd Ed.

Brady, Ross (1984). "Depth Relevance of Some Paraconsistent Logics", *Studia Logica*.

- (1996). "Relevant implication and the case for a weaker logic", *Journal of Philosophical Logic*, 25, pp.151-83.

- (2000). "Entailment, Negation and Paradox Resolution", in: Batens et al. (2000), pp.113-36.

Bremer, Manuel (1998). *Wahre Widersprüche*. Einführung in die parakonsistente Logik. Sankt Augustin.

- (1999). "Can Contradictions Be Asserted?", *Logic and Logical Philosophy*, 7, pp. 167-77.

- (1999a). "Truth in Internal Realism", in: Nida-Rümelin, Julian (Ed.). *Rationality, Realism and Revision,* Paderborn.

- (1999b). "Die Welt ist die Gesamtheit der Tatsachen, nicht der Dinge", *Grazer Philosophische Studien*, pp. 111-32.

- (2000). "Wahrheit im Internen Realismus", *Philosophisches Jahrbuch*, pp.30-46.

- (2000a). "Possibilia. Notwendig, möglich – oder überflüssig?", *Metaphysica*, Special Issue 1, pp. 49-72.

- (200x). "Hypercontradictions".

- /Cohnitz, Daniel (2004). *Information and Information Flow*. An Introduction. Frankfurt a.M.

Brendel, Elke (1992). *Die Wahrheit über den Lügner*. Eine philosophisch-logische Analyse der Antinomie des Lügners. Berlin/New York.

Brewka, Gerhard (1991). *Nonmonotonic Reasoning*: Logical Foundations of Commonsense. Cambridge.

Bromand, Joachim (2001). *Philosophie der semantischen Paradoxien*. Paderborn.

Bueno, Otávio (2002). "Can a Paraconsistent Theorist Be a Logical Monist?", in: (Carnielli/Coniglio/Ottavanio 2002), pp. 525-51.

Carnap, Rudolf (1933). *Die logische Syntax der Sprache*. Wien.

Carnielli, Walter (2000). "Possible-Translation Semantics for Paraconsistent Logics", in: (Batens et. al. 2000), pp. 149-64.

- /Coniglio, Marcelo/D'Ottavanio, Itala (2002). (Eds.) *Paraconsistency*. The Logical Way to the Inconsistent. New York/Basel.

- /Marcos, Joao (2002). "A Taxonomy of C-sytems", in: (Carnielli/Coniglio/D'Ottavanio 2002), pp.1-94.

Cherniak, Christopher (1986). *Minimal Rationality*. Cambridge/MA.

Church, Alonzo (1974). "Set Theory with a Universal Set", *Proceedings of Symposia in Pure Mathematics*, 25, pp.297-308.

Da Costa, Newton (1974). "On the Theory of Inconsistent Formal Systems", *Notre Dame Journal of Formal Logic*, 15, pp. 497-510.

Damásio, Carlos (1996). *Paraconsistent Extended Logic Programming with Constraints*. Thesis, University of Lissabon.

- /Pereira, Luís. (1998). "A Survey of Paraconsistent Semantics for Logic Programs", in: (Gabbay/Smets 1998), pp. 241-320.Davidson, Donald (1967). "Truth and Meaning", *Synthese*, 17, pp.304-23.

Devlin, Keith (1991). *Logic and Information*. Cambridge/MA.

Epstein, Richard (1995). *The Semantic Foundations of Logic*. Propositional Logics. New York, 2nd Edition.

Essler, Wilhelm/Martinez, Rosa (1991). *Grundzüge der Logik*. Vol. I. Das Schließen. Frankfurt a.M., 4th Ed.

Everett, Anthony (1993). "A Note on Priest´s 'Hypercontradictions'", *Logique et Analyse*, pp. 39-43

Fuhrmann, Andre (1985). "Ein relevanzlogischer Dialogkalkül Erster Stufe", *Conceptus*, 19, pp. 51-65.

- (1991). "Theory Contraction Through Base Contraction", *Journal of Philosophical Logic*, 20.

Gabbay, D./Smets, P. (1998). (Eds.) *Handbook of Defeasible Reasoning and Uncertainty Management Systems*. Vol. 2. Dordrecht.

Gärdenfors, Peter (1988). *Knowledge in Flux*. Cambridge/MA.

Geach, Peter (1954/55). "On Insolubilia", *Analysis*, 15.

Gentzen, G. (1934/35). "Untersuchungen über das logische Schließen", *Mathematische Zeitschrift*, pp.176-210, pp. 405-31.

Gibbins, P. (1981). "Putnam on the Two-Slit Experiment", *Erkenntnis*, 16, pp. 235-41.

Goble, Lou (2001). (Ed.) *The Blackwell Guide to Philosophical Logic*. Oxford.
Goldblatt, Robert (1992). *Logics of Time and Computation*. Standford, 2nd Ed.
Goodship, Laura (1996). "On Dialethism", *Australasian Journal of Philosophy*, 74.
Grim, Patrick (1991). *The Incomplete Universe*. Totality, Knowledge and Truth. Cambridge/MA.
- (1993). "Operators in the Paradox of the Knower", *Synthese*, 94, pp. 409-28.
Günther, Arnold (1995). "Paradoxien und parakonsistente Logiken", *Zeitschrift für Semiotik*, 17, pp. 379-403.
Hack, Susan (1978). *Philosophy of Logics*. Cambridge et al.
Harman, Gilbert (1986). *Change in View*. Principles of Reasoning. Cambridge/MA.
Hintikka, Jaakko (1970). "Surface Information and Depth Information", in: Hintikka, J./Suppes, P. (eds.) *Information and Inference*. Dordrecht.
- (1973). *Logic, Language-Games and Information*. Oxford.
Hughes, G./Cresswell, M. (1990). *An Introduction to Modal Logic*. London/New York, 7th Ed.
Hunter, Geoffrey (1996). *Metalogic*. An Introduction to the Metatheory of Standard First Order Logic. Berkeley, 6th Ed.
Jacquette, Dale (2002). (Ed.) *A Companion to Philosophical Logic*. Oxford.
Jaskowski, S. (1969). "Propositional Calculus for Contradictory Deductive Systems", *Studia Logica*, 24, pp. 143-57.
Kaplan, David/Montague, Richard (1960). "A Paradox Regained", *Notre Dame Journal of Formal Logic*, 1, pp. 79-90.
Koons, Robert (1992). *Paradoxes of Belief and Strategic Rationality*. Cambridge/MA.
Kripke, Saul (1975). "Outline of a Theory of Truth", *Journal of Philosophy*, 72, pp. 690-716.
Lambert, Karel (1983). *Meinong and the Principle of Independence*. Cambridge et al.
- (1991). (Ed.) *Philosophical Applications of Free Logic*. New York/Oxford.
Lavine, Stephen (1998). *Understanding the Infinite*. Cambridge/MA, 2nd Ed.
Lenzen, Wolfgang (1980). *Glauben, Wissen und Wahrscheinlichkeit. Systeme der epistemischen Logik*. Berlin/New York.
- (1998). "Necessary Conditions for Negation-Operators (with Particular Applications to Paraconsistent Negation)", in: (Gabbay/Smets 1998), pp. 211-39.
Lorenzen, Paul/Lorenz, Kuno (1978). *Dialogische Logik*. Darmstadt.
Marquis, Pierre/Coste-Marquis, Sylvie (2002). "Complexity Results for Paraconsistent Inference Relations", in: Fensel, Dieter et. al. (Eds.): *Proceedings of the Eights International Conference on Principles and Knowledge Representation and Reasoning*, (KR-02), Toulouse, pp. 61-72.
Meheus, Joke (2002) (Ed.). *Inconsistency in Science*. Dordrecht.

Meyer, R./Slaney, J. (1989). "Abelian Logic (from A to Z)", in: Priest/Routley/Norman (1989), pp. 259-71.
Miller, Arthur (2002). "Inconsistent Reasoning Towards Consistent Theories", in: Meheus (2002), pp. 35-41.
Milne, Peter (1996). "On Tennant's Intuitionist Relevant Logics", *Australasian Journal of Philosophy*, 74, pp. 175-81.
Moore, A.W. (1990). *The Infinite*. London/New York.
Nelson, David (1949). "Constructible Falsity", *The Journal of Symbolic Logic*, 14, pp. 16-26.
- (1959). "Negation and Separation of Concepts in Constructive Systems", in: Heyting, A. (Ed.) *Constructivity in Mathematics*. Amsterdam, pp. 208-25.
Pardey, Ulrich (1994). *Identität, Existenz und Reflexivität*. Weinheim.
Paoli, Francesco (2003). "Quine and Slater on Paraconsistency and Deviance", *Journal of Philosophical Logic*, 32, pp. 531-48.
Pena, Lorenzo (1996). "Graham Priest's ‚Dialectheism' – Is it Altogether True?", *Sorites*.
Petersen, Uwe (1992). "Dialetheism and Paradoxes of the Berry Family", *Logique et Analyse*, pp. 273-89.
Popov, V.K. (1988). "Paraconsistent Sequential Calculi", *Bulletin of the Section of Logic*, pp. 148-59.
Putnam, Hilary (1968). "Is Logic Empirical?", *Boston Studies in the Philosophy of Science*, 5.
Priest, Graham (1979). "The Logic of Paradox", *Journal of Philosophical Logic*, 8, pp. 219-41.
- (1980). "Sense, Entailment and Modus Ponens", *Journal of Philosophical Logic*, 9, pp. 415-35.
- (1982). "To Be and Not to Be: Dialectical Tense Logic", *Studia Logica*, pp. 249-68.
- (1984). "Hyper-Contradictions", *Logique et Analyse*, 27, pp. 237-43.
- (1984a). "Semantic Closure", *Studia Logica*, pp. 117-29.
- (1987). *In Contradiction*. A Study of the Transconsistent. Dordrecht.
- (1989). "Reductio ad Absurdum et Modus Tollendo Ponens", in: (Priest/Routley/Norman 1989), pp. 613-626.
- (1991). "Intensional Paradoxes", *Notre Dame Journal of Symbolic Logic*, 32, pp. 193-211.
- (1991a). "Minimally Inconsistent LP", *Studia Logica*, 50, pp. 321-33.
- (1993). "Can Contradictions Be True", *Proceedings of the Aristotelian Society*, pp. 35-54.
- (1994). "Is Arithmetic Consistent?", *Mind*, 103, pp. 337-49.
- (1994a). "What Could the Least Inconsistent Number Be?", *Logique et Analyse*, 145, pp.3-12.
- (1995). *Beyond the Limits of Thought*. Cambridge.
- (1996). "Everett's Triology", *Mind*, 105, pp. 631-48.

- (1996a). "On Inconsistent Arithmetics: A Reply to Denyer", *Mind*, 105, pp. 649-59.
- (1997). "Inconsistent Models of Arithmetic. Part I: Finite Models", *Journal of Philosophical Logic*, 26, pp. 223-35.
- (1997a). "On a Paradox of Hilbert and Bernays", *Journal of Philosophical Logic*, 26, pp. 45-56.
- (1999). "Semantic Closure, Descriptions and Non-Triviality", *Journal of Philosophical Logic*, pp. 549-58.
- (2000). "Could Everything Be True?", *Australasian Journal of Philosophy*, 78, pp. 189-95.
- (2001). *An Introduction to Non-Classical Logic*. Cambridge.
- (2002). "Inconsistency and the Empirical Sciences", in: Meheus (2002), pp. 119-28.
-/Routley,Richard (1983). *On Paraconsistency*. Research Report 13. Australian National University.
-/Routley, Richard/Norman, Jean (1989). (Eds.) *Paraconsistent Logic*. Essays on the Inconsistent. Munich et al.
Quine, Willard Van Orman (1937). "Logic based on inclusion and abstraction", *Journal of Symbolic Logic*, 2.
- (1974). *Methods of Logic*. London, 3rd Edition.
Raspa, Venanzio (1999). "Lukasiewicz on the Principle of Contradiction", *Journal for Phenomenological Research*, 24, pp. 57-112.
Rescher, Nicholas (1979). *Cognitive Systematization*. Oxford.
- /Brandom, R. (1980). *The Logic of Inconsistency*. A Study in Non-Standard Possible Worlds Semantics and Ontology. Oxford.
Routley, Richard (1978). "Semantical Analysis of Arruda-da Costa P Systems and Adjacent Non-Replacement Relevant Systems", *Studia Logica*, pp. 301-20.
- (1979). "Dialectical Logic, Semantics and Metamathematics", *Erkenntnis*, 14, pp. 301-31.
- (1979a). *Exploring Meinong's Jungle and Beyond*. Canberra.
-/Brady, Ross (1989). "The Non-Triviality of Extensional Dialectical Set Theory", in: (Priest/Routley/Norman 1989), pp. 415-36.
-/Loparic, A. (1980). "Relevant Logics Without Replacement", in: Arruda, A./Da Costa, N./Sette, A. (Eds.) *Proceedings of the Third Brasilian Conference on Mathematical Logic*. Estadual de Campinas, pp. 263-80.
-/Meyer, J. (1976). "Dialectical logic, classical logic and the consistency of the world", *Studies in Soviet Thought*, 16.
-/Plumwood, V. (1989). "Moral Dilemmas and the Logic of Deontic Notions", in: (Priest/Routley/Norman 1989), pp. 653-90.
Russell, Bertrand (1905). "On Some Difficulties in the Theory of Transfinite Numbers and Order Types", *Proceedings of the London Mathematical Society*, 4, pp.29-53.
Sainsbury, R. (1988). *Paradoxes*. Cambridge.

Schotch, P./Jennings, R. (1989). "On Detonating", in: (Priest/Routley/Norman 1989), pp. 306-27.
Schurz, Gerhard (1991). "Relevant Deduction", *Erkenntnis*, 35, pp.391-437.
Shapiro, Steward (1991). *Foundations without Foundationalism*. A Case for Second-Order Logic. Oxford.
Sidorenko, Evgenij (1997). "Binary Relational Semantics of Entailment", manuscript, 7 pp.
Slater, B. (1995). "Paraconsistent Logics?", *Journal of Philosophical Logic*, 24, pp. 451-54.
Smiley, Timothy (1993). "Can Contradictions Be True?", *Proceedings of the Aristotelian Society*, pp. 16-33.
Smullyan, Raymond (1992). *Gödel's Incompleteness Theorems*. Oxford/New York.
Sneed, Joseph (1979). *The Logical Structure of Mathematical Physics*. Dordrecht, 2nd Ed.
Stalnaker, Robert (1968). "A Theory of Conditionals", *Studies in Logical Theory*, American Philosophical Quarterly, Monograph 2, pp. 98-112.
Stegmüller, Wolfgang (1986). *Die Entwicklung des neuen Strukturalismus*. Probleme und Resultate der Wissenschaftstheorie und Analytischen Philosophie, Bd. II, Dritter Teilband. Berlin et al.
Stoll, Robert (1963). *Set Theory and Logic*. New York, 2nd Ed.
Sylvan, Richard (1992). "Grim Tales Retold: How to Maintain Ordinary Discourse About – and Despite – Logically Embarassing Notions and Totalities", *Logique et Analyse*, pp. 349-74.
Tarski, Alfred (1936). "Der Wahrheitsbegriff in den formalisierten Sprachen", *Studia Philosophica*, 1.
Tennant, Neil (1984). "Perfect Validity, Entailment and Paraconsistency", *Studia Logica.*
- (1987). *Anti-Realism and Logic*. Truth as Eternal. Oxford.
- (1992). *Natural Logic*. Edinburgh, 3rd Ed.
Thagard, Paul (1978). "The Best Explanation. Criteria for Theory Choice", *The Journal of Philosophy*, 75, pp.76-92.
Urchs, Max (1995). "Discursive Logic: Towards a Logic of Rational Discourse", Studia Logica, 54, pp. 231-49.
van Inwagen, Peter (1995). *God, Knowledge, and Mystery*. Essays in Philosophical Theology. Ithaca/London.
Wansing, Heinrich (2001). "Negation", in: (Goble 2001), pp. 415-36.
Weingartner, Paul (1999). "Reasons for Filtering Classical Logic", in: Batens et. al. (1999), pp. 315-28.
Wolenski, Jan (1995). "Logic and Falsity", in: Childers, T./Majer, O. (Eds.) *Logica '94*. Prague, 1995, pp. 95-106.
Wormell, C. (1958). "On the Paradoxes of Self-Reference", *Mind*, 67.
Yablo, Stephen (1993). "Paradoxes without Self-Reference", *Analysis*, 53, pp. 251-52.

www.ingramcontent.com/pod-product-compliance
Ingram Content Group UK Ltd.
Pitfield, Milton Keynes, MK11 3LW, UK
UKHW020121290926
15471UKWH00003B/211

9 783631 534137